IMAGES
of America

VINTAGE TAMPA SIGNS AND SCENES

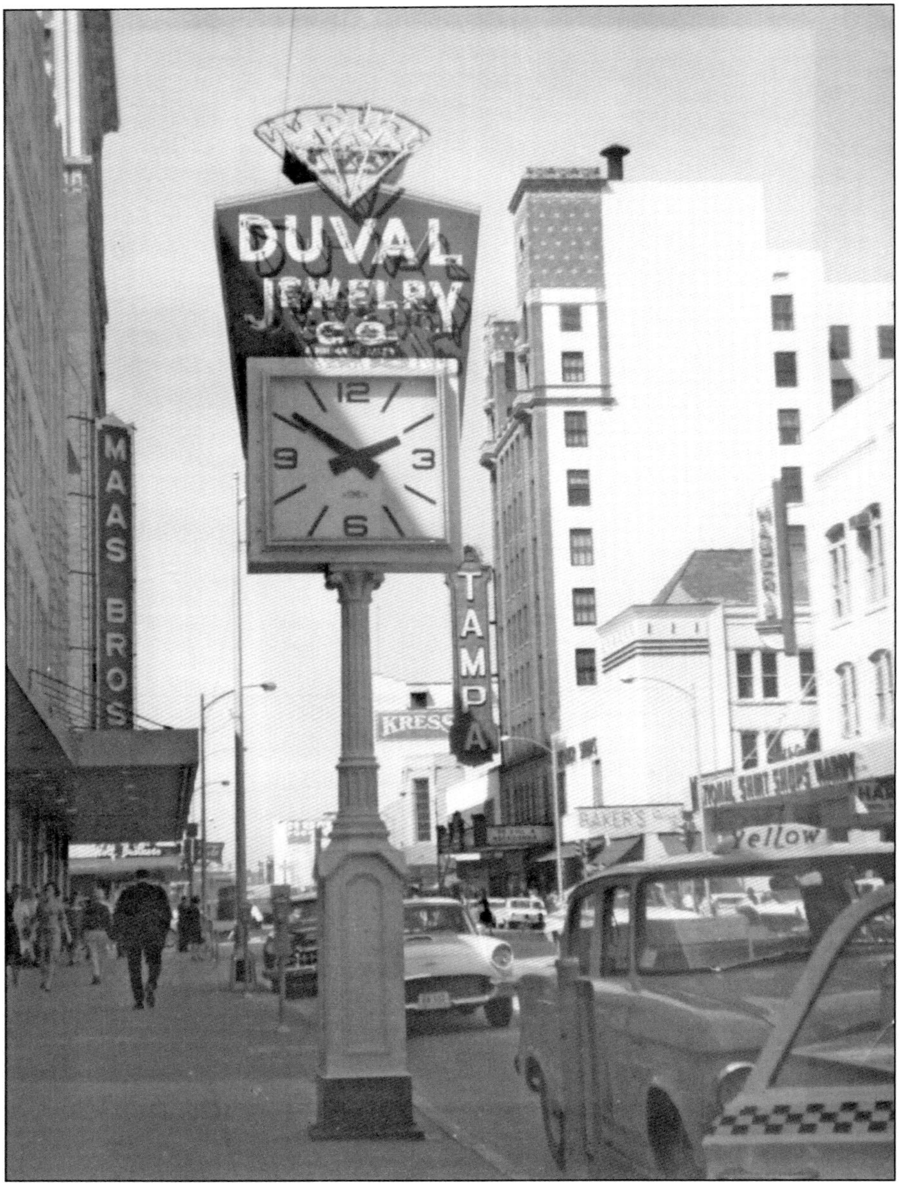

Here is a spectacular 1961 view of Franklin Street looking north from Twiggs Street, and among the many shops and stores are the well-known Maas Brothers, Kress, and Tampa Theatre buildings. Notice the great detail in the neon diamond for the Duval Jewelry Company—quite a work of art created by the Cinchett Neon Sign Company.

ON THE COVER: This 1949 photograph was taken in downtown Tampa for several businesses with sign work completed by Cinchett Neon Signs along Franklin Street between Polk and Cass Streets. Among the stores is Pollers Dress Shop, one of Tampa's most popular shops at the time. This area on Franklin Street was always busy with shoppers during the 1950s with several department stores nearby, including Newberry's and Grants. The car parked out front is a 1946 Chevrolet Aerosedan.

IMAGES
of America

VINTAGE TAMPA SIGNS AND SCENES

John V. Cinchett

ARCADIA
PUBLISHING

ISBN 978-0-7385-6836-2

Published by Arcadia Publishing
Charleston, South Carolina

Printed in the United States of America

Library of Congress Catalog Card Number: 2008938677

For all general information contact Arcadia Publishing at:
Telephone 843-853-2070
Fax 843-853-0044
E-mail sales@arcadiapublishing.com
For customer service and orders:
Toll-Free 1-888-313-2665

Visit us on the Internet at www.arcadiapublishing.com

This book is dedicated to my beloved mother, Delia Cinchett,
whose loving radiance and sparkling personality
shine on you like a flashy neon sign!

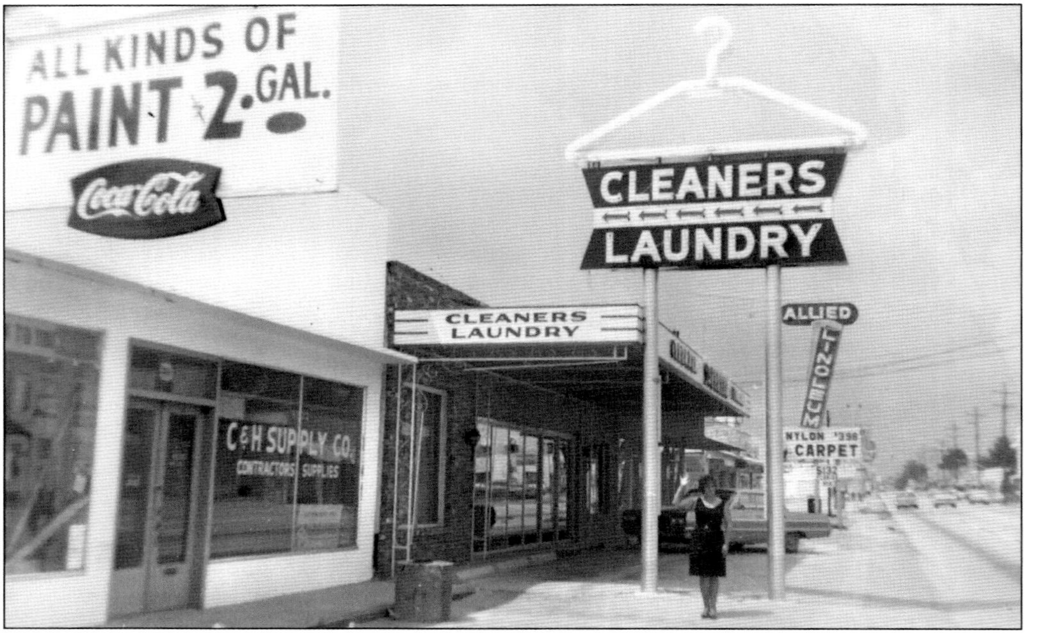

In this 1963 photograph, Delia Cinchett poses with one of the sign company's animated creations, a giant flashing neon hanger on Florida Avenue for Sterling Cleaners. Delia took many pictures of her husband's neon sign work around Tampa when she was secretary at the company from 1956 to 1964.

CONTENTS

ACKNOWLEDGMENTS

The author would like to extend sincerest appreciation to the following individuals for their assistance with the research and restoration project of this photographic collection.

Tampa historians Prof. Gary Mormino of University of South Florida (USF)-St. Petersburg, Leland Hawes, and Rodney Kite-Powell (curator of the Tampa Bay History Museum) have all been very helpful to me in my research. Additionally, the editors of the *Penny Saver News*, Sulphur Springs historian Linda Hope, and Gail Hope are gratefully acknowledged.

In appreciation of restoration work, Bob Baggett and Kenneth Meysan of Baggett Photography and the friendly staff of Walgreens Restoration Service on Kennedy Boulevard are all acknowledged for their professional assistance.

Sincerest appreciation goes to the Tampa–Hillsborough County Public Library, who assisted with several Burgert Brothers photographs that captured neon work included herein. Those eight images will be followed by the credit HCPLC. The USF-Tampa Special Collections Library is acknowledged for their assistance with one picture followed by the credit USFSCL. All other photographs are the property of John V. Cinchett.

My dear circle of friends and coworkers are graciously acknowledged for tolerating my endless stories of growing up in Tampa and appreciating my nostalgic tendencies. My mother, Delia, certainly must be mentioned here because it was her foresight in taking many of these photographs during the 1950s that has allowed us to take this journey into Tampa's past and appreciate that well-loved era.

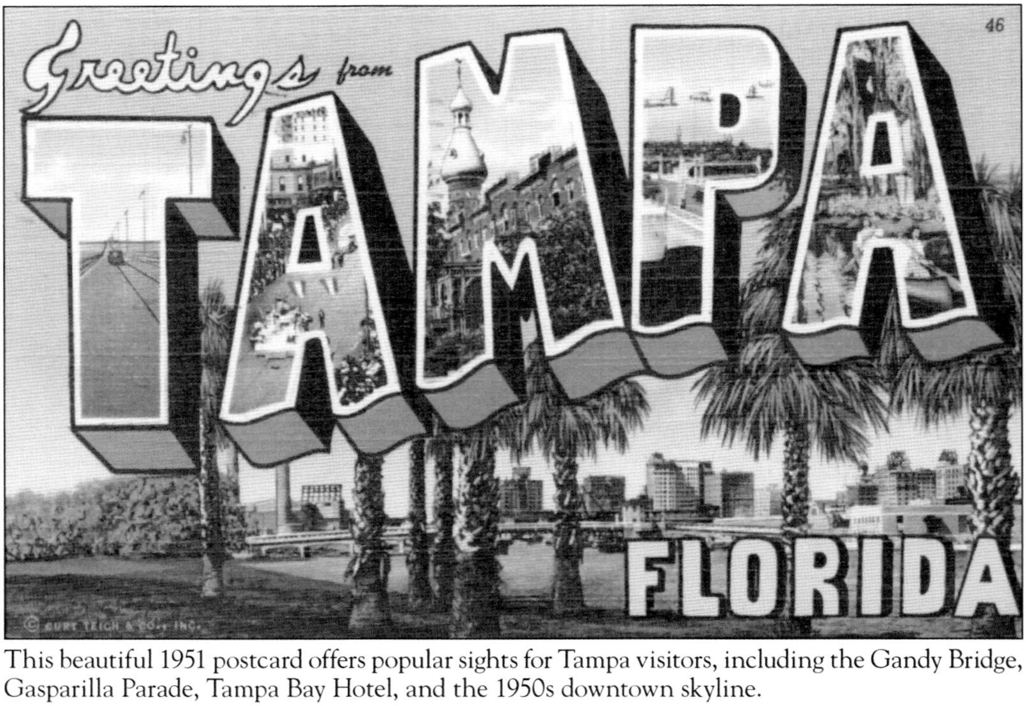

This beautiful 1951 postcard offers popular sights for Tampa visitors, including the Gandy Bridge, Gasparilla Parade, Tampa Bay Hotel, and the 1950s downtown skyline.

INTRODUCTION

You have been invited on a nostalgic journey through Tampa's glory years, the 1950s. During this period, Tampa was experiencing a record-setting population increase that had never been seen before. Within 10 years, Tampa's population more than doubled, and the cityscape was transformed with new highways, bridges, and a brand new interstate system all making their way into Tampa during this era. The residents of Tampa enjoyed a bustling downtown shopping mecca. All of the most popular stores of the time were there, like JCPenney, Grants, Sears, Woolworth's, and Kress; the list goes on and on. Everyone wanted a flashy new neon sign to direct patrons into their establishment, and neon signs began appearing on every street corner and storefront.

Frank Cianchetta was a pioneer of the sign industry, establishing his first sign shop in Philadelphia in 1927. He knew that neon signs were becoming increasingly popular on busy city streets that were seeing more cars than ever before. Frank had a passion for his trade and used his artistic talents to achieve great success in his sign business. The creator of neon is an artist because it is the design of the sign taken from a drawn pattern that the neon glass is formed upon. By 1947, Frank was doing well in Philadelphia, but he had heard that there were more new business opportunities in Tampa. He visited Tampa and immediately fell in love with the city's climate and potential. One year later, he decided to move his family and the sign company to Tampa with one profound concession: he was changing his name.

Frank Cianchetta wanted to have great success opening his neon sign shop in Tampa, and he had heard that most business owners were white Southerners. He was concerned that the Italian family name might somehow deter business or be difficult to pronounce, so he changed his name (and all of his children's) to "Cinchett," and thus was born Cinchett Neon Signs, a name that would be synonymous with the sign industry in Tampa for five decades.

Frank and his son, John F. Cinchett, became masters of their trade and were considered among the most knowledgeable and creative experts in the neon sign industry. Many of their neon creations became familiar landmarks in vivid hues that changed the landscape of Tampa's streets into brightly colored scenes. They created beautiful neon signs that lit up the city for every type of business from diners to dress shops, and from churches to nightclubs. They documented their work through photographs and proudly displayed them in the sign shop office. These magnificent pictures came about for one simple reason: to create examples of the company's neon designs for prospective customers. What better way to sell someone a neon sign than to have pictures of your completed work displayed on the front office wall?

In 1956, Frank's son, John, married West Tampa girl Delia Collera, and the couple began to take over the photographer duties from Frank. Delia became secretary of the company and loved to take pictures of her husband's neon sign handiwork. She often included the street scene around the building when taking the photographs. This was for the benefit of the prospective customer, so they could see how the sign appeared to the patron walking down the street or driving by.

This brings us now to the pictorial collection you are about to see. This selection of nostalgic photographs is from the archives of the Cinchett Neon Sign Company that operated in Tampa during the 1950s and 1960s. During this era, the neon sign industry reached new heights of success. Along with Cinchett Neon Signs were several other shops sharing Tampa's wealth of new commerce, including Acme Signs, Badia Signs, the Neon Service Company, and the well-known Dixie Neon, whose creative work is also fondly remembered among some of these Tampa street scenes. Many of these neon signs became local landmarks and artistic creations for drivers to enjoy along city boulevards. This extraordinary collection of pictures represents that spirit of entrepreneurship that led to the success of hundreds of Tampa businesses and provides a pictorial documentary of the most successful time period in the city's history for new business development and growth. These captivating images truly capture the changing landscape of the city during these prosperous years in her long history. In creating this publication, it is the author's hope that these pictures will bring back nostalgic memories for some and present scenes of vintage Tampa to others who may enjoy the glimpses of a bygone era well loved and cherished by all.

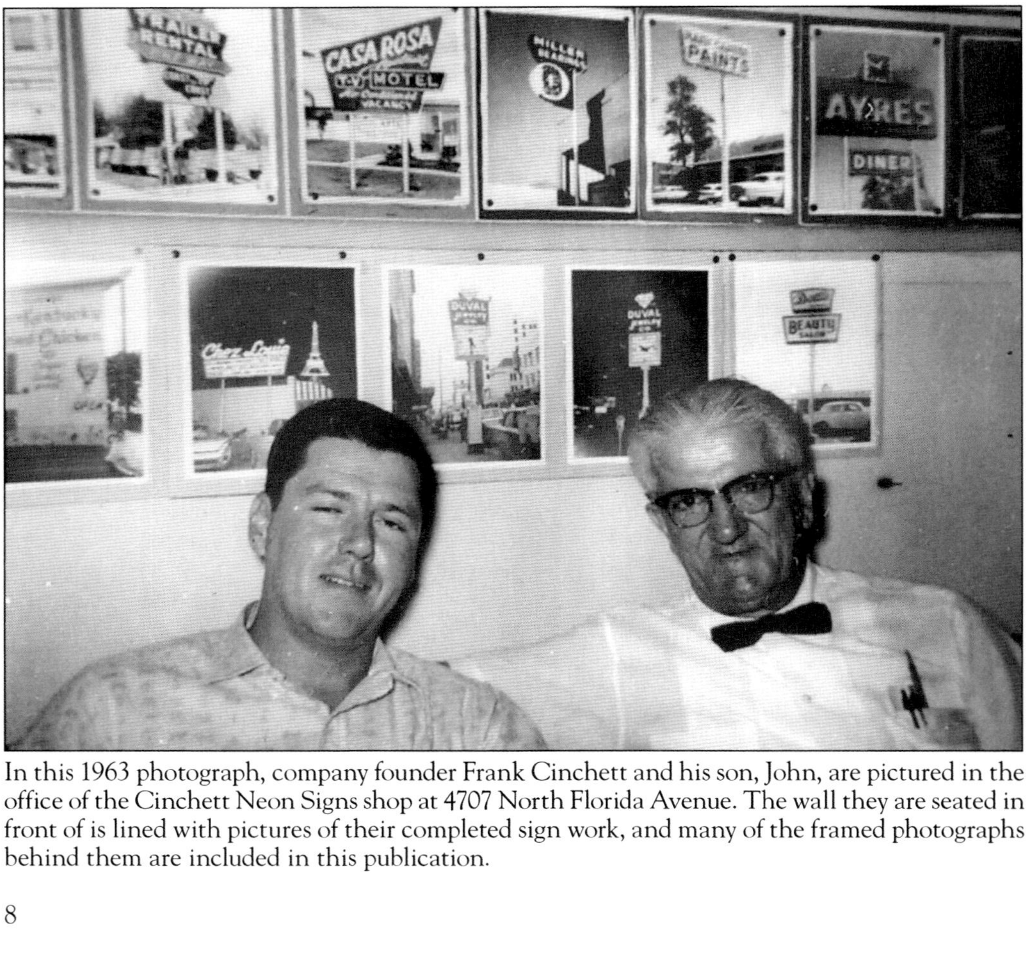

In this 1963 photograph, company founder Frank Cinchett and his son, John, are pictured in the office of the Cinchett Neon Signs shop at 4707 North Florida Avenue. The wall they are seated in front of is lined with pictures of their completed sign work, and many of the framed photographs behind them are included in this publication.

One

Neon Nifties for the Fabulous Fifties

Welcome to downtown Tampa's glory years, the 1950s. Before the arrival of shopping centers around the city, downtown was the place to be for all one's shopping needs. Tampa residents flocked downtown looking for bargains at places like Newberry's and Kress. All of the favorite department stores were there too, like JCPenney, Grants, Sears, and Maas Brothers, where shoppers could find a special gift for Mother's Day or just a new pair of shoes. There was something for everyone, and it was not uncommon for folks to spend a good portion of the day shopping downtown.

This chapter walks along the streets of downtown Tampa during this wonderful period in the city's history. These captivating photographs show the busy sidewalks of a bustling city's retail and business district among the many well-known Tampa shops that folks frequented for decades in the city's central shopping destination. Places like Mangel's and Wolf Brothers became local favorites for shoppers needing to select a new hat or pair of gloves. Downtown shopping was an event not taken lightly; ladies would dress up, and gentlemen donned their hats before heading out. It was an enjoyable affair that everyone looked forward to.

Downtown Tampa was a shining model of the American landscape in the 1950s. On every corner, one could find the best jewelry stores, hat shops, and restaurants that Tampa had to offer. Some of these places had been around long enough to see three generations of families shopping at their store. It was an exciting place to be, and everyone enjoyed shopping visits downtown. Within these scenic images are great details to enjoy—not only in the designs of the neon signs, but also in the scene around each business and street corner. Many hidden treasures can be found in these amazing images, like the common attire of the day and those fabulous cars parked along the street.

These images of Tampa's bustling downtown go back in time to those wonderful days of shopping trips with friends, visiting favorite stores, and stopping in the luncheonette for a slice of apple pie before heading home. There might be a new show playing at the theater or a sale going on at Maas Brothers—it was all there downtown, and these glorious scenes have captured that moment in time.

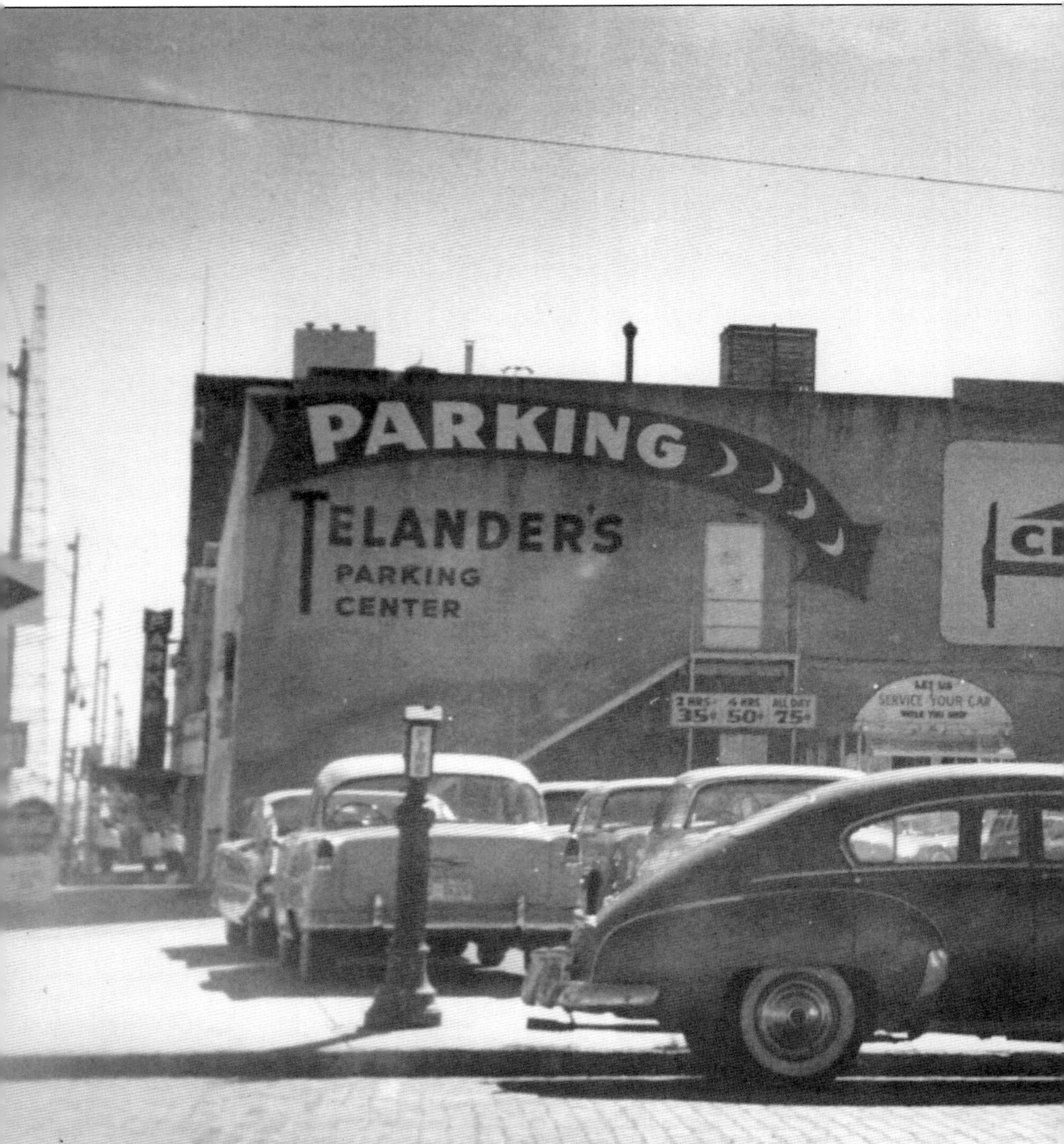

This classic, nearly 20-foot-tall neon Pepsi-Cola bottle cap was created by Cinchett Neon Signs in a Las Vegas style and was placed at Tampa and Twiggs Streets in 1958. Several of these flashy giant bottle caps were placed on downtown rooftop billboards and featured elaborate displays

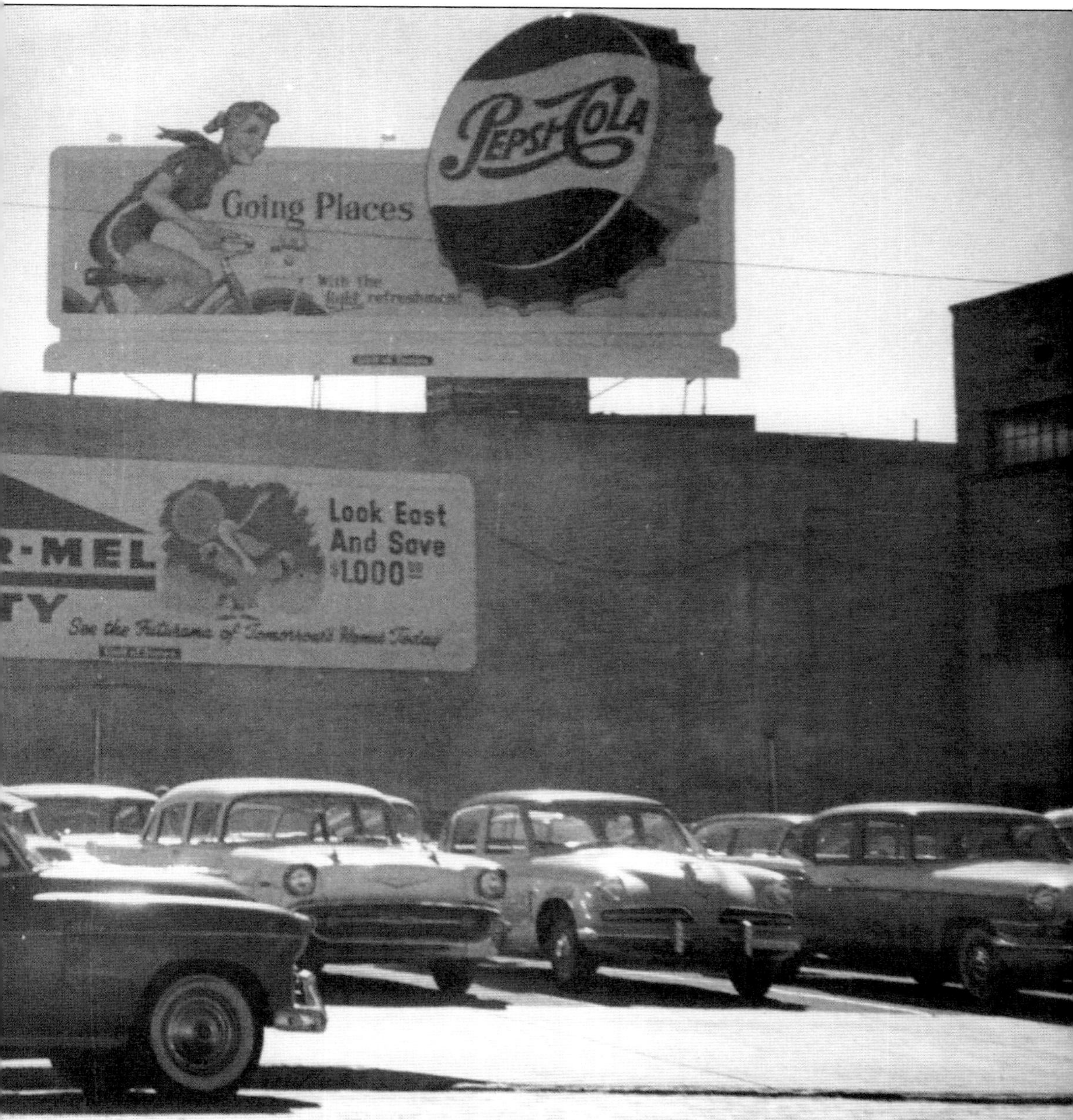

of neon that created a light show for passing traffic. Notice that the sign above the attendant's booth says "Let us service your car while you shop." A close look to the lower left of the picture reveals a vintage fire-alarm call box on the corner.

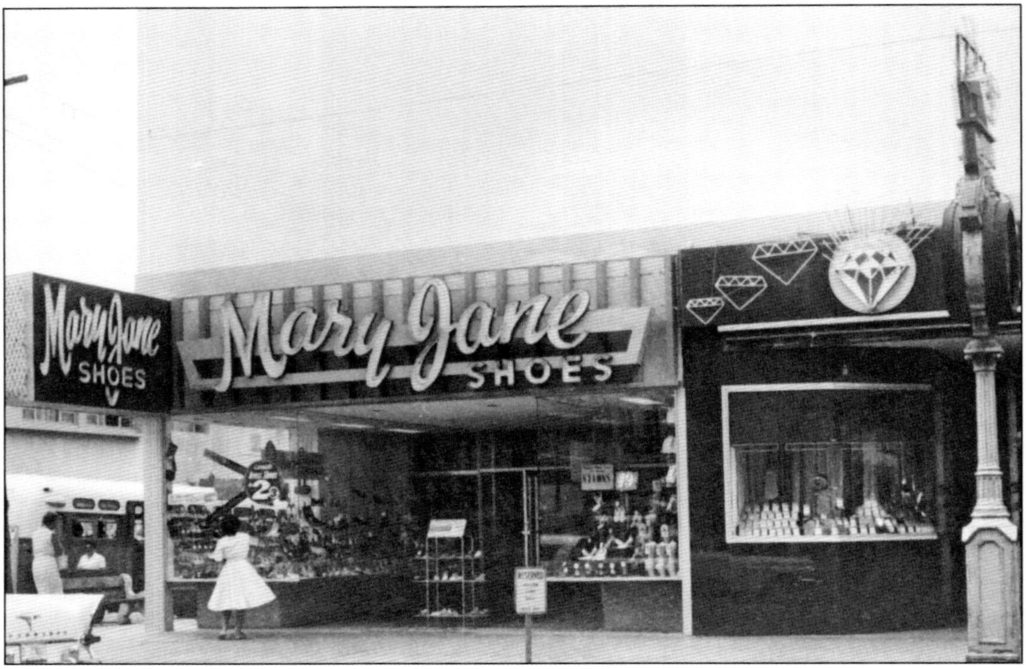

Here is the Mary Jane Shoe Shop at Franklin and Twiggs Streets in 1957. This spectacular photograph captures the typical downtown shopping scene of the 1950s. Take notice of the beautiful neon diamonds for the jewelry shop next door.

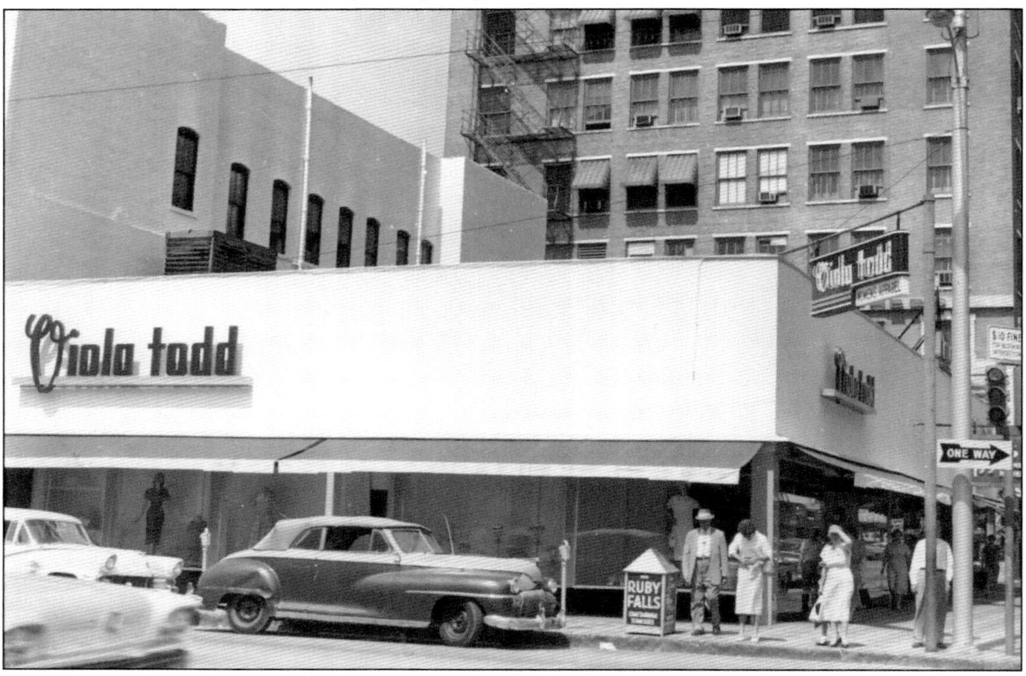

Welcome to Tampa's finest ladies dress shop, Viola Todd at the corner of Tampa and Zack Streets in 1957. Shopping for an evening gown? This is where Tampa's ladies looked for just the right dress and matching gloves.

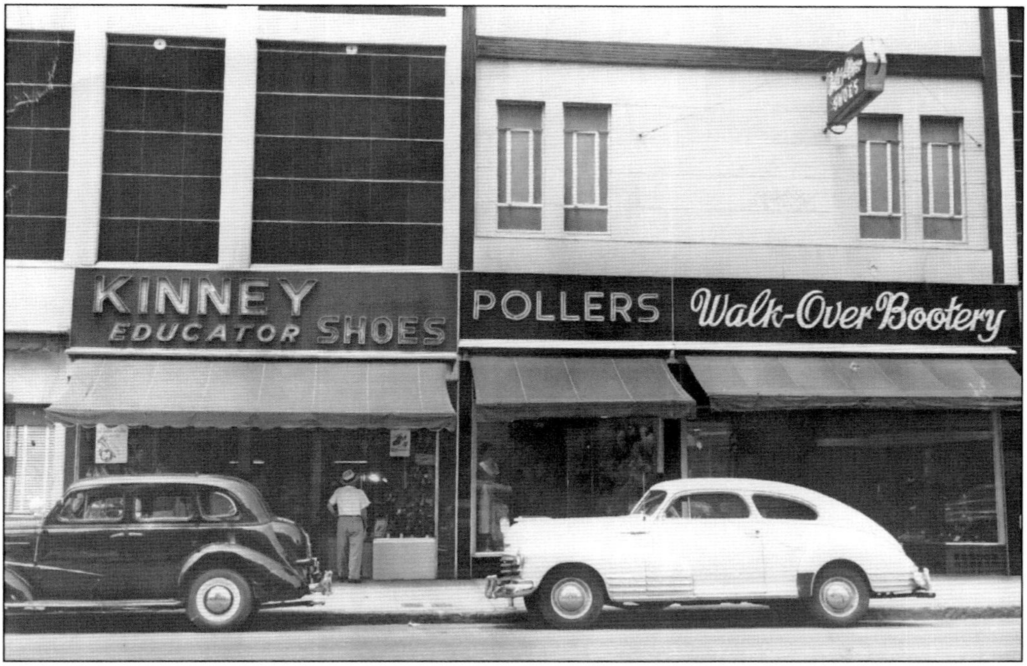

This vintage 1949 photograph of Franklin Street was taken for three signs designed by Cinchett Neon Signs: Pollers Dress Shop, Kinney Shoes, and the Walk-Over Bootery. This photograph was taken from across the street in front of the Kress Building between Polk and Cass Streets.

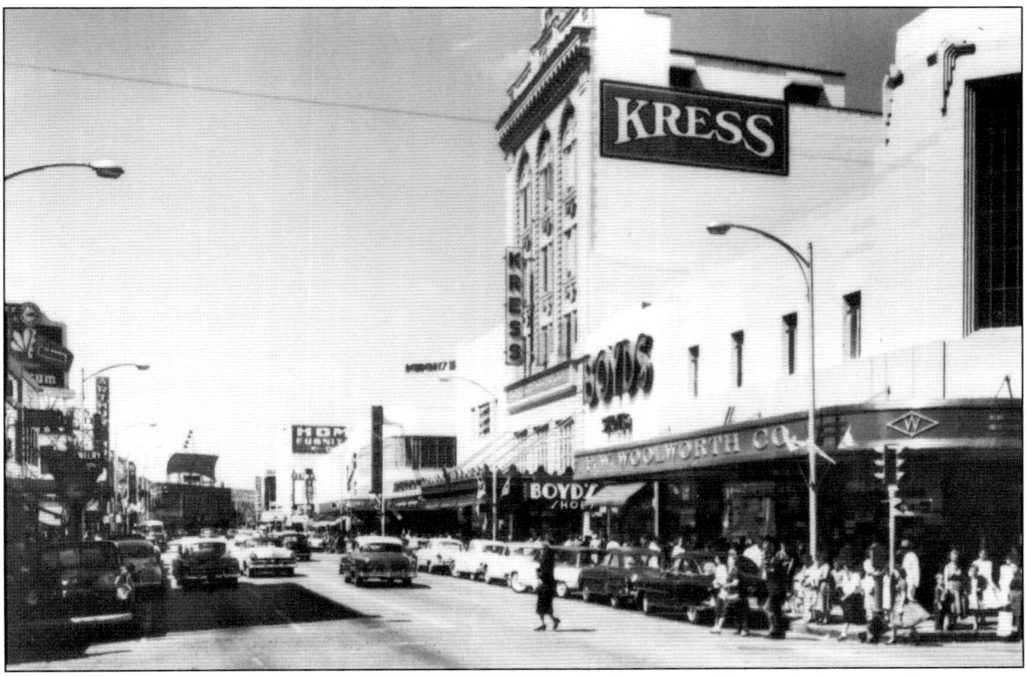

The above 1956 scene shows Woolworth's on Franklin Street, one of Tampa's favorite dime stores, with a luncheonette that served hot meals for folks needing a break from their shopping trip. (Courtesy HCPLC.)

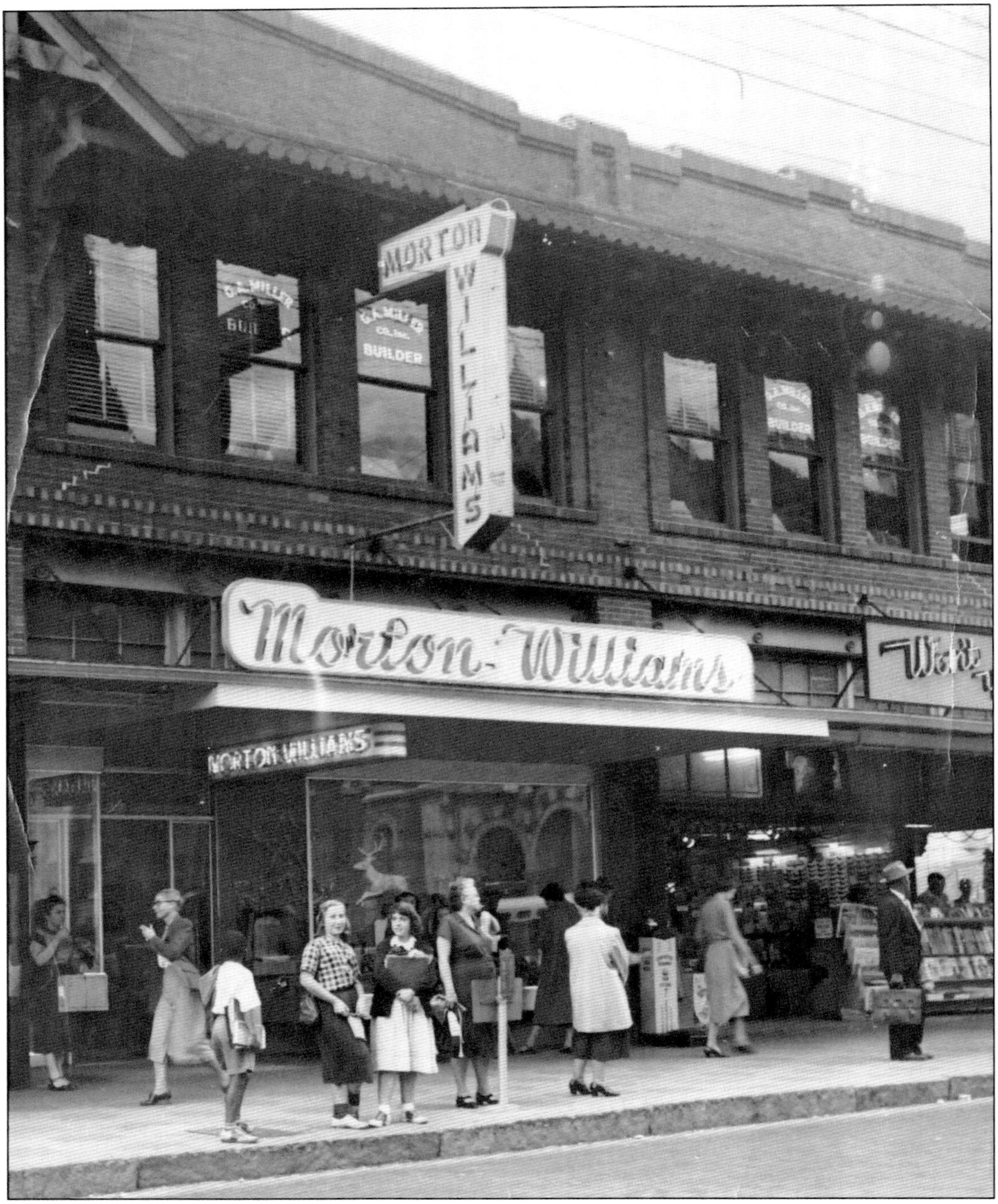

These shoppers know where to find a bargain in 1951 at Morton-Williams on Florida Avenue at Twiggs Street. The detail in this image of the crowd gathered is truly amazing; it is a vintage busy Tampa street scene. Notice the newspaper stand on the corner, another nostalgic time-stamp.

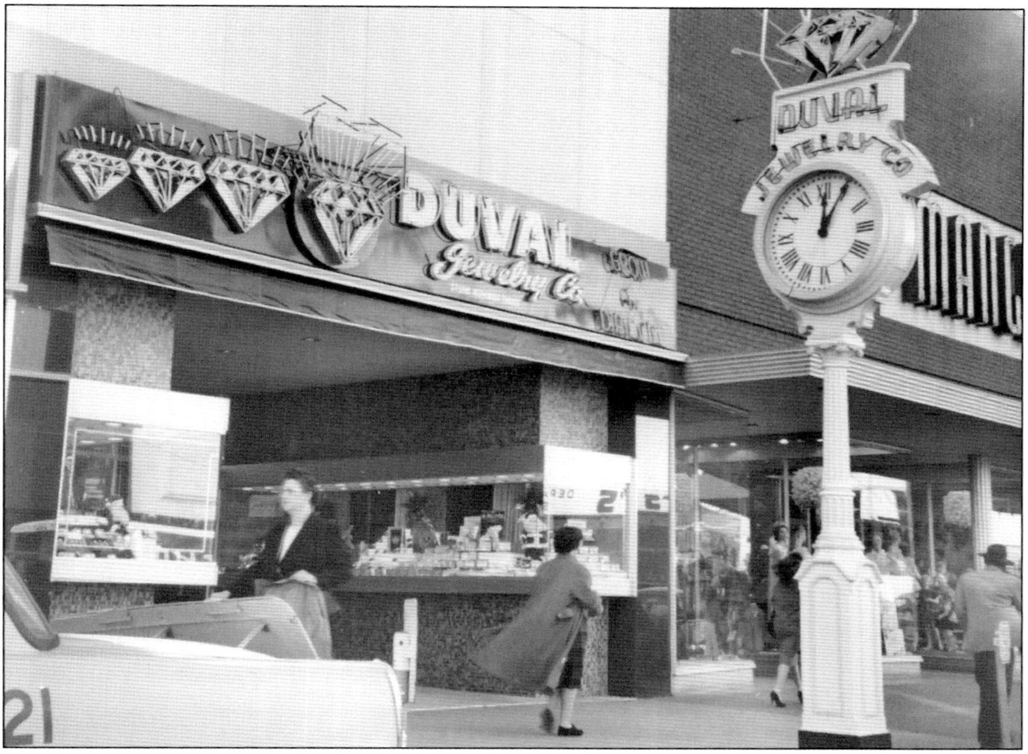

Here is another stunning scene on Franklin Street near the Duval Jewelry Company and Mangel's in 1958. Looking closely, one can see in the window dressings. In the 1957 scene below is Wolf Brothers, one of Tampa's best-known downtown department stores, which specialized in fine menswear.

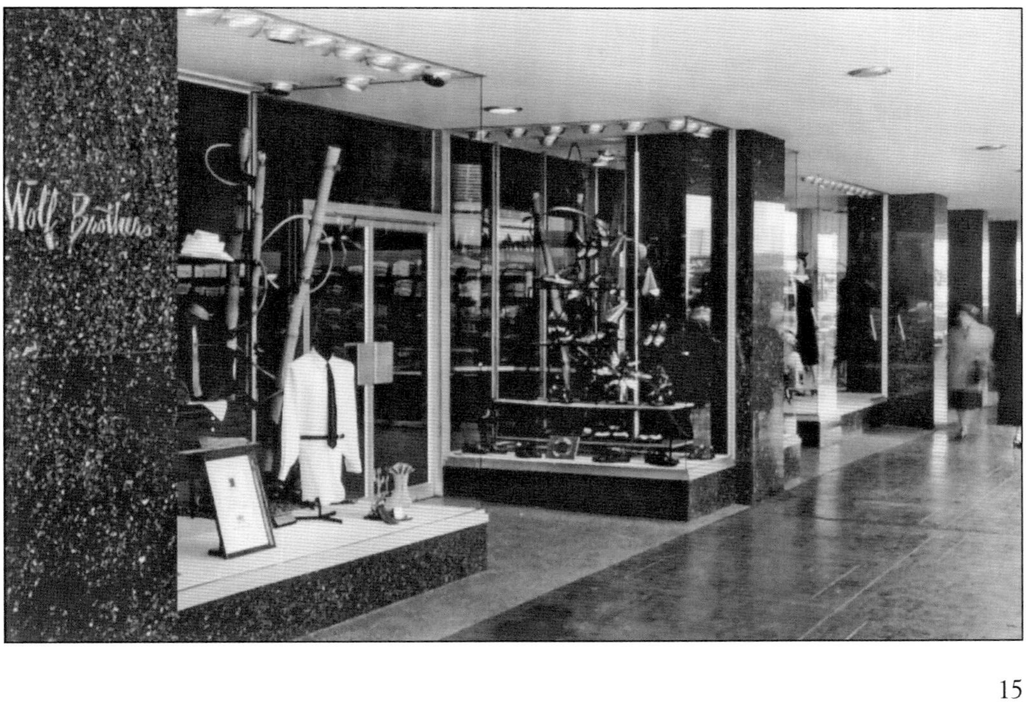

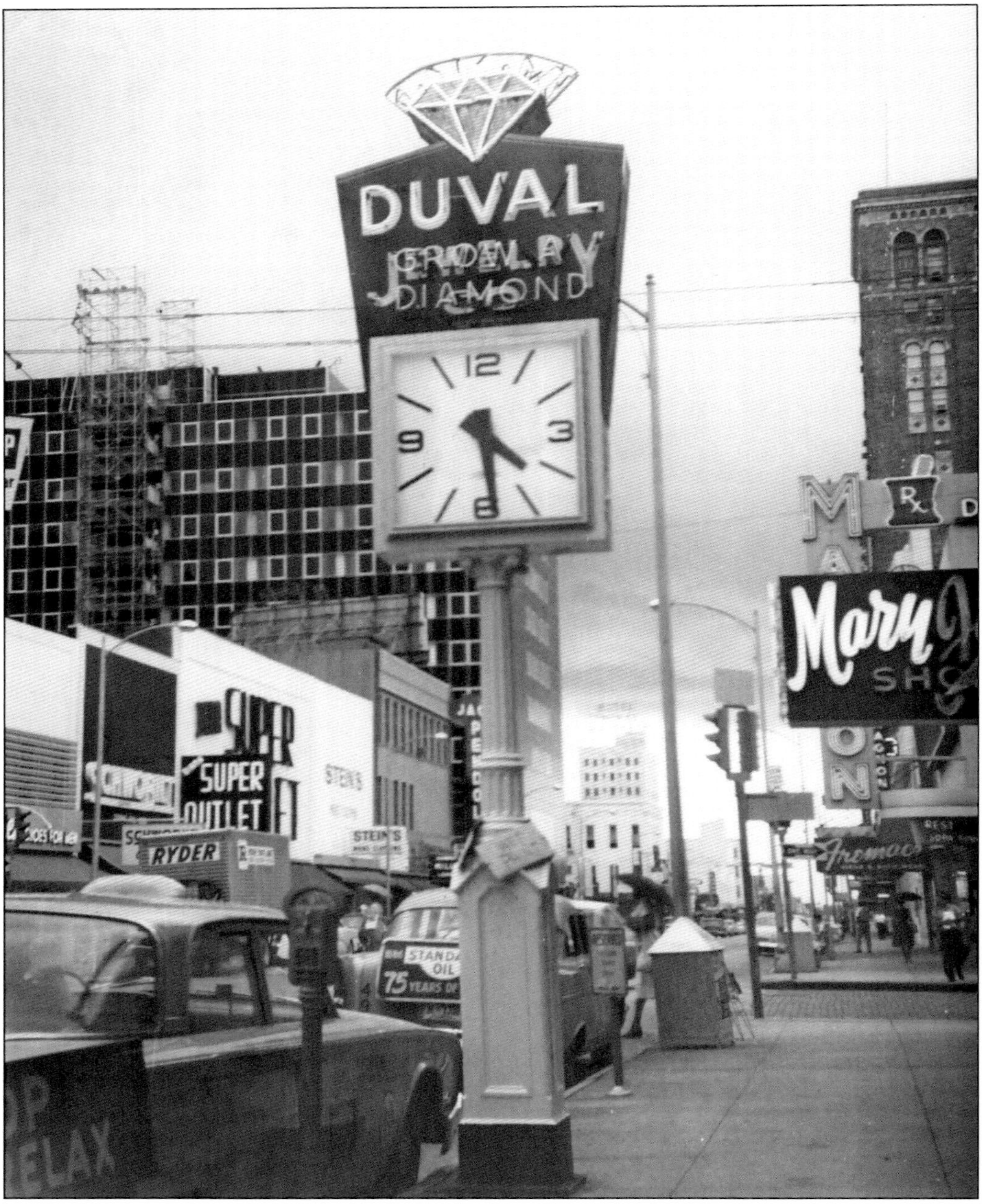

This 1961 image captures the bustling scene of Franklin Street looking south at Twiggs Street. The Duval Jewelry Company has just replaced an older version of its clock sign, and this new neon sign flashes "Grow A Diamond" at night. Having a clock in front of a business was a clever way to impress locals, who would see the shop's name when they checked the time.

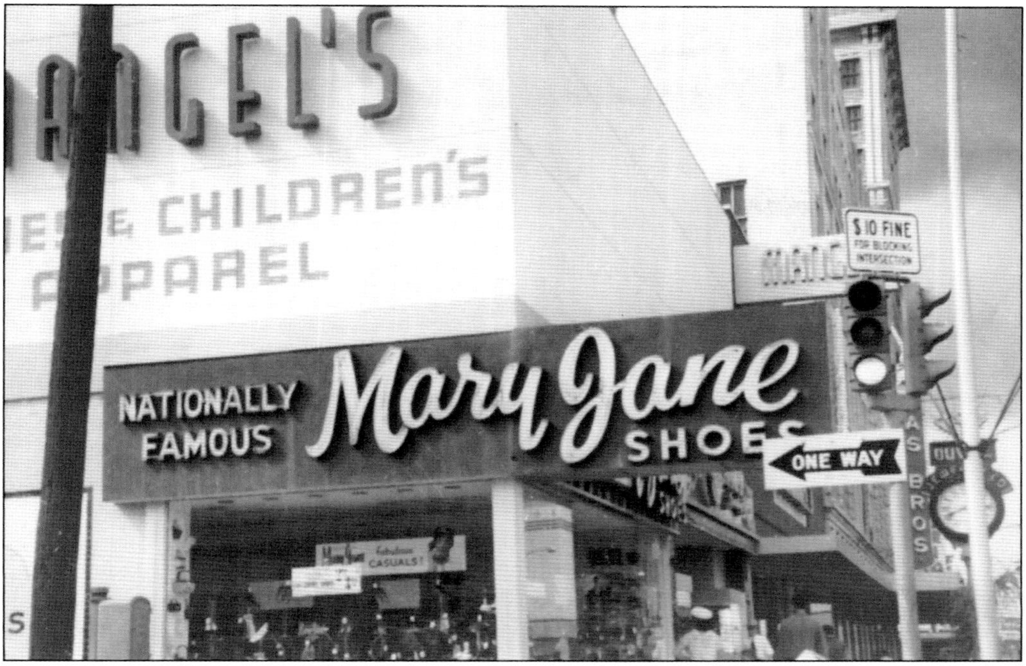

Here is the storefront window at the Mary Jane Shoe Shop on Franklin at Twiggs Streets in 1958. The store advertises children's shoes for 99¢, and this was considered one of downtown's finer shoe stores.

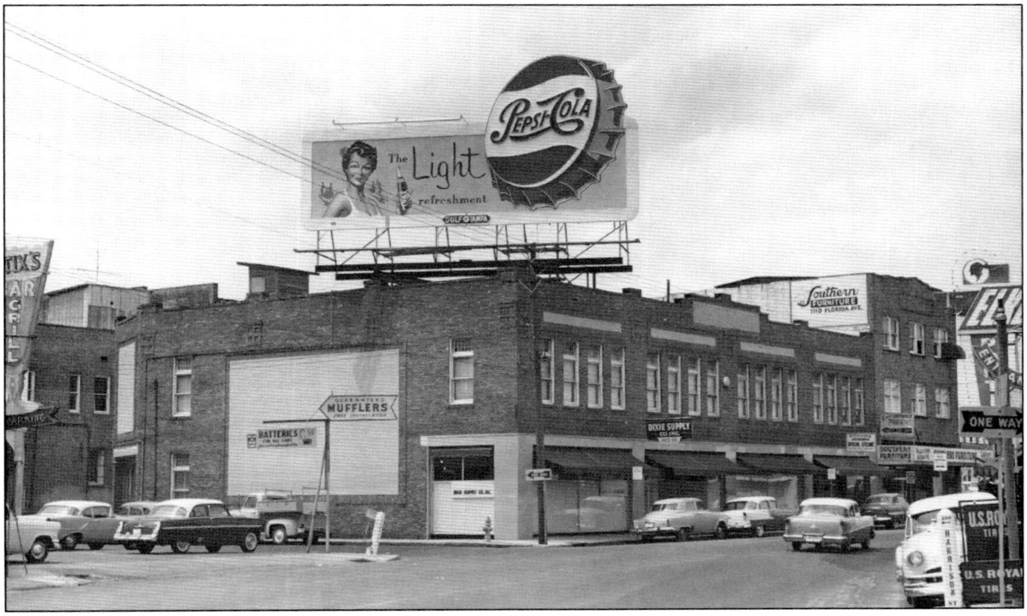

This magnificent 1957 image captures the typical Tampa city street scene of the 1950s. This view looks north on Florida Avenue at Harrison Street. These neon Pepsi-Cola bottle caps were something never seen before in the city. Created by Cinchett Neon Signs, the flashy animated signs were modeled after the Broadway-style signage seen at Times Square. Many Tampa citizens were amazed at the sight of these neon wonders.

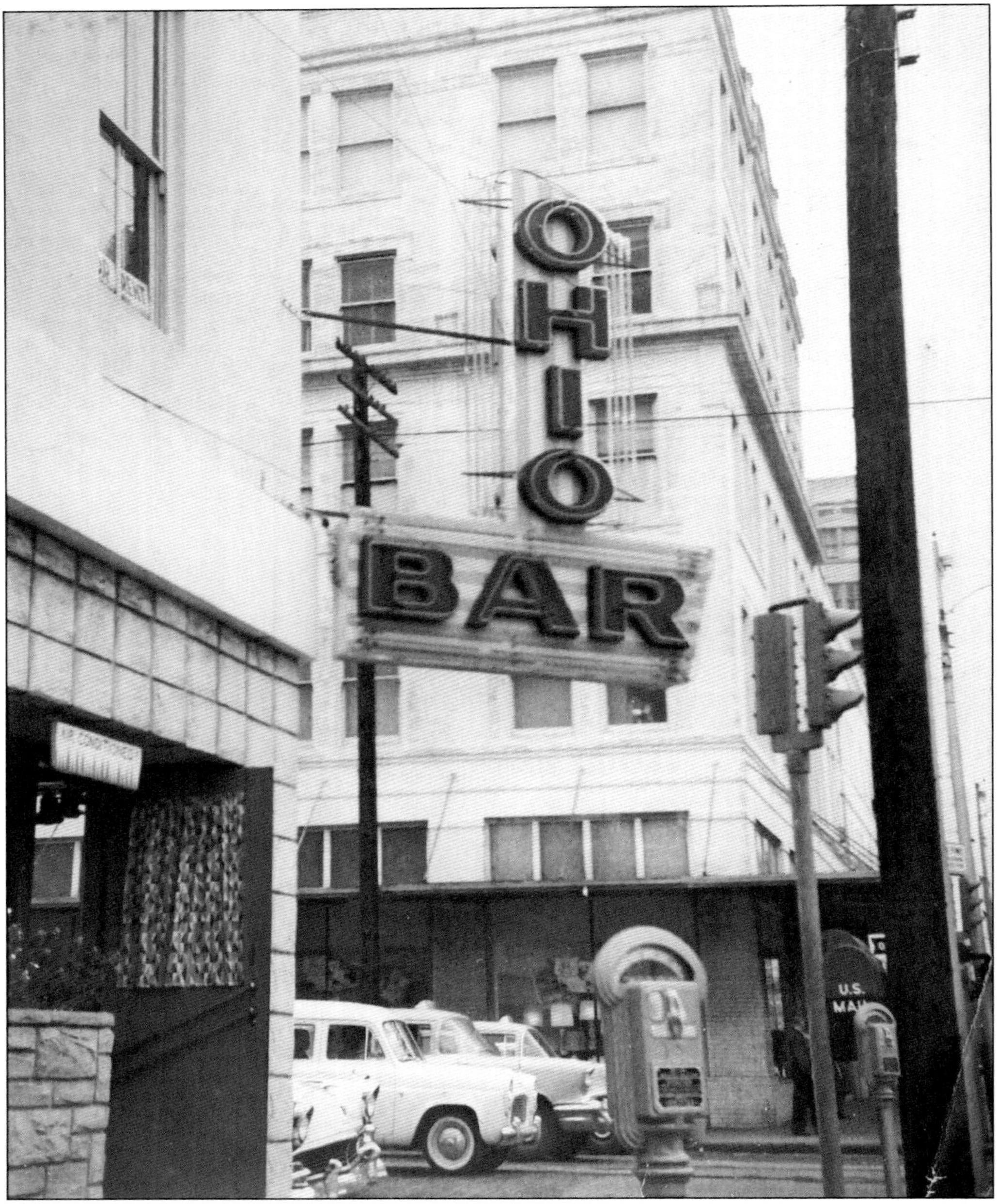

Here is the Ohio Bar at the corner of Tampa and Polk Streets in 1958 looking south. Notice the icicle sign above the doorway that announces "Air-Conditioned." This was a common feature for Tampa bars and restaurants to welcome folks out of the tropical temperatures.

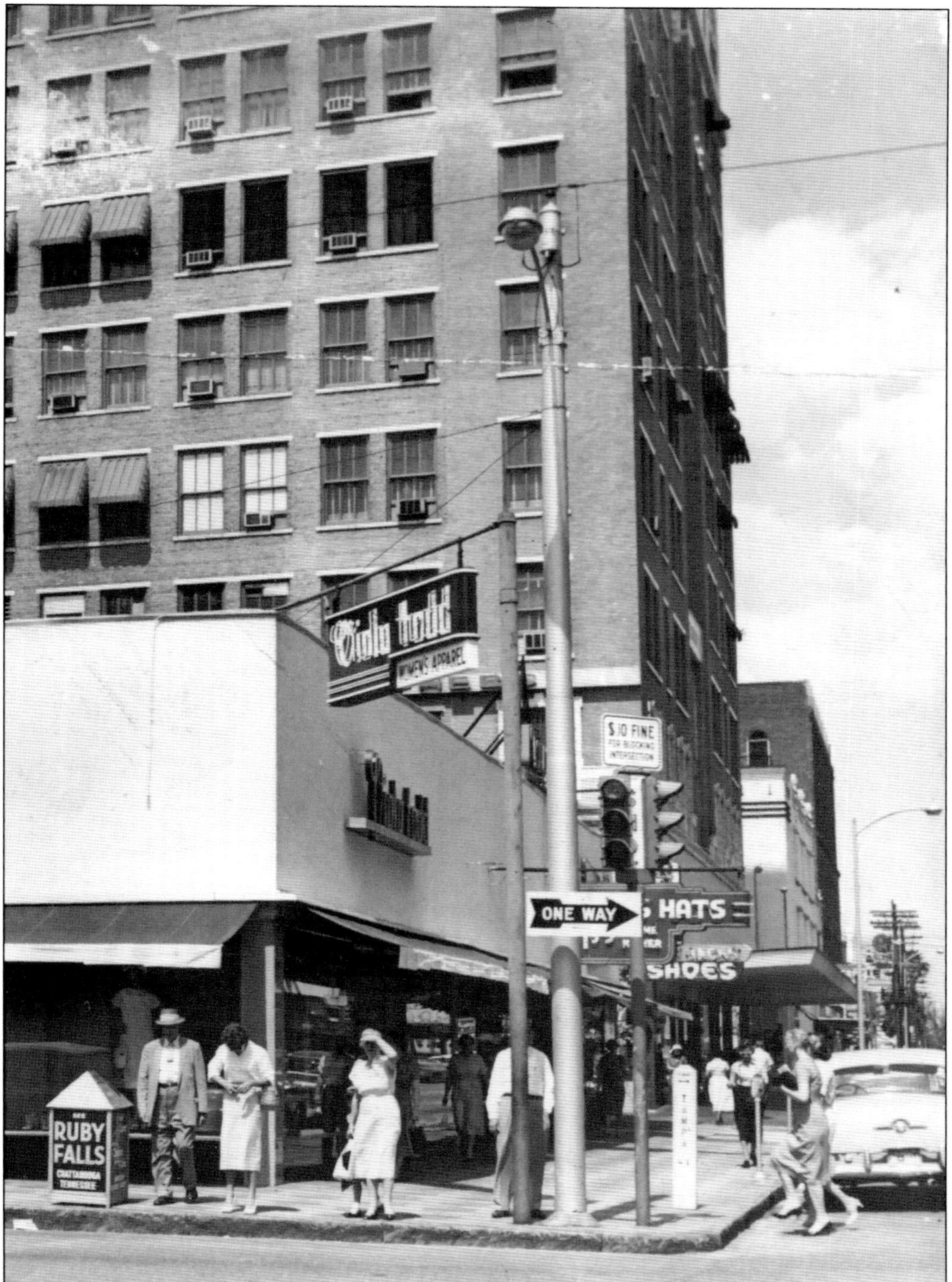

In this busy 1957 downtown shopping scene in front of the Viola Todd dress shop, observe the gentlemen wearing hats and the young girl in a poodle skirt holding her grandmother's hand. One of Tampa's meter maids is also making her rounds to check the cars parked along Zack Street. Notice the monument-style concrete street marker on the corner.

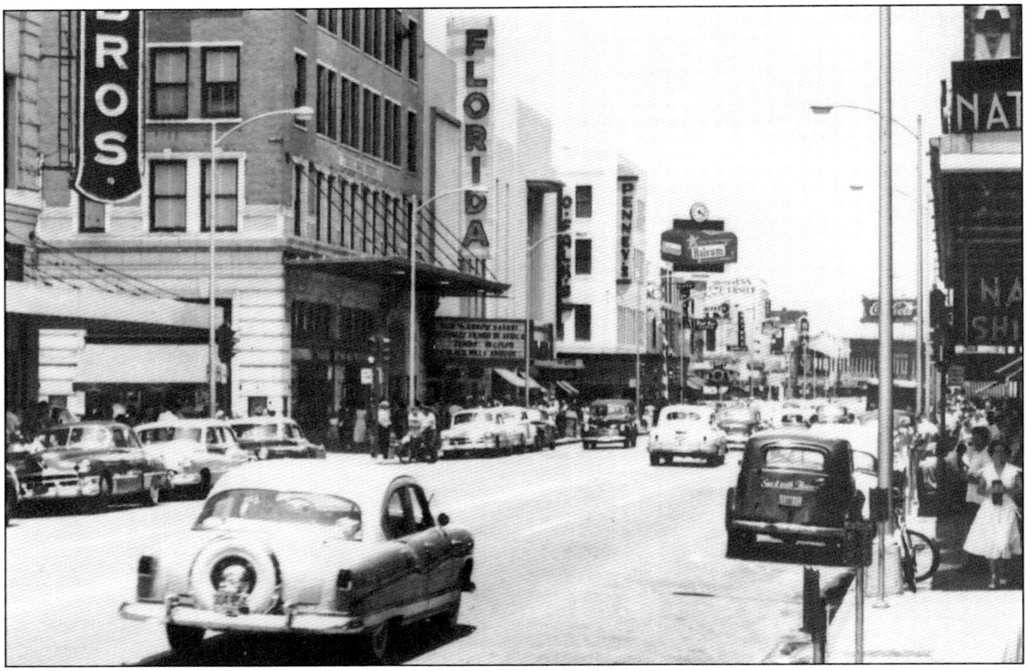

This 1956 scene captures the west side of Franklin Street looking north from Twiggs Street. Among the many familiar places are the Florida Theatre and JCPenney. Cinchett Neon Signs lit up almost the entire city block of storefronts between JCPenney and Cass Street during the 1950s.

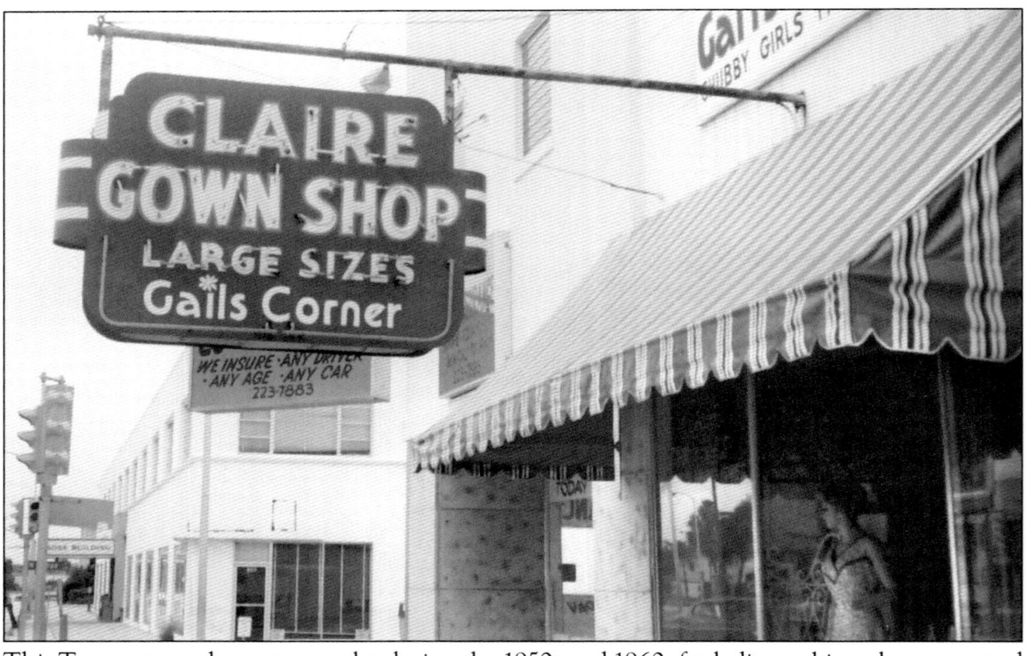

This Tampa gown shop was popular during the 1950s and 1960s for ladies making plans to attend one of Tampa's formal affairs. The store was located at the corner of Tampa and Cass Streets, and this vintage building still stands today.

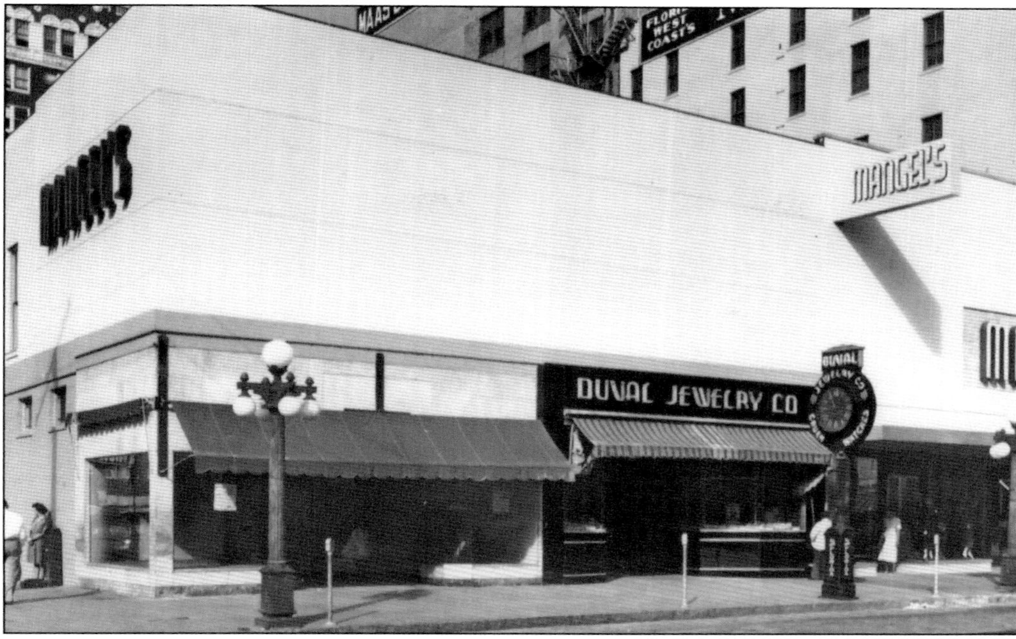

In this 1950 scene, the Mangel's building has been refurbished with a sleek new appearance. Compare this photograph to the one below to see what a different look the facade took on after Cinchett Neon Signs dressed up the storefronts with flashy new neon signs several years later. (Courtesy HCPLC.)

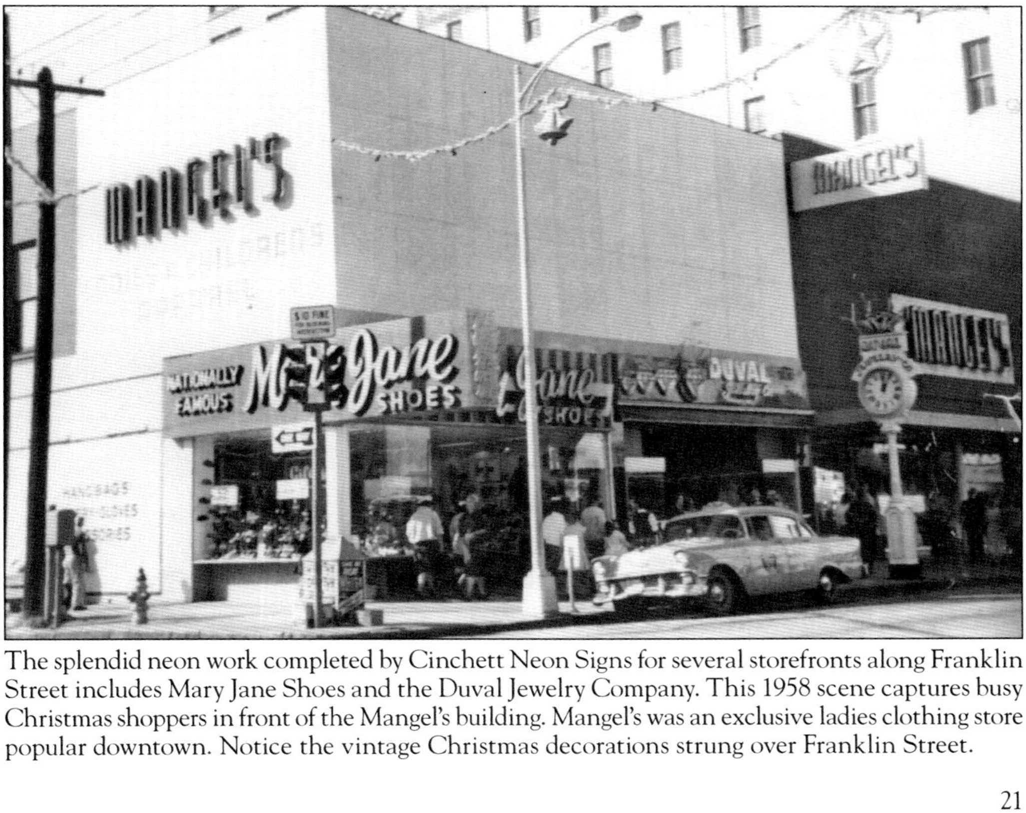

The splendid neon work completed by Cinchett Neon Signs for several storefronts along Franklin Street includes Mary Jane Shoes and the Duval Jewelry Company. This 1958 scene captures busy Christmas shoppers in front of the Mangel's building. Mangel's was an exclusive ladies clothing store popular downtown. Notice the vintage Christmas decorations strung over Franklin Street.

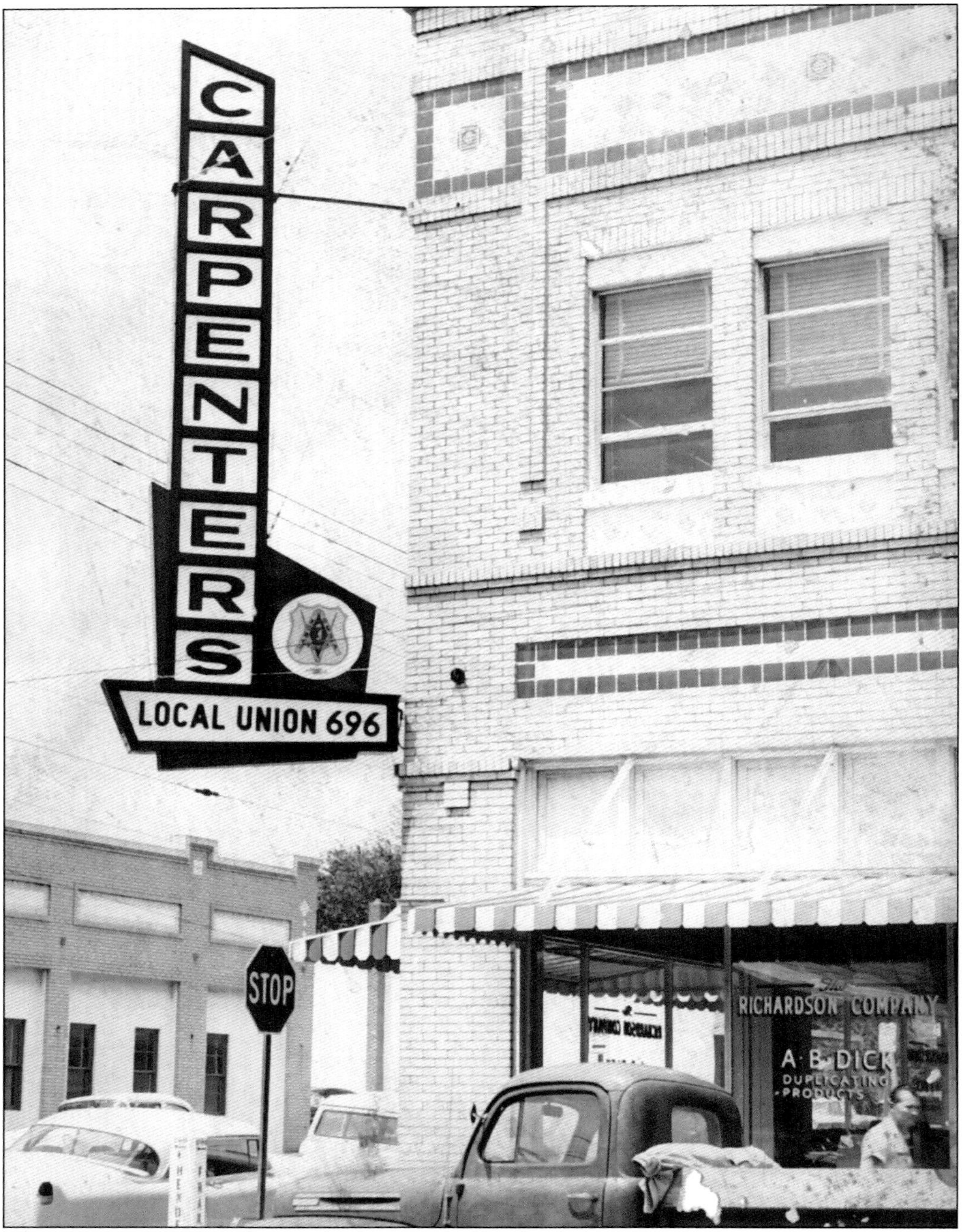

This is the Carpenters Union in the Farris Building on the north end of downtown at Franklin Street and Henderson Avenue in 1955. The top half of the vintage concrete street marker is just visible. This vintage 1920s building was restored into a popular nightclub a few years ago.

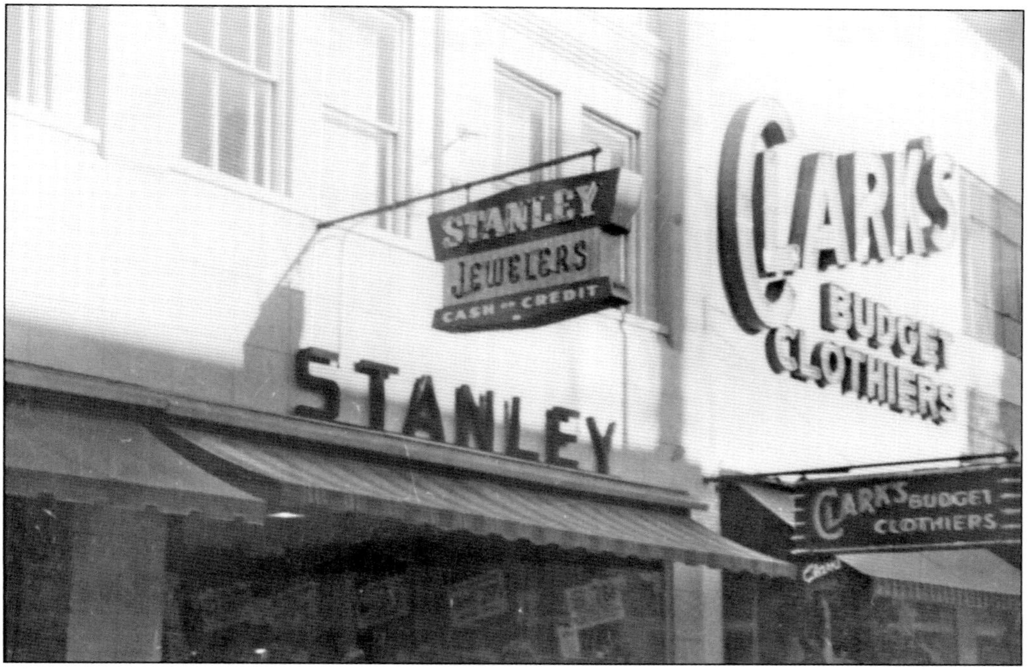

This is the well-known Stanley Jewelers at 910 Franklin Street in 1960. This jewelry store in later years made its way into several popular Tampa shopping centers.

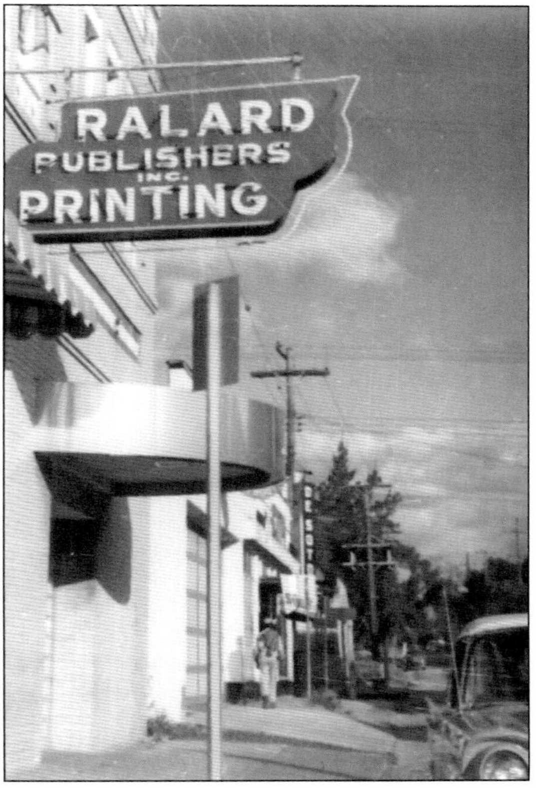

The Ralard Printing Company in the historic Farris Building is seen in this *c.* 1955 view on Henderson Avenue between Franklin Street and Florida Avenue looking east.

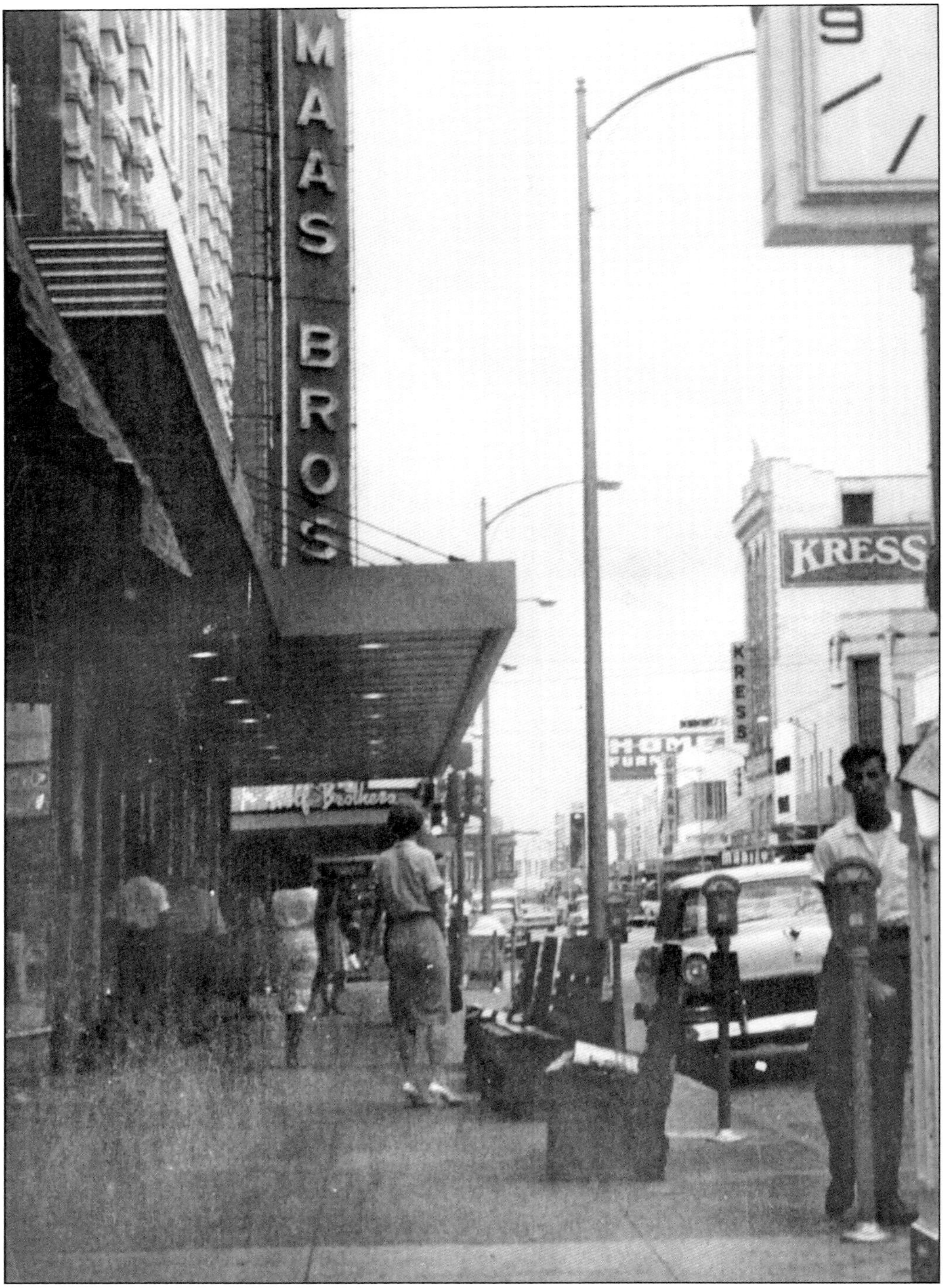

Maas Brothers was Tampa's best-known department store and a busy place, as seen in this 1960 photograph. The department store was around so long that many generations of families shopped there. This view looks north on Franklin Street between Twiggs and Zack Streets. Take notice of the well-dressed shoppers in their Sunday best.

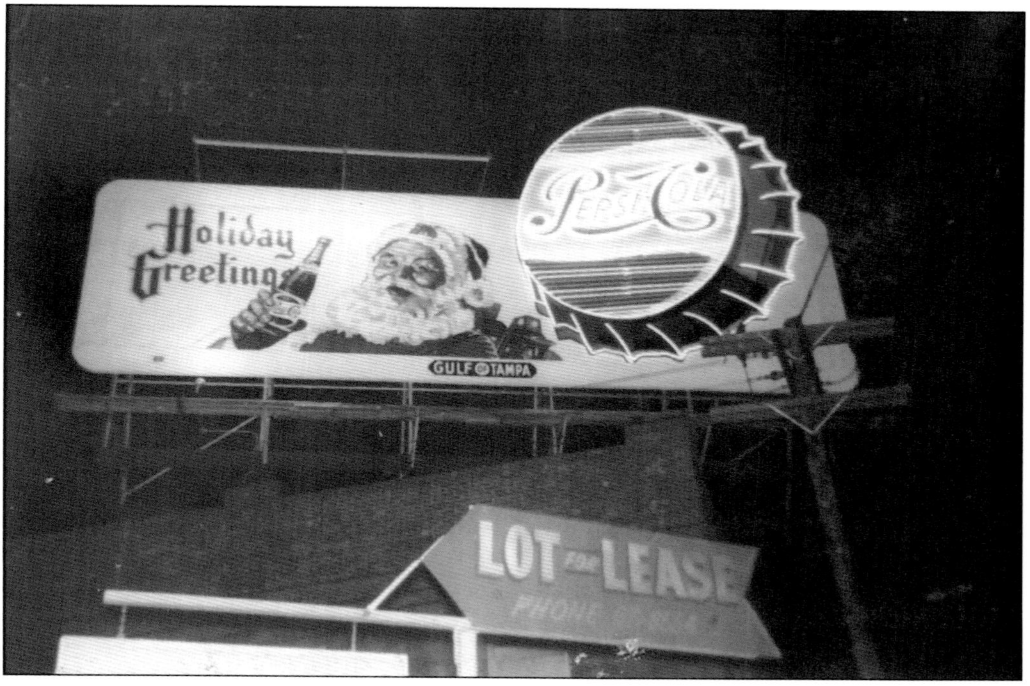

Rooftop billboards are another symbol of nostalgic city scenes from the past. Here is another animated Pepsi-Cola neon bottle cap sign made for the Christmas season in 1958 at Florida Avenue and Royal Street. This is the original world-famous Pepsi-Cola logo, and this neon marvel stood nearly 20 feet tall. The image below looks west along Lafayette Street (now Kennedy Boulevard) in front of the University of Tampa in 1954.

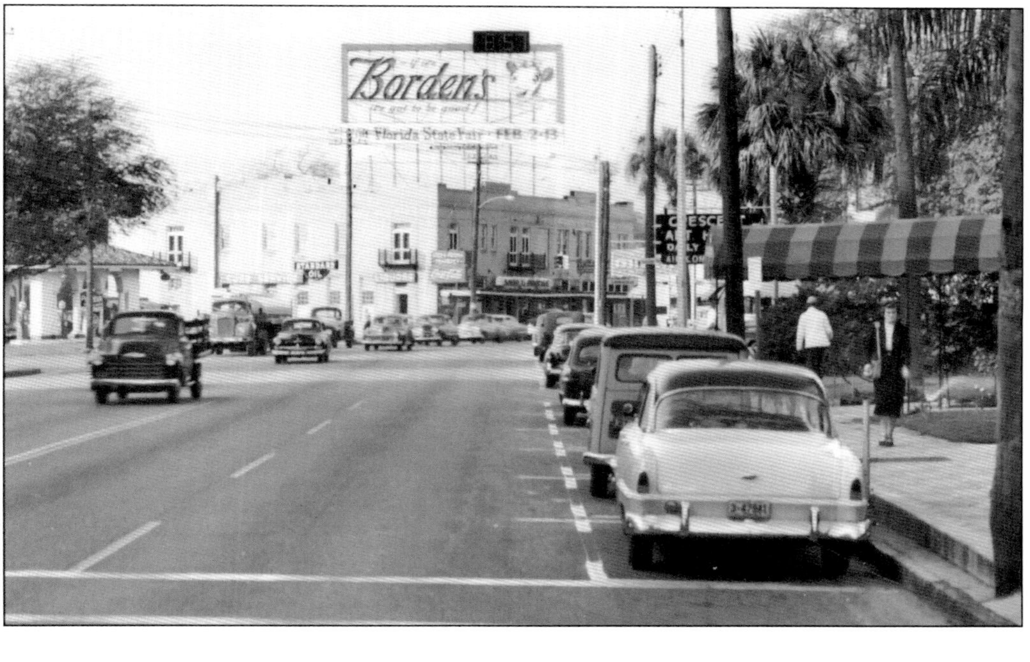

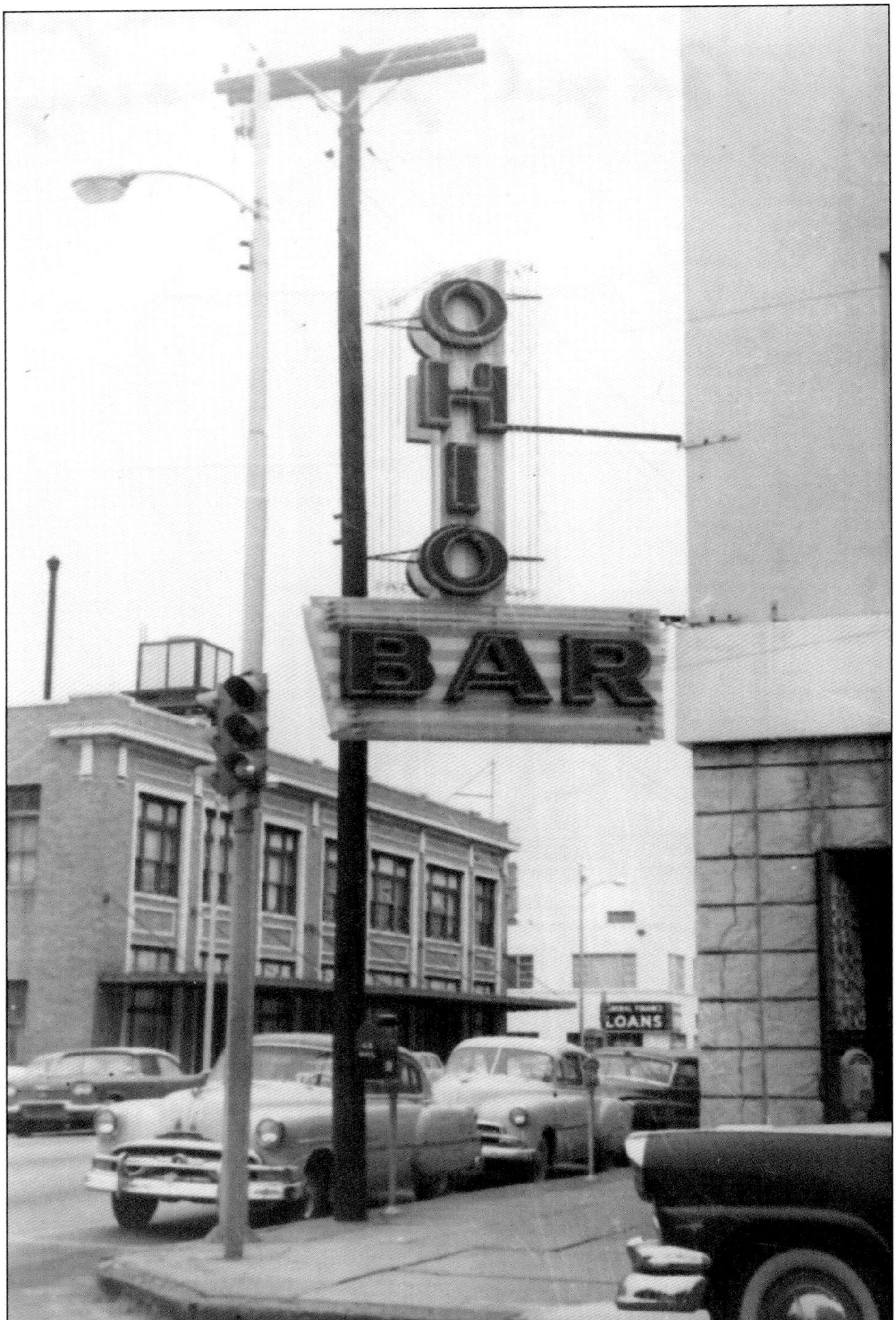

Here is another view of the Ohio Bar in 1958. This scene is looking north on Tampa Street from Polk Street. The owner proudly named his new downtown venture after his home state. This bar was a popular downtown fixture for many years.

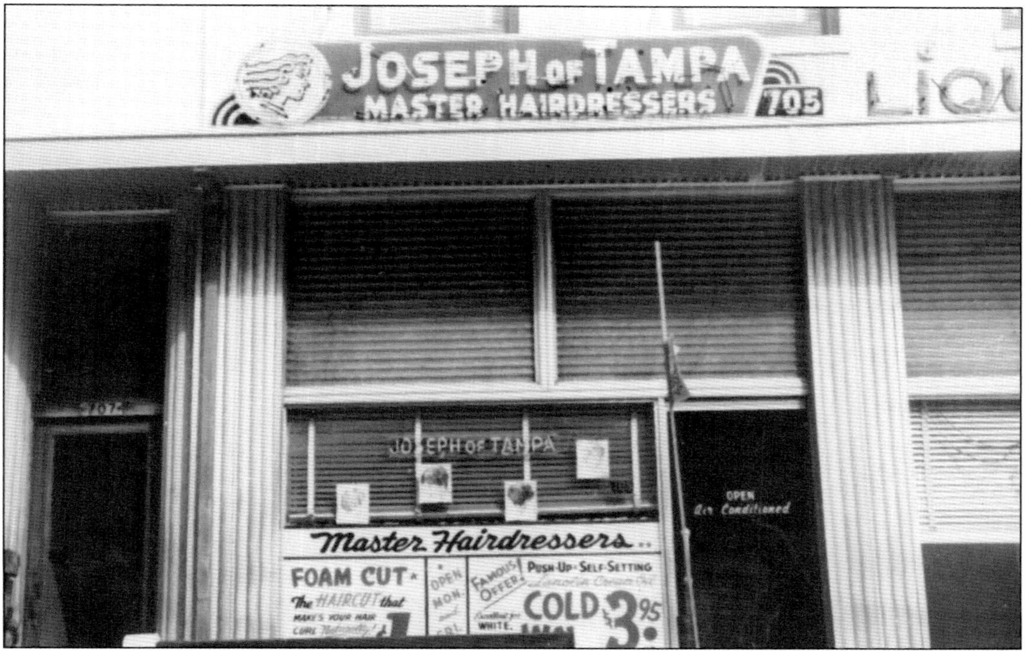

Look at that neon blond in the sign above this popular downtown beauty parlor in 1959. Haircuts were $1 at the salon on North Florida Avenue. Notice that the front door says "Air Conditioned."

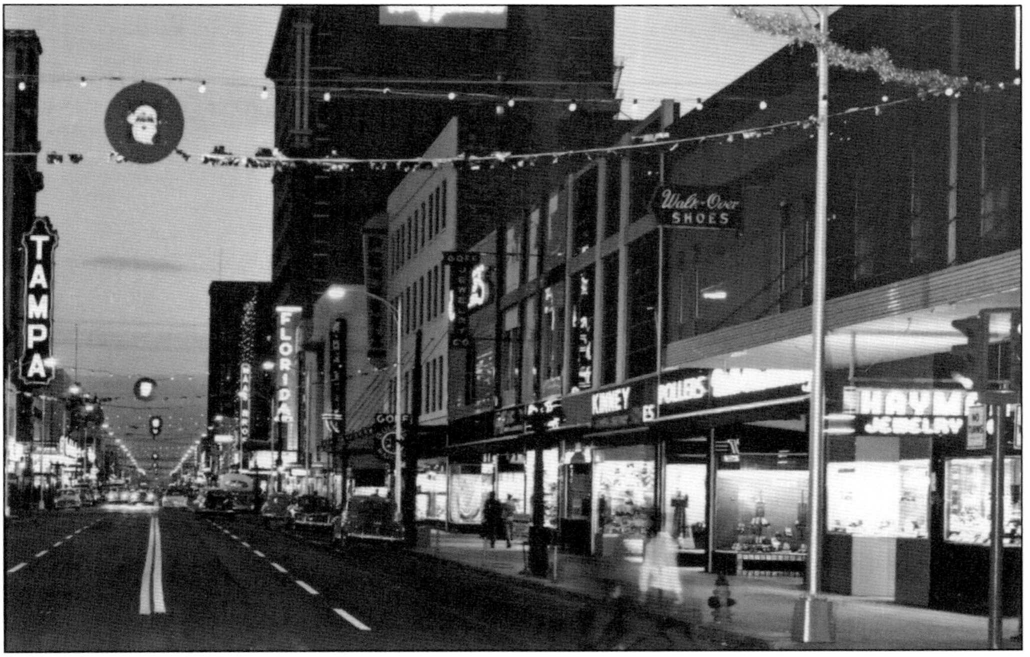

This beautiful 1950 scene along Franklin Street looks south from Cass Street. With lights aglow and those glorious flashing theater marquees, downtown Tampa had a very different look to it during the 1950s. Among the many businesses with colorful signage by Cinchett Neon Signs are Pollers Dress Shop, Kinney Shoes, and the Walk-Over Bootery, all on the west side of Franklin Street. (Courtesy HCPLC.)

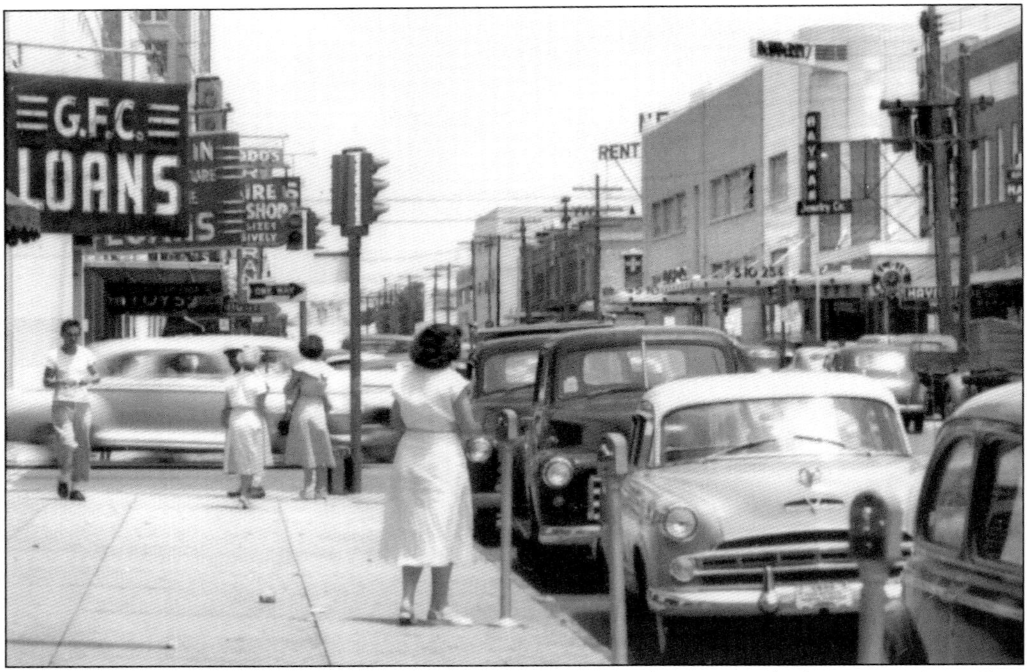

Here is another busy day in 1953 for downtown shoppers. This view is looking east along Cass Street. At the corner of Franklin Street is the Hayman Jewelry Company, where many happy couples made their way with wedding plans in mind. This was one of Tampa's best-known jewelers for over four decades.

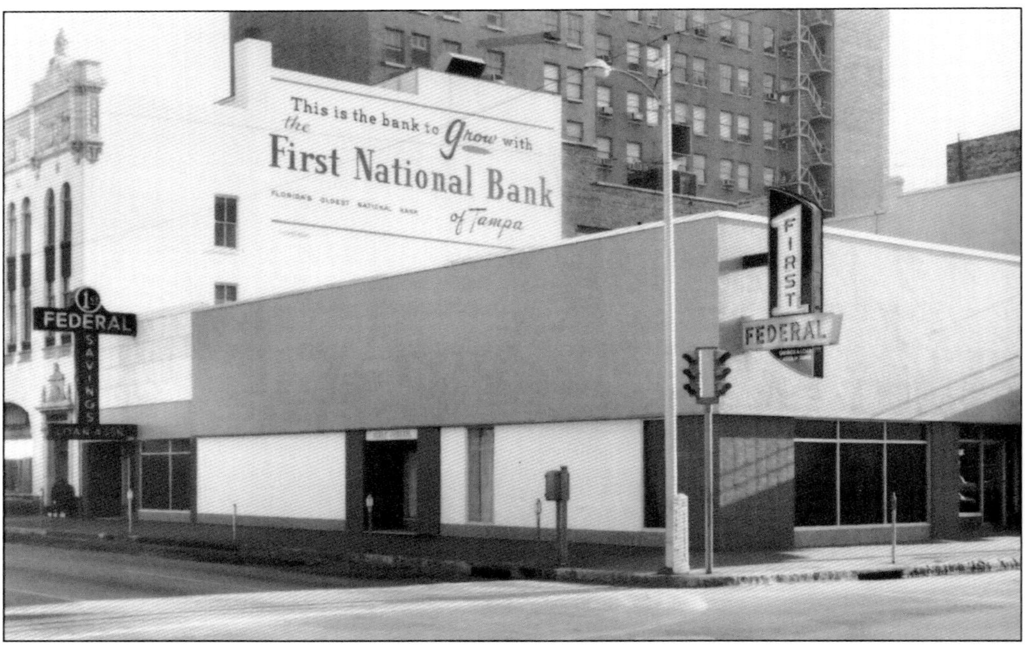

The new neon sign for First Federal proudly appears in this 1958 corner scene at Lafayette and Tampa Streets. Take notice of the monument-style marker that Tampa had installed on street corners designed for pedestrian traffic as well as cars. (Courtesy HCPLC.)

Looking south, this neon "cool-cat" is for the Siamese Cat Lounge, one of downtown's new nightclubs in 1960 at 1118 Franklin Street. This club had no problems with mice, with that giant neon cat guarding the entrance!

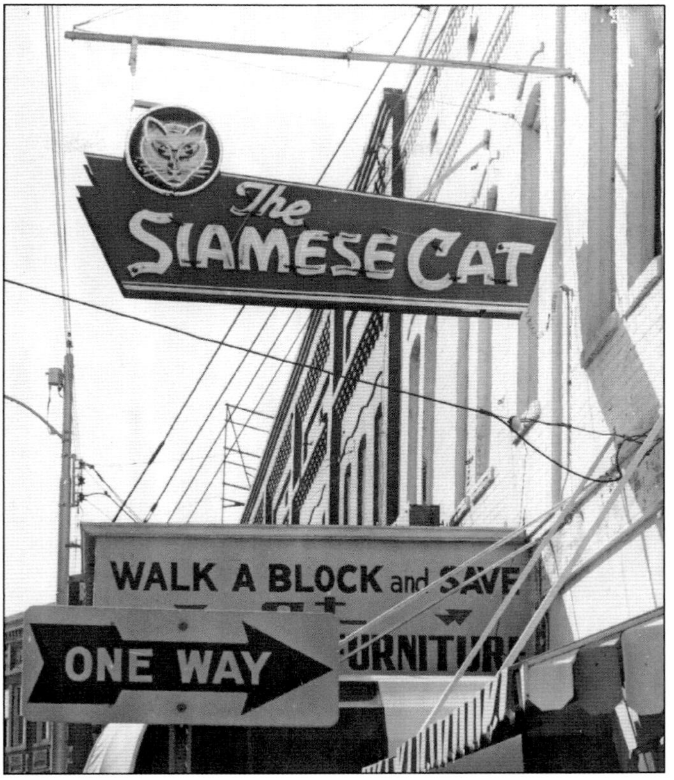

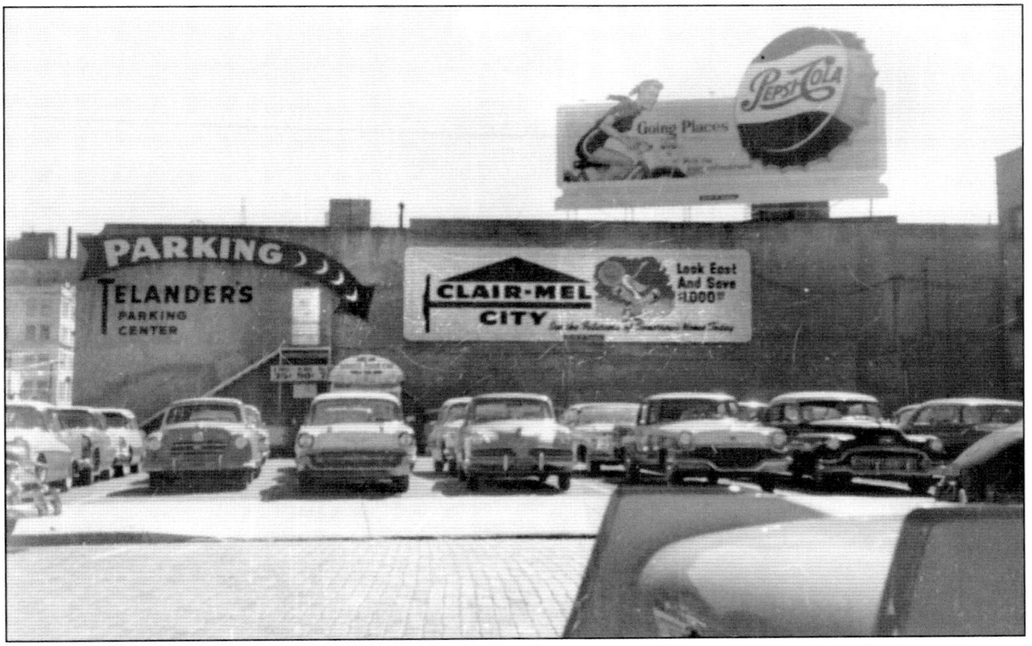

Here is another view of the neon Pepsi-Cola bottle cap in 1958 near Telander's Parking Center on Twiggs Street. The giant neon arrow for Telander's was another landmark for decades. Notice that the vintage Pepsi-Cola design is the original still used during the 1950s.

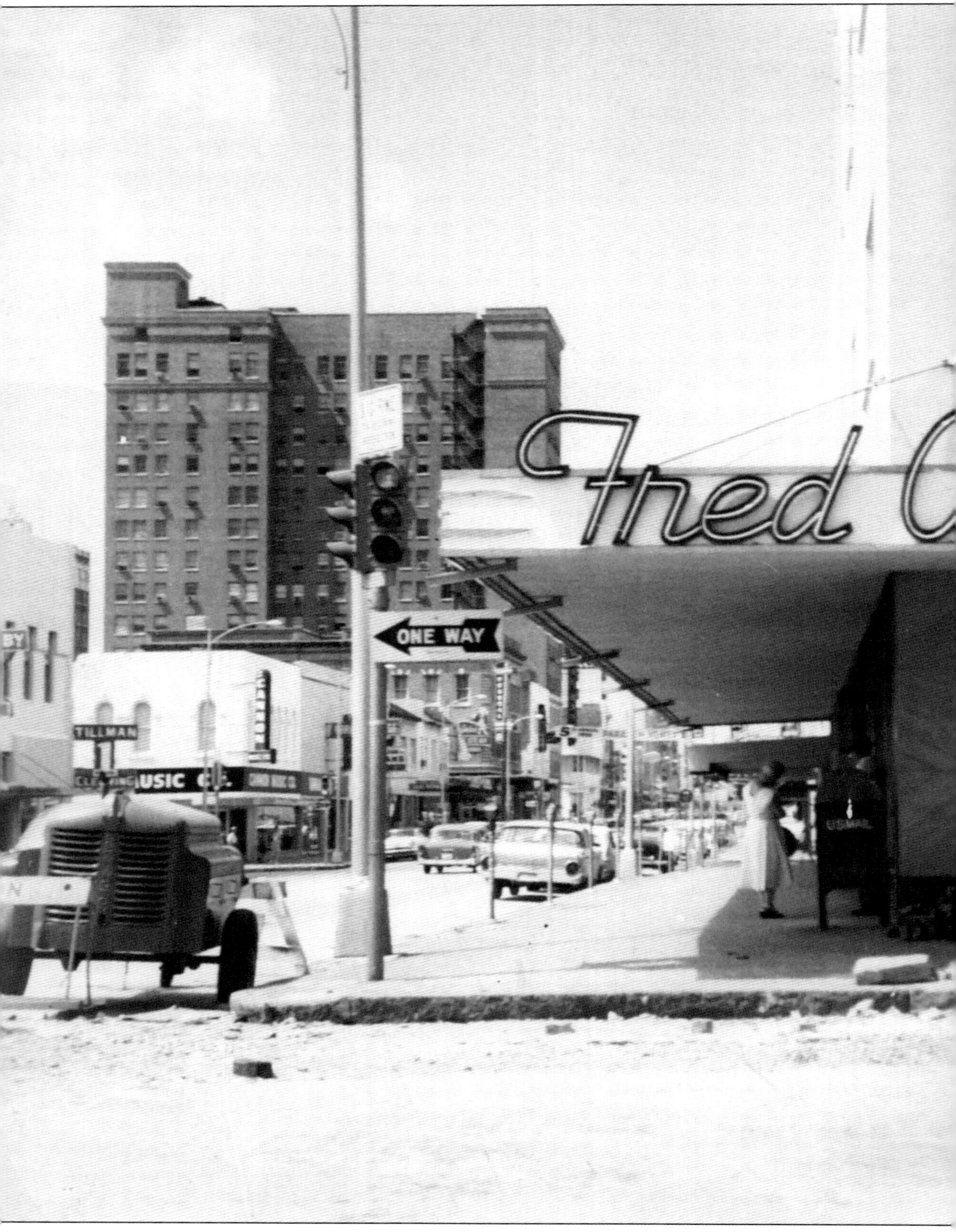
Fred
ONE WAY
TILLMAN
MUSIC CO.

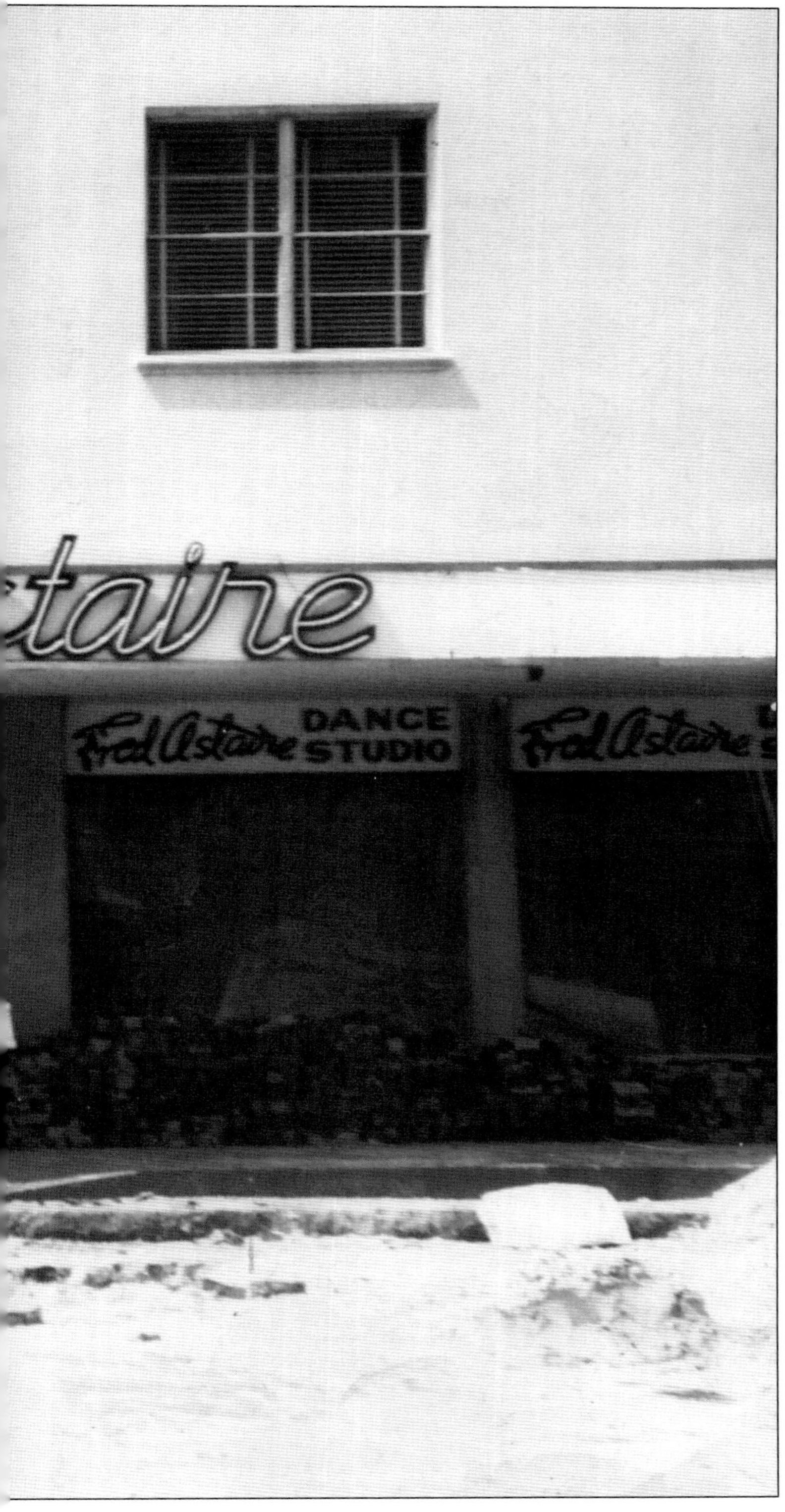

Here is the Fred Astaire Dance Studio on South Franklin Street at Washington Street looking north toward Lafayette Street (now Kennedy Boulevard) in 1957. This was a popular chain of dance studios around the country during the 1950s named after the Hollywood legend. Many popular shops are across the street, including Canon Music, Quinby Electric, and Tillman Cleaners, all well-known, family-owned businesses. Farther down the block is Licata's Steakhouse on the left.

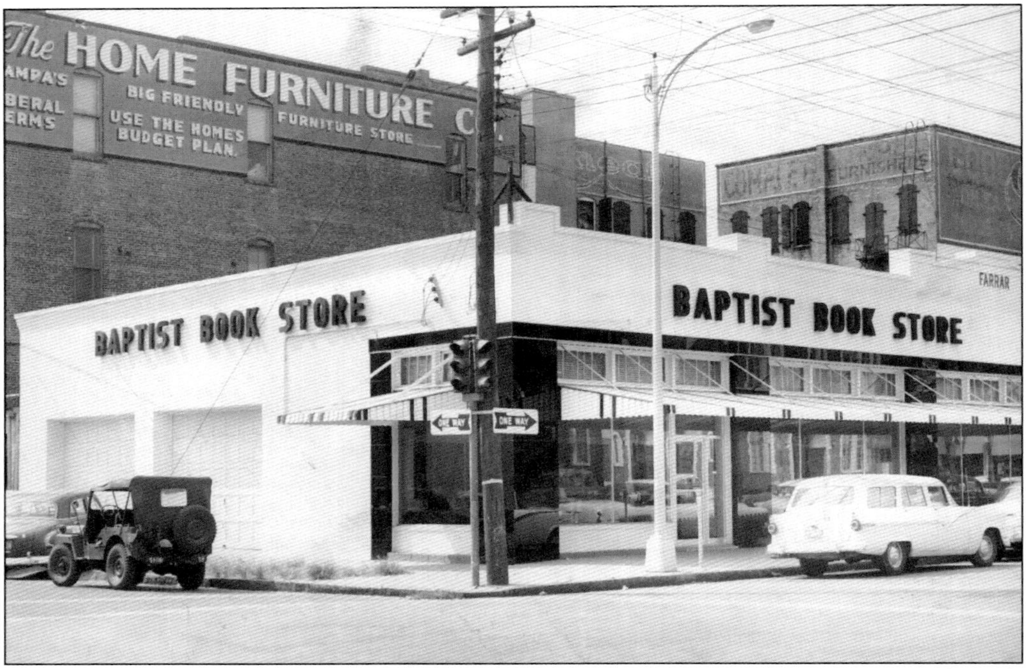

Here is the Baptist Book Store in the old Farrar Tire Company Building at the corner of North Florida Avenue and Tyler Street. This photograph was taken in 1956, and this beautiful building still stands today.

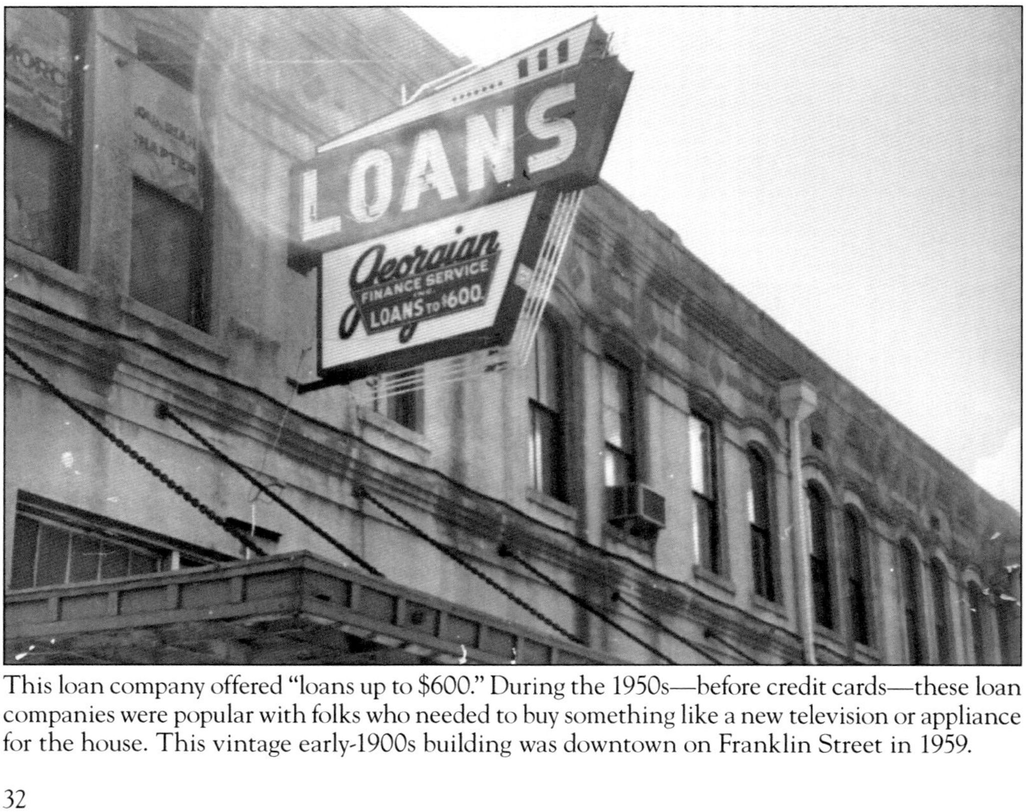

This loan company offered "loans up to $600." During the 1950s—before credit cards—these loan companies were popular with folks who needed to buy something like a new television or appliance for the house. This vintage early-1900s building was downtown on Franklin Street in 1959.

Two

Tampa Has an Appetite for Neon

Neon signs became synonymous with diners and nightclubs all across America in the 1950s. Those flashing roadside arrows were as popular as 1957 Chevys, lighting up the highways and sending drivers into busy burger joints along city boulevards. As folks fell in love with their cars and the highways expanded, so did local drive-ins, roadside cafés, and cocktail lounges. These were the glory days for curb-service restaurants and diners lining Tampa's ever-expanding highways. Tampa restaurant owners were enjoying the rewards of the city's record growth, and many of them established local family-owned places that would continue providing enjoyable dinners to hungry Tampa folks for decades. Popular neighborhood cafés established a loyal following; families would often plan a weekly outing for dinner and came to know the owners on a first-name basis. That warm and friendly service became a trademark for Tampa's family-owned restaurants offering every type of dish, from devil crabs to sirloin steaks.

Many of these nostalgic photographs will bring back happy memories of days gone by, when families would pack into the Buick and head out for dinner to their favorite dining spots. Some of these places became local institutions where Tampa lawyers met to discuss trials over lunch or young couples made wedding plans over dinner. Everywhere along Tampa's city streets, neon signs lit the way into favorite local gathering spots and greasy spoons. The designs of these neon signs were extraordinary—they were bright shining works of art that actually became local landmarks in some neighborhoods.

These amazing pictures hearken back to those glorious days of carhops and poodle skirts. Memories of visiting the ice cream stand to cool off after hot summer days at the swimming hole might flood back as these captivating images stir up fond remembrances of fun times and lazy afternoons. This nostalgic collection of photographs takes one back to simpler days and friends gathering for shakes at the corner soda fountain or an after-school meeting with buddies at one of the burger joints around town.

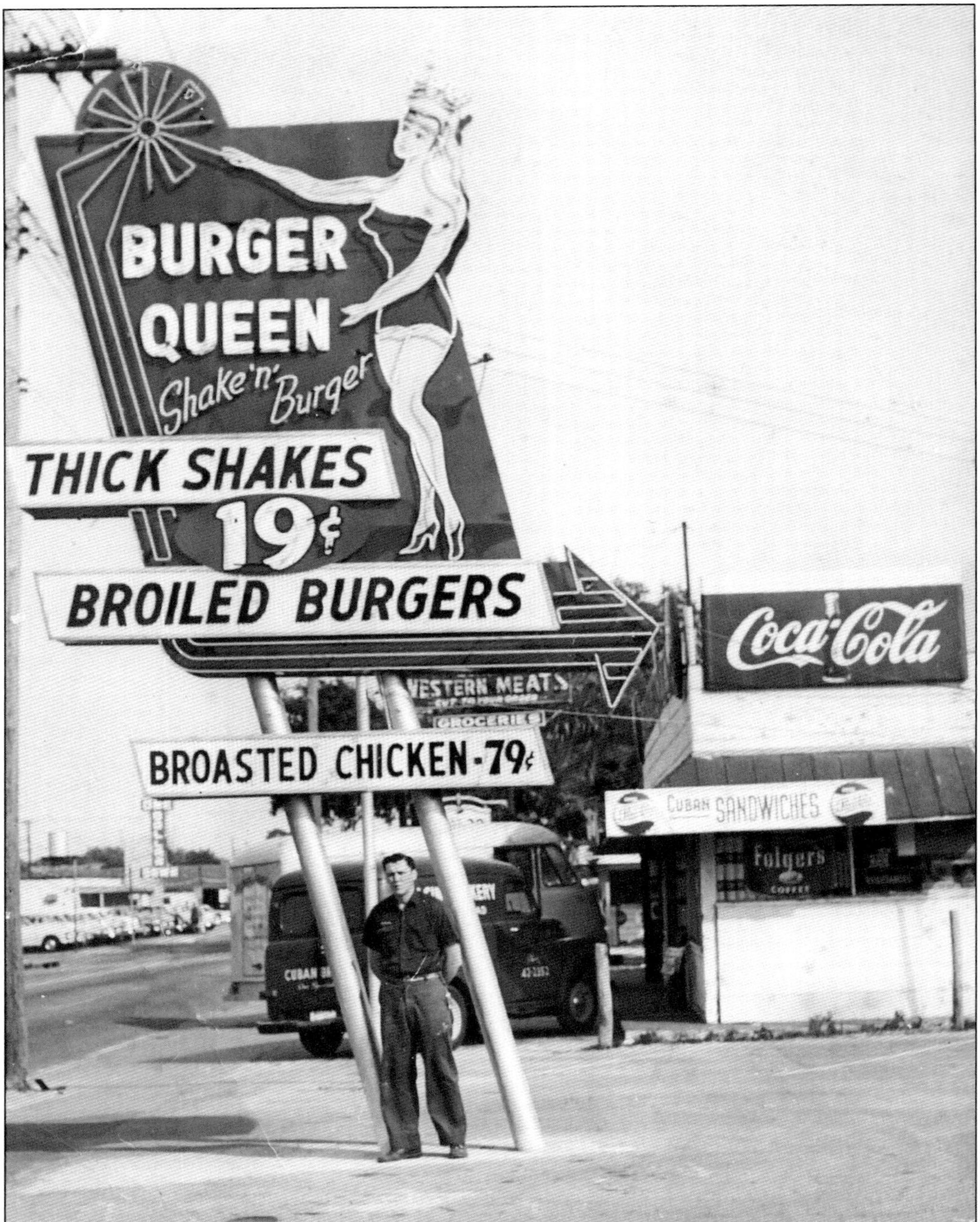

Burger Queen was one of the first established chain restaurants in Tampa. The "broasted chicken" was a popular feature of this restaurant, and the owner declared it to be the wave of the future. This neon beauty was completed in 1958 on Florida Avenue. Across the street, a used-car lot advertises "One-Dollar-Down." In this photograph looking north at Osborne Avenue, John F. Cinchett poses with his creation.

Licata's Steakhouse was one of Tampa's most famous restaurants during the 1950s and 1960s with an elegant flair for fine dining. The restaurant was actually located in the basement of the building down a long stairwell off the street level, where the maître d' waited to seat customers. This legendary gathering spot was at 108 Jackson Street at Franklin Street in the Knight-Wall building.

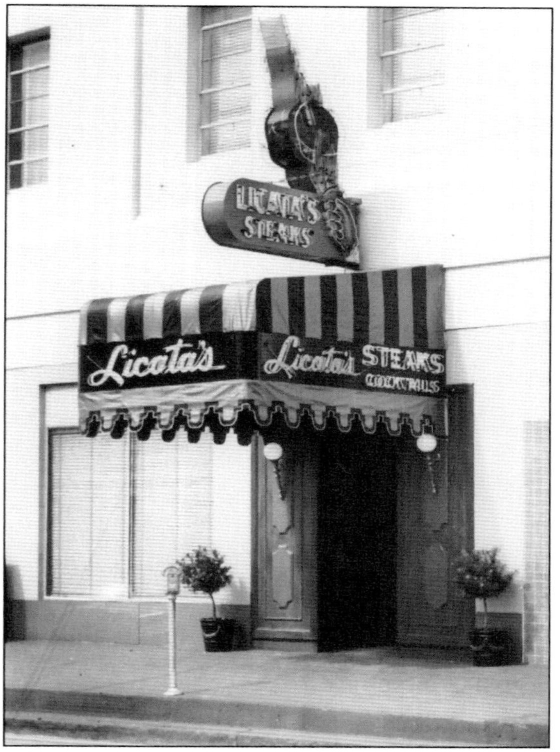

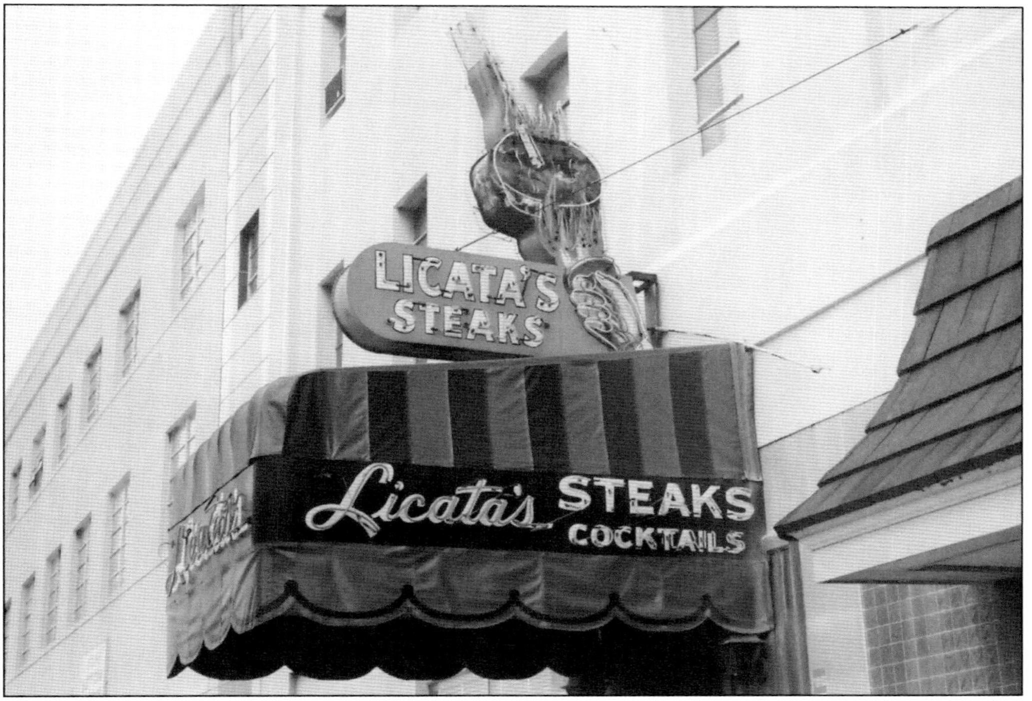

Here is another view of the Licata's restaurant sign, a spectacular flaming neon steak skewer. This was Tampa's most popular downtown restaurant in the 1950s.

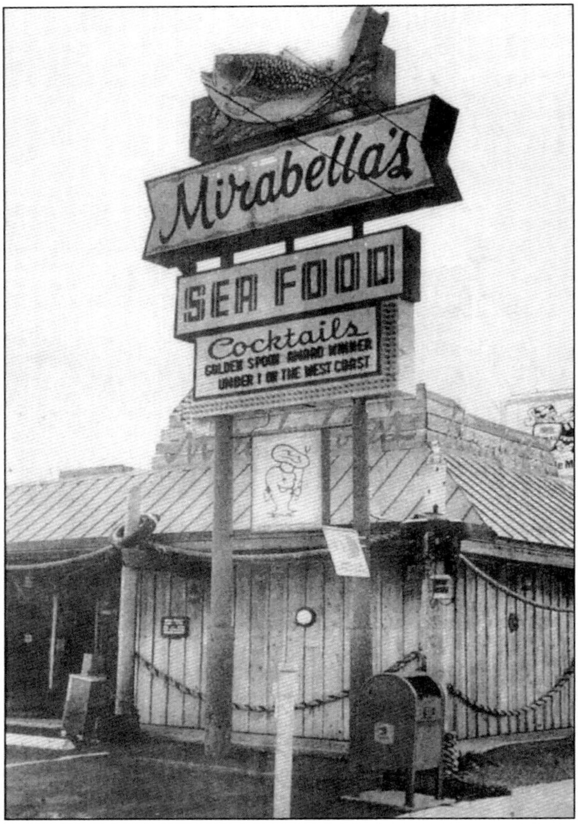

The Mirabella family's Tampa legacy began in the 1920s with their downtown seafood company, which later became a riverside market and restaurant where patrons enjoyed fresh fish on picnic tables alongside the river. In 1952, Frank Mirabella opened this restaurant at 327 North Dale Mabry Highway, and it became Tampa's best-known restaurant for seafood dinners. Buster and Frank Mirabella created another legendary family-owned business success story that Tampa folks still recall today.

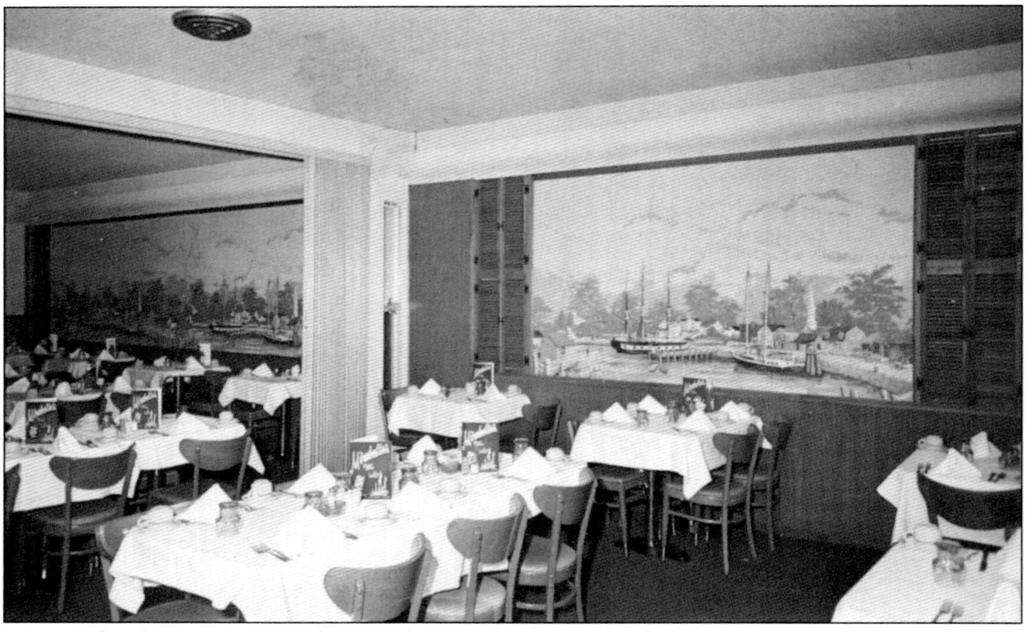

Here is the dining room at the popular Mirabella's seafood restaurant in 1952. Tampa diners enjoyed the city's best grouper sandwiches and hushpuppies here for almost 40 years.

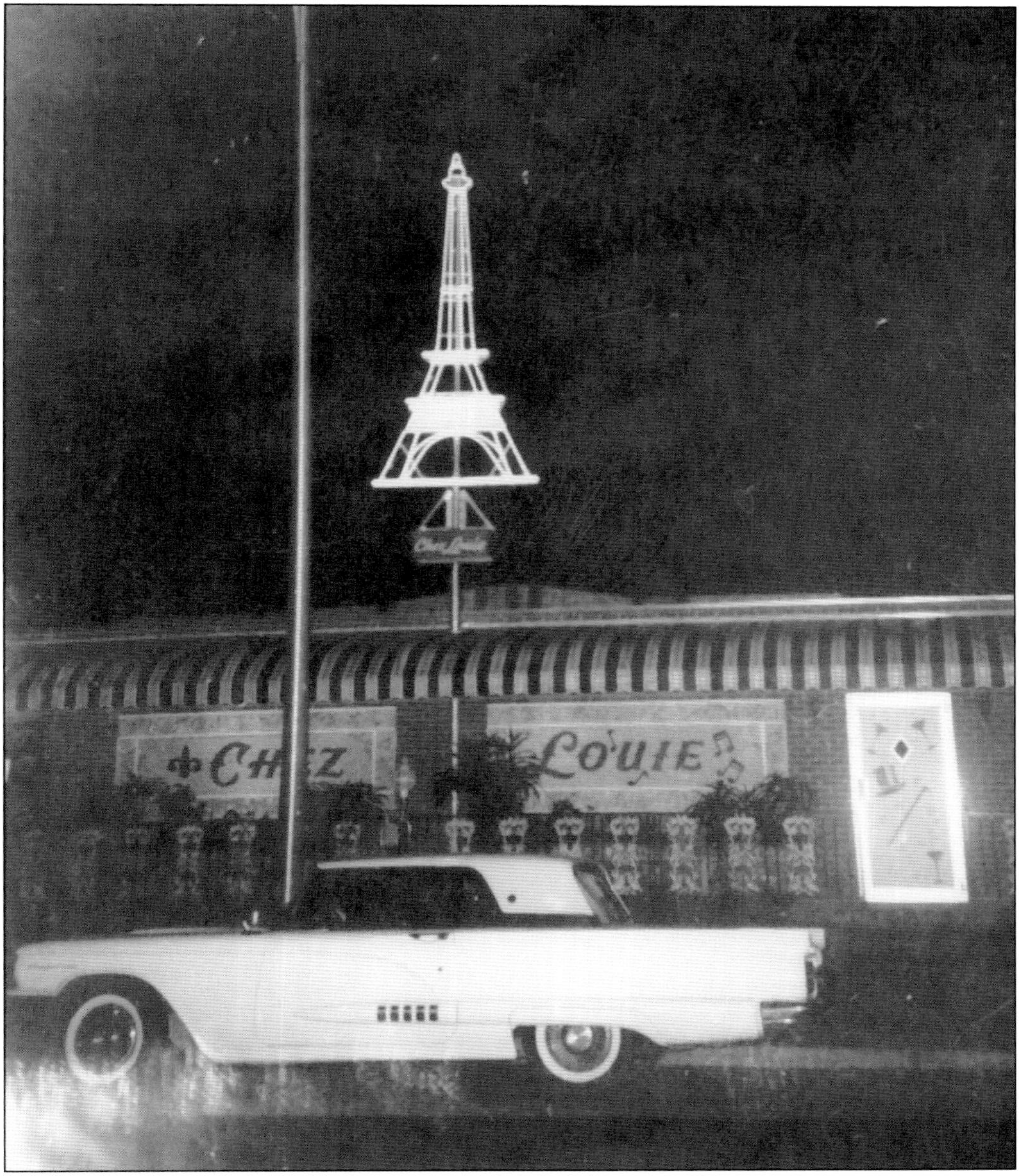

This spectacular neon Eiffel Tower, nearly 15 feet tall, directed patrons into the Chez Louie, Tampa's finest nightclub, in 1960. This neon masterpiece was at 4407 West Grand Central Avenue (now Kennedy Boulevard). The neon tower, another marvel by Cinchett Neon Signs, actually rotated above the roof of the building. The car parked out front is a brand new 1960 Thunderbird.

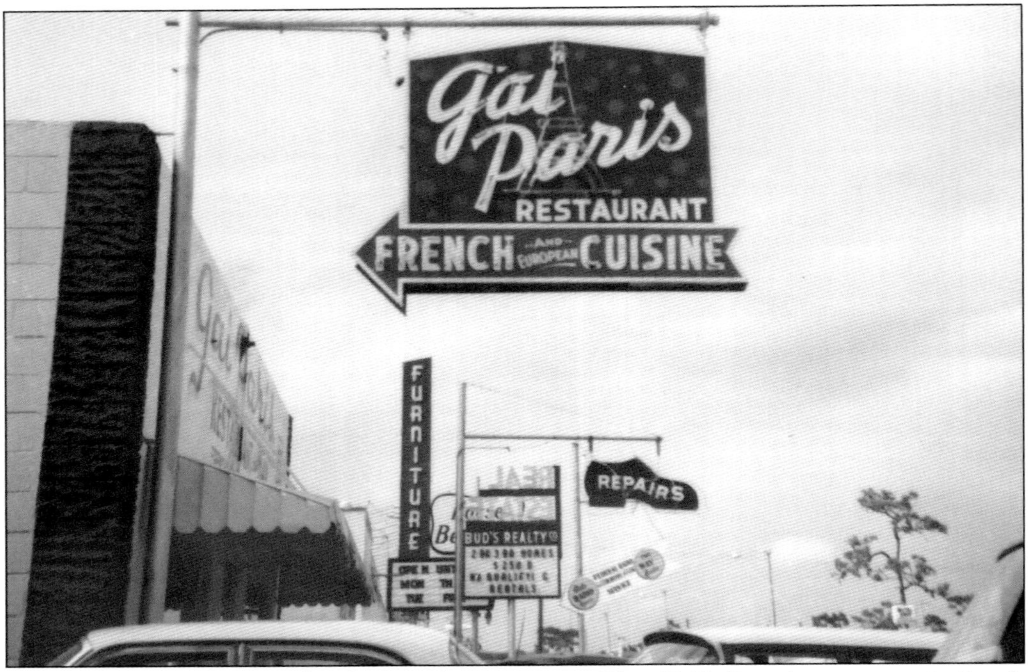

Look closely—there are polka dots on this neon sign. This 1960s French restaurant in South Tampa welcomed patrons with another neon Eiffel Tower. Notice the shoe shop next door with its neon shoe hanging over the sidewalk.

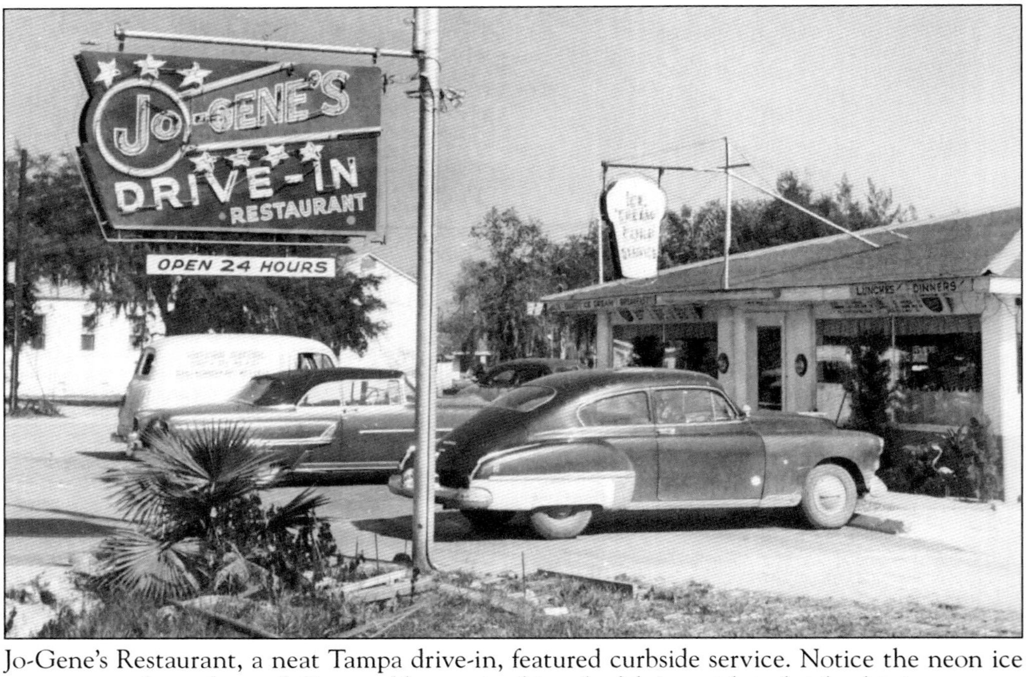

Jo-Gene's Restaurant, a neat Tampa drive-in, featured curbside service. Notice the neon ice cream cone above the roof. One could not miss this colorful sign with its bright shining stars on Nebraska Avenue at Linebaugh Avenue in 1956. This was also a popular hangout for kids leaving the nearby swimming hole to have an ice cream cone on the way home.

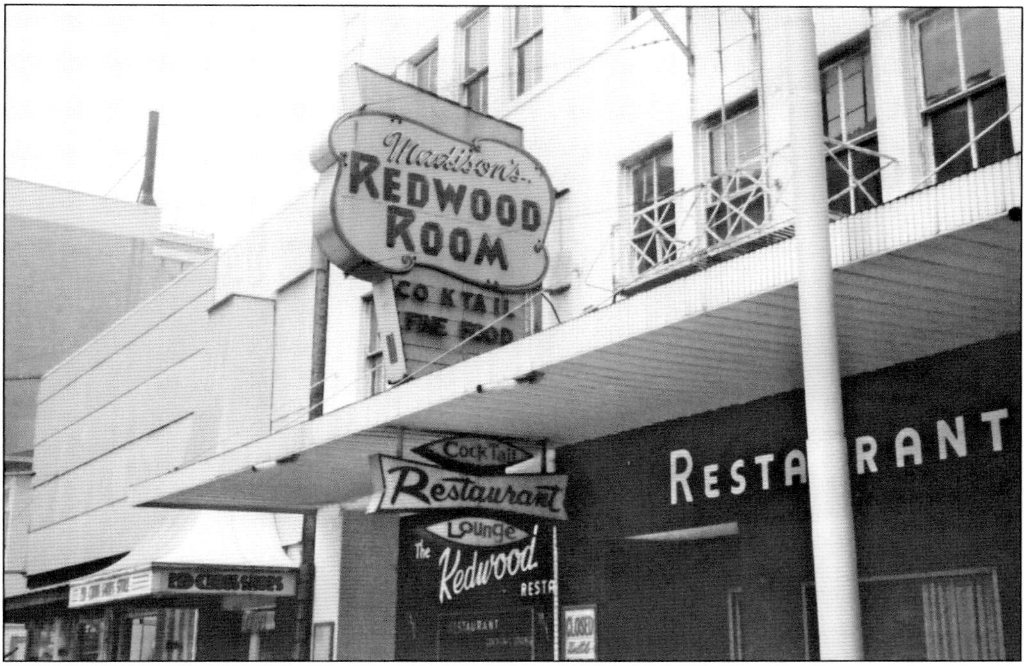

The Redwood Room was another popular restaurant and friendly cocktail lounge during the 1950s and 1960s at 513 Tampa Street downtown. Today another popular restaurant occupies this vintage building.

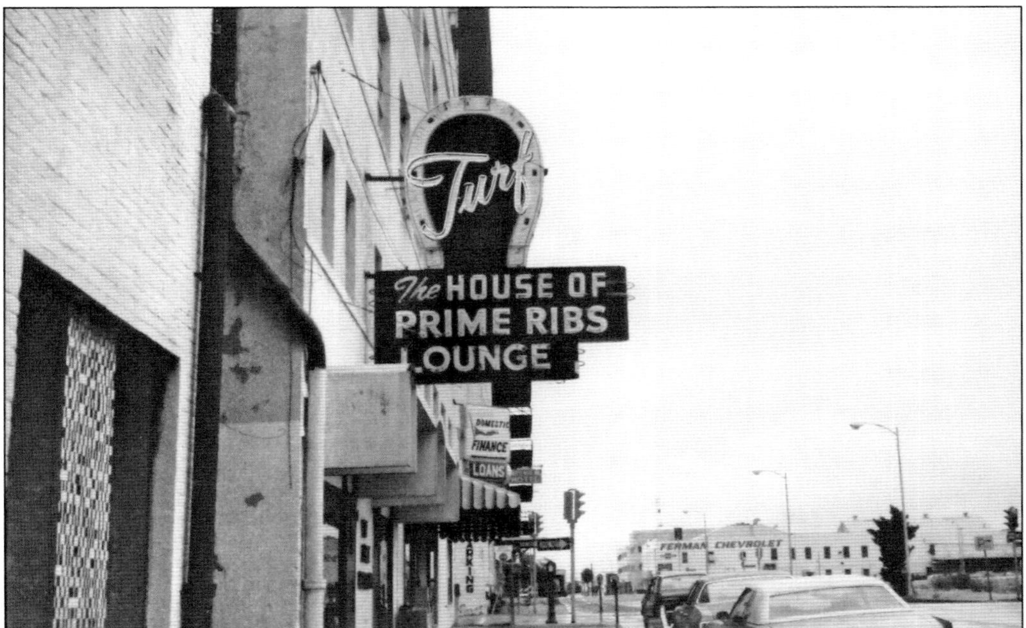

During the 1950s and 1960s, patrons of this popular restaurant must have felt lucky to enter beneath the giant flashing horseshoe pictured here. The Turf Bar and Grill was a downtown fixture for decades at 106 Jackson Street near the Bay View Hotel. Looking east, one can see Ferman Chevrolet still at its original downtown location in this 1968 scene.

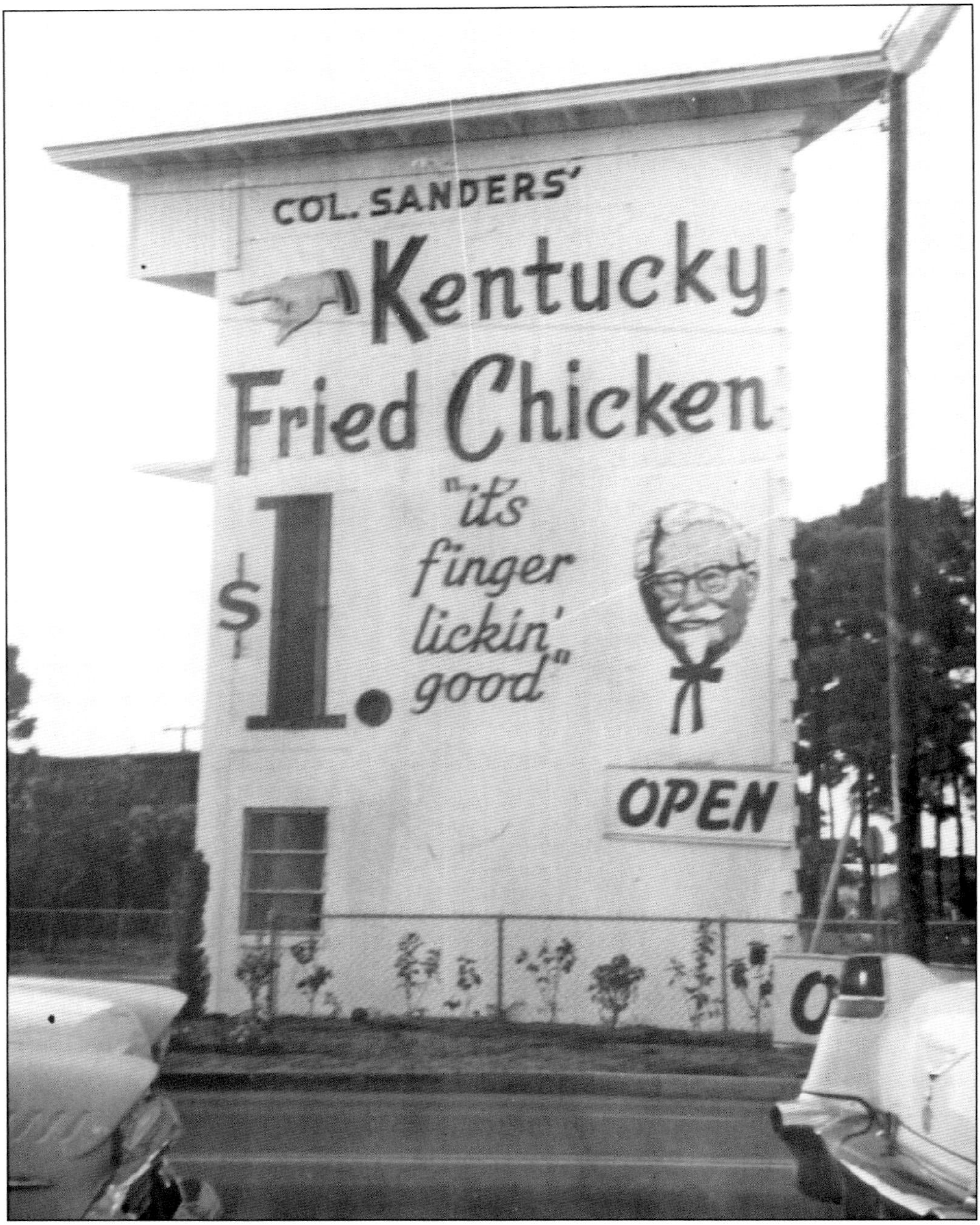

In 1962, Col. Harland Sanders arrived in Tampa and contracted Cinchett Neon Signs to complete the work on his first two Kentucky Fried Chicken locations in West Central Florida. This giant neon edifice was a landmark for the location at Dale Mabry Highway and Henderson Boulevard for over three decades. This view looks across Dale Mabry. The other location was on North Florida Avenue in North Tampa.

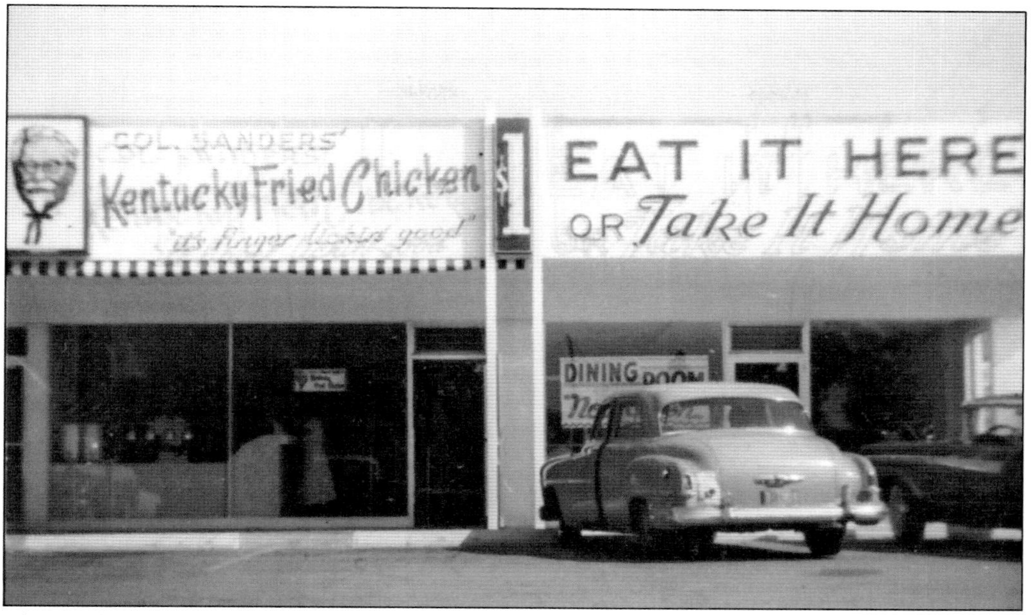

This is the first Kentucky Fried Chicken restaurant in West Central Florida, which opened in 1962 on North Florida Avenue at Fairbanks Street. Colonel Sanders knew that Tampa was having a population boom, and he wanted to be one of the successful businesses enjoying the city's growth. Notice the giant neon $1 sign. The below scene looks north along Florida Avenue, and this was one of the first revolving bucket signs ever created. Notice the prices: $1 for a fish or chicken dinner and 25¢ more for shrimp.

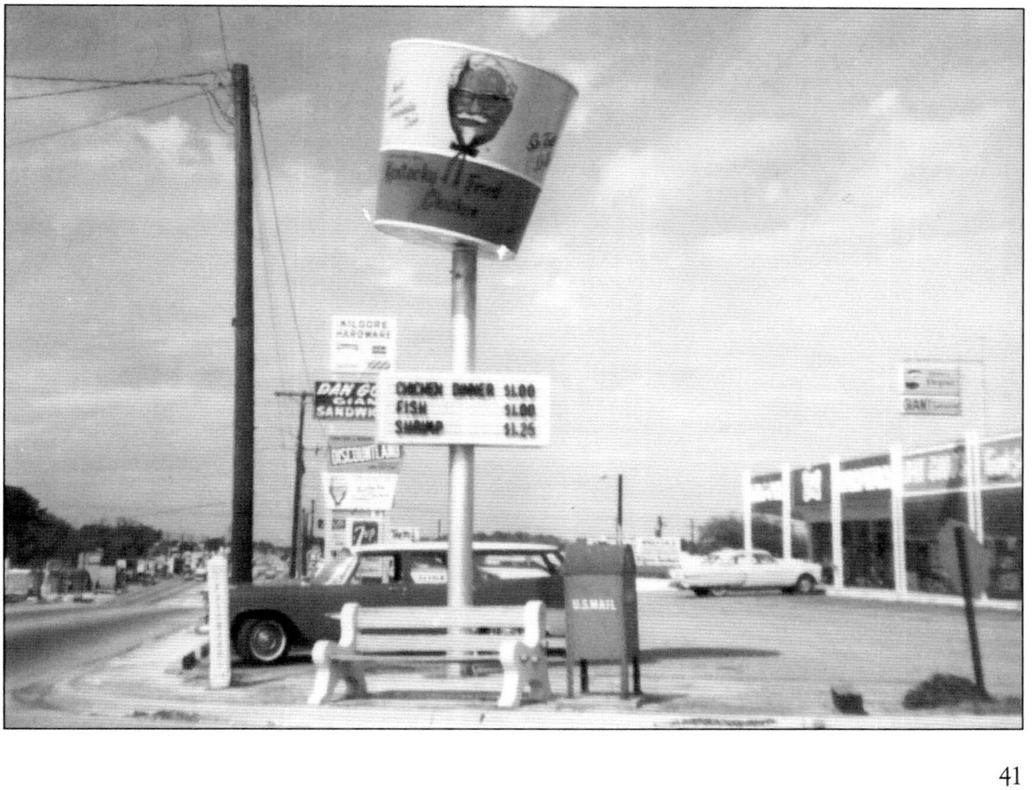

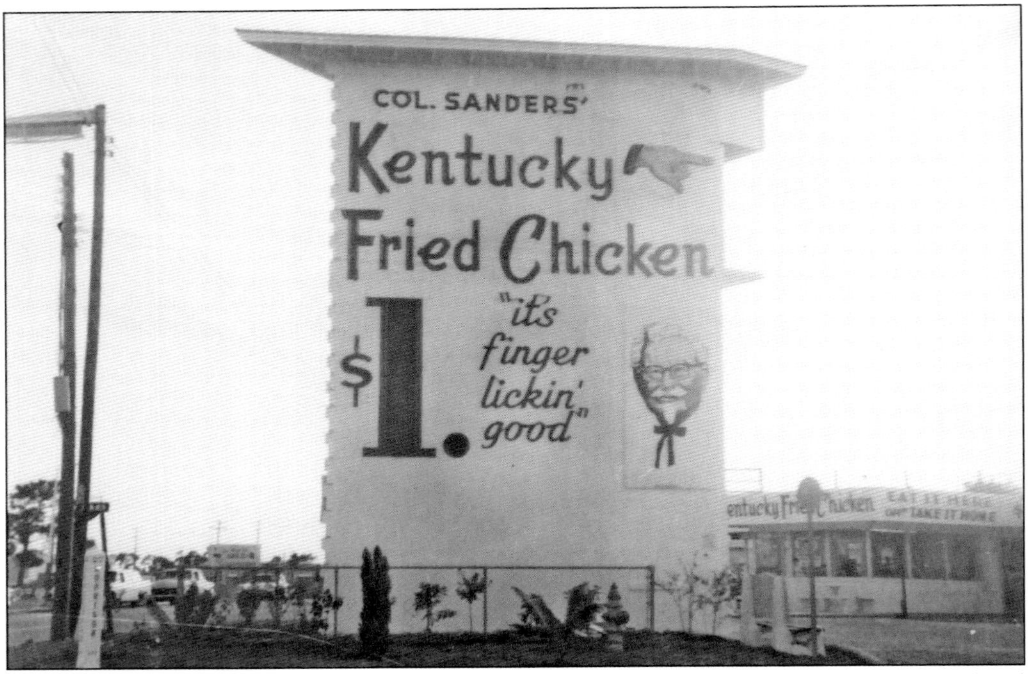

Here is the giant Kentucky Fried Chicken sign looking south along Dale Mabry Highway. Colonel Sanders liked to do business with local family-owned shops, so when he passed the Cinchett Neon Signs Company on Florida Avenue, he decided to stop in and introduce himself. He liked the proposed designs so much that he awarded the sign company his contract for neon signage at both of his first locations in Tampa.

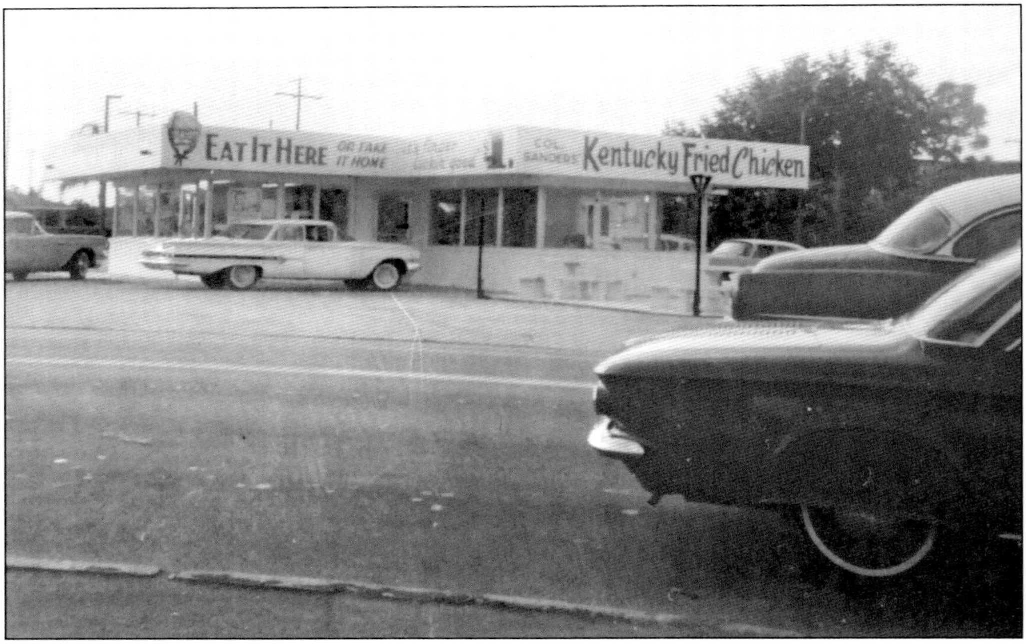

This is the Kentucky Fried Chicken restaurant on Dale Mabry Highway at Henderson Boulevard in 1962. Notice the sign says $1 for a whole chicken dinner.

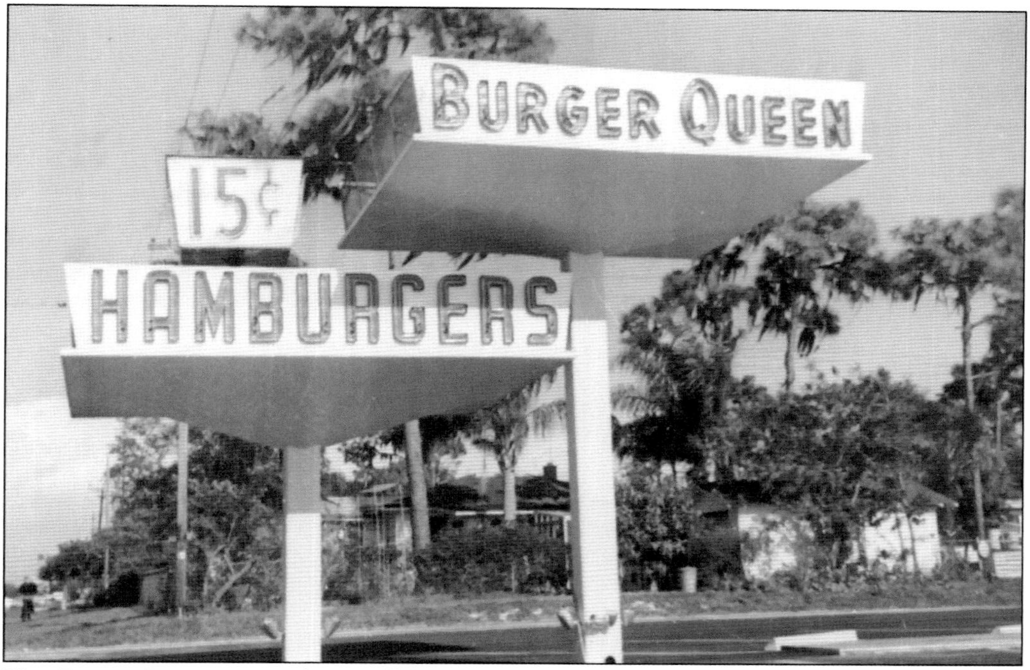

This Burger Queen was on busy Hillsborough Avenue. One could stop here and pick up some burgers on the way to the Hillsboro Drive-In or Fun-Lan Drive-In, both within a couple of miles in either direction of this burger palace. The picture above was taken on Hillsborough Avenue looking east, just east of Rome Avenue, in 1960. In the photograph below is the revolving 15¢ sign—that is all one needed for a burger.

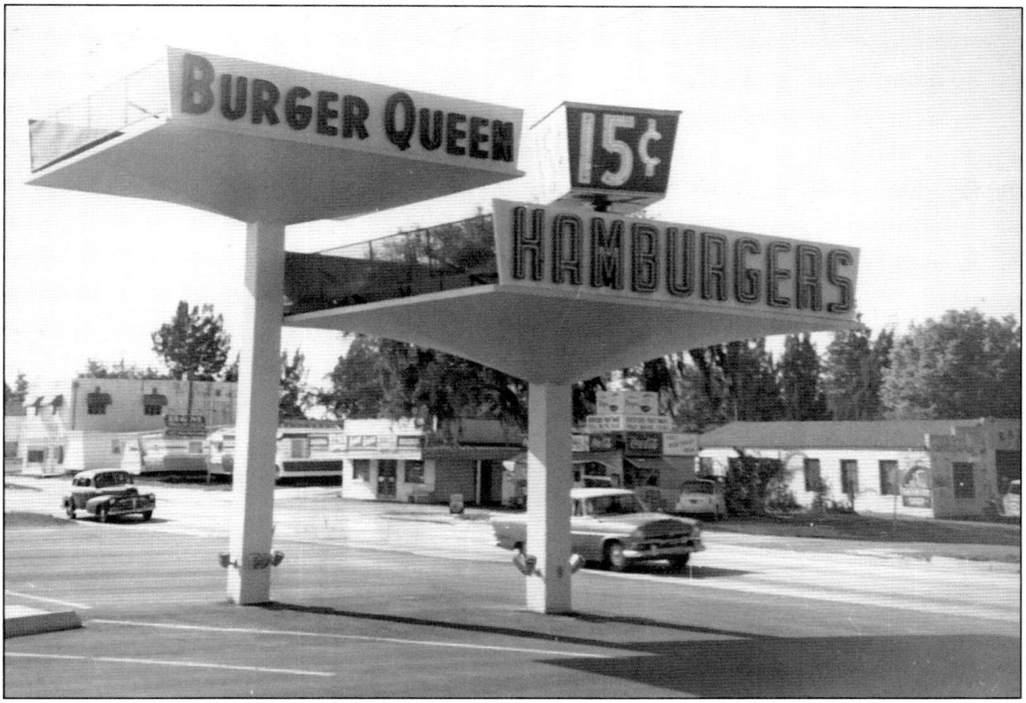

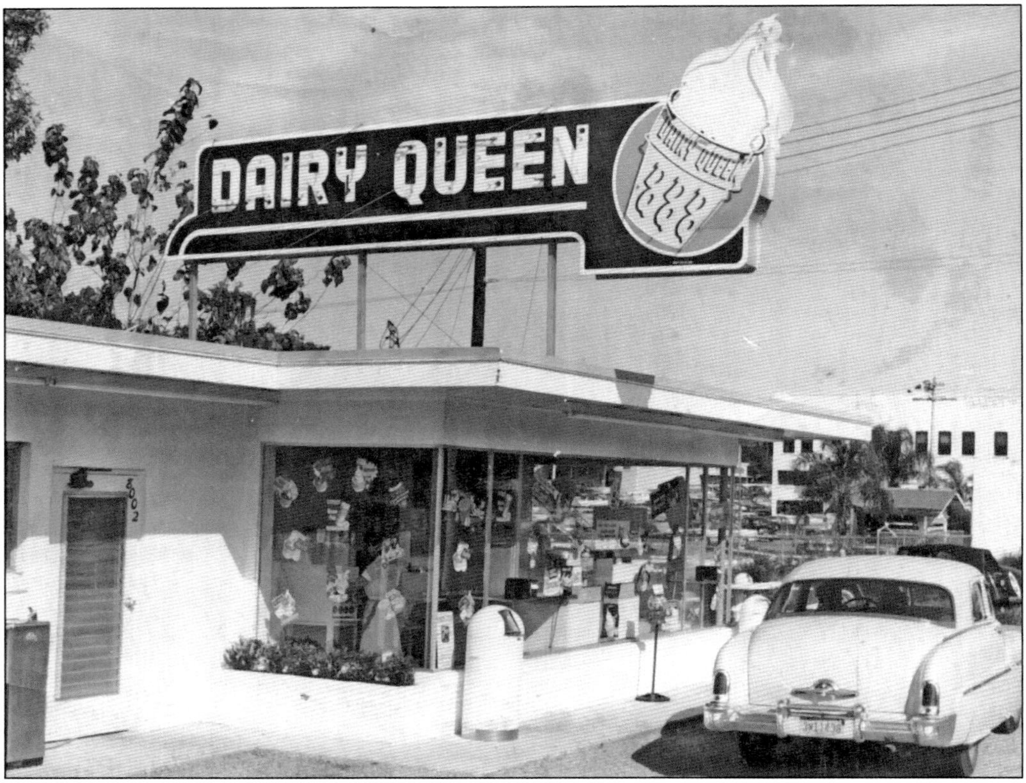

This Dairy Queen, one of Tampa's first, was located in Sulphur Springs on Nebraska Avenue at the bridge near the Sulphur Springs pool, a popular gathering spot for decades. Looking north in this 1956 photograph, one can also see the Sulphur Springs Arcade.

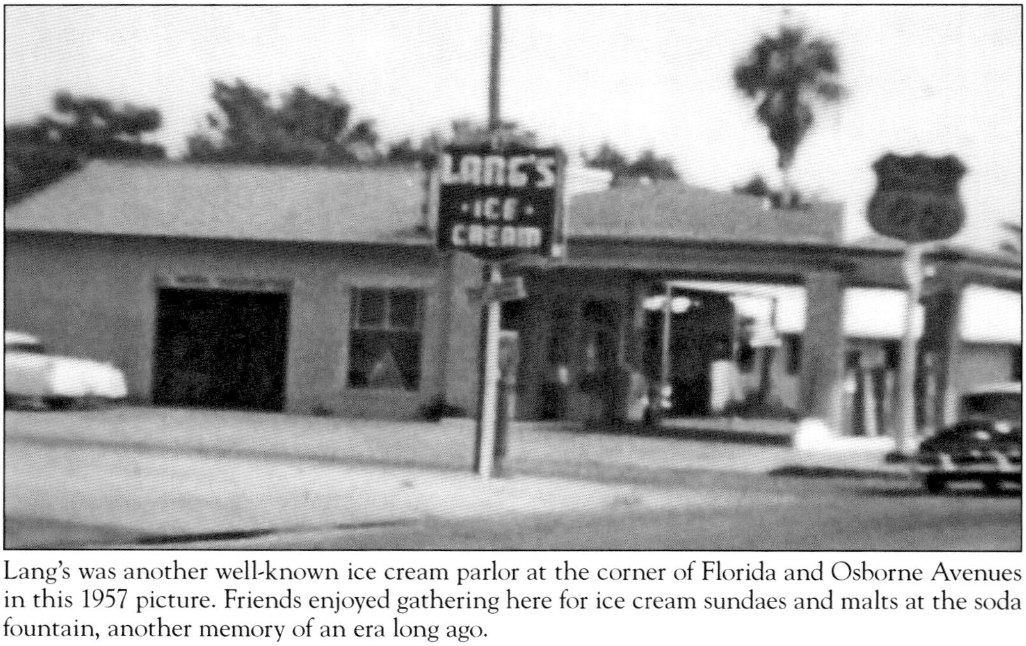

Lang's was another well-known ice cream parlor at the corner of Florida and Osborne Avenues in this 1957 picture. Friends enjoyed gathering here for ice cream sundaes and malts at the soda fountain, another memory of an era long ago.

This neon sign lit up the entire street corner in 1958 for Burger Queen on Florida Avenue, where shakes only cost 19¢. This Seminole Heights location was a popular spot for teenagers attending nearby Hillsborough High and was another great Friday night hangout on the way to the movies.

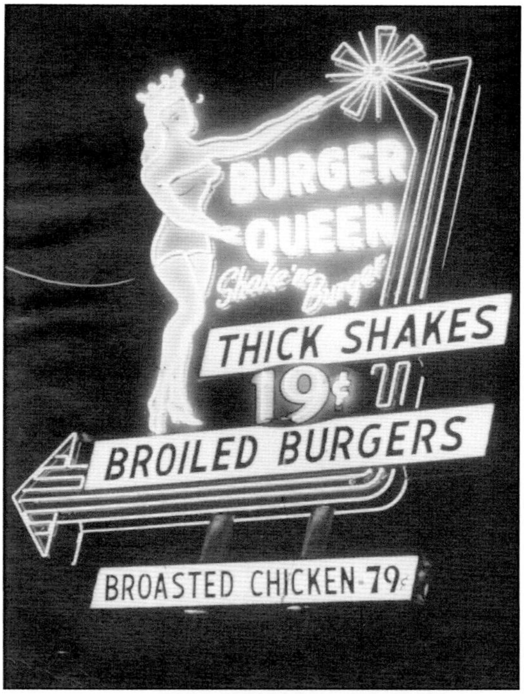

Welcome to the Chicken Pit at 4718 Gandy Boulevard, a popular stop for folks on the way to the beach. This photograph looks west on Gandy Boulevard in 1965. Notice the sign says "Take-Out or Eat-Here." Another vintage find in this photograph is next door at the gas station, the S&H Green Stamp sign. It looks like gas was on sale for 33¢ a gallon.

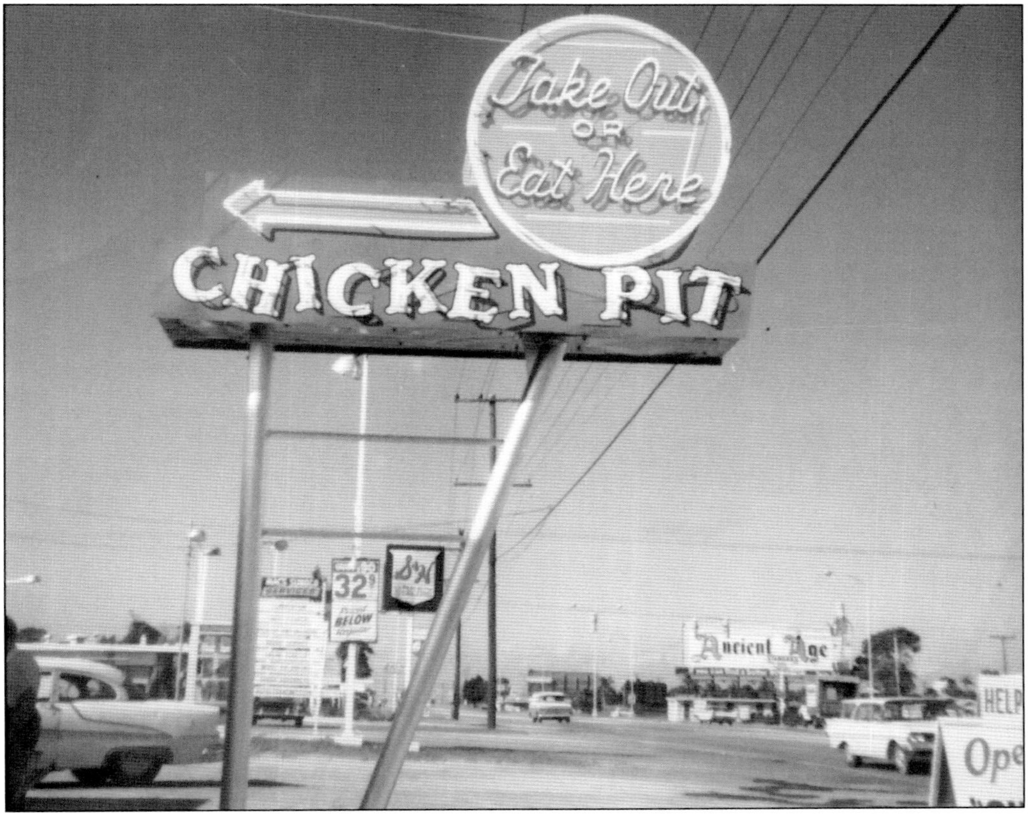

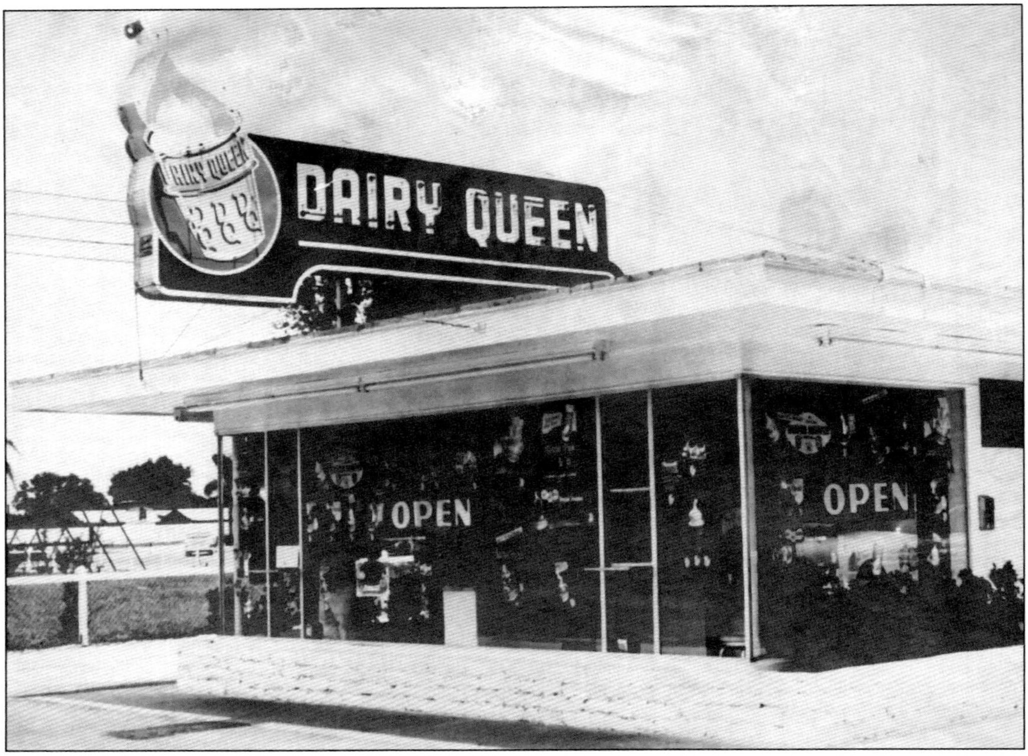

This Dairy Queen opened on Hillsborough Avenue just east of Nebraska Avenue in 1956. Notice the playground offered for children just left of the restaurant.

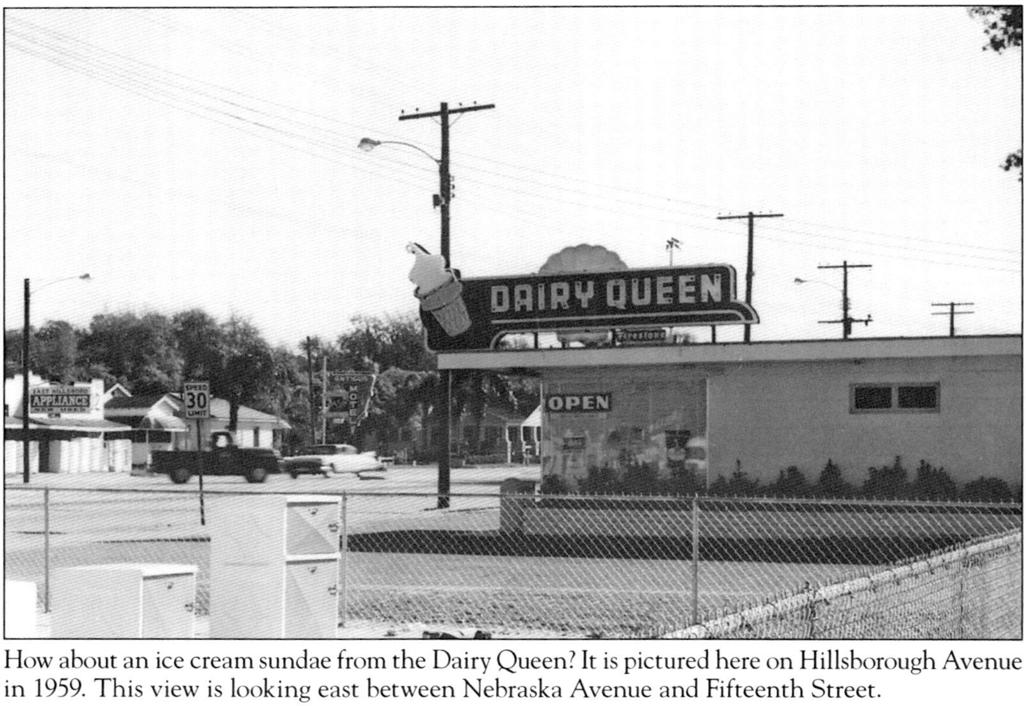

How about an ice cream sundae from the Dairy Queen? It is pictured here on Hillsborough Avenue in 1959. This view is looking east between Nebraska Avenue and Fifteenth Street.

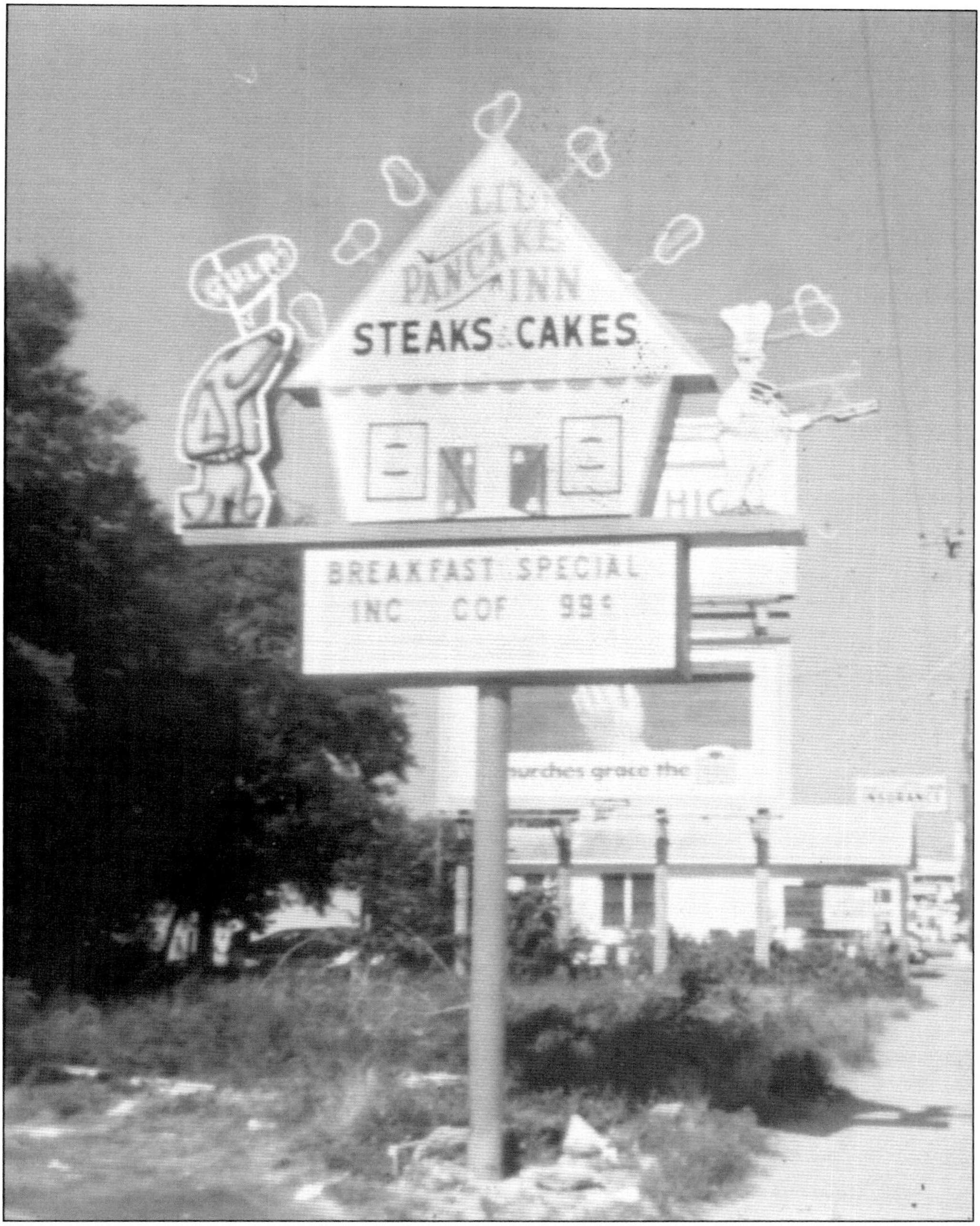

The neon sign for this restaurant is truly a step back in time. This was a popular breakfast destination for Seminole Heights residents on East Hillsborough Avenue near Fifteenth Street in the late 1960s. This sign featured a neon chef flipping pancakes over a doghouse to the hungry pup. When he catches it, the neon sign says "GULP!"

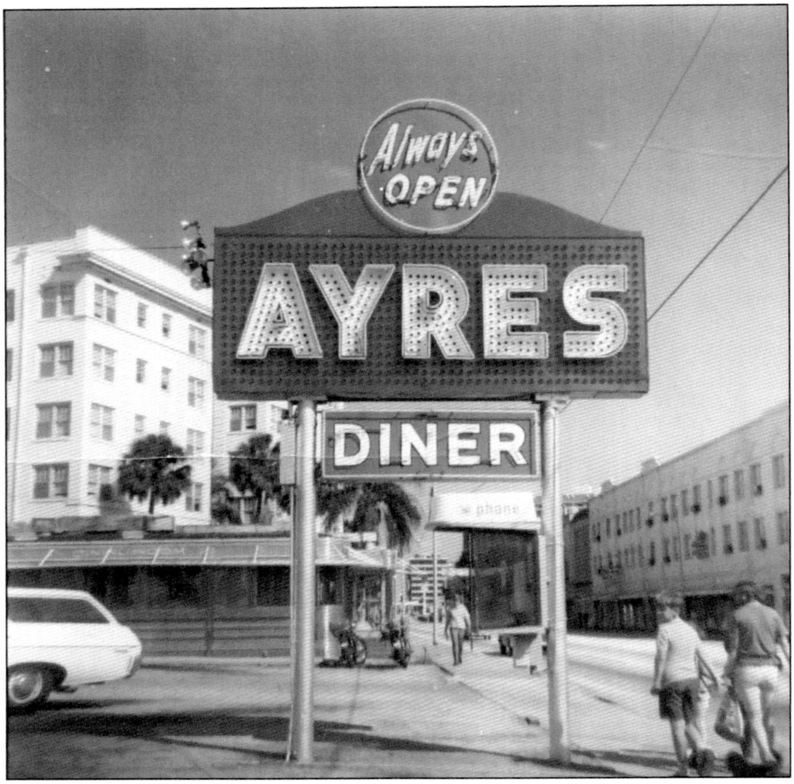

The Ayres Diner, at 603 Lafayette Street (now Kennedy Boulevard) near the University of Tampa, was popular during the 1950s. This was one of several dining-car style diners around Tampa. Notice that the top of the sign reads "Always Open" in neon. Diners could stop in anytime to enjoy a hot cup of coffee and a sandwich on their favorite stool at the counter.

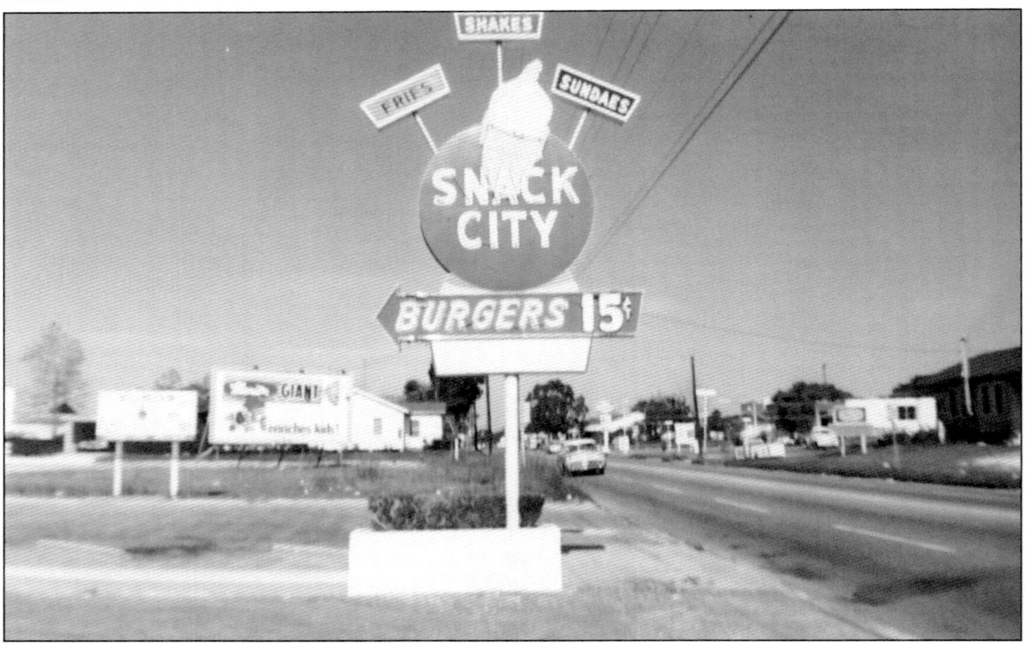

Welcome to Snack City, West Tampa's most popular drive-in for ice cream and burgers. This 1960s hangout was on Columbus Drive just west of Armenia Avenue. It still serves snacks today, but the lollipop sign is just a memory.

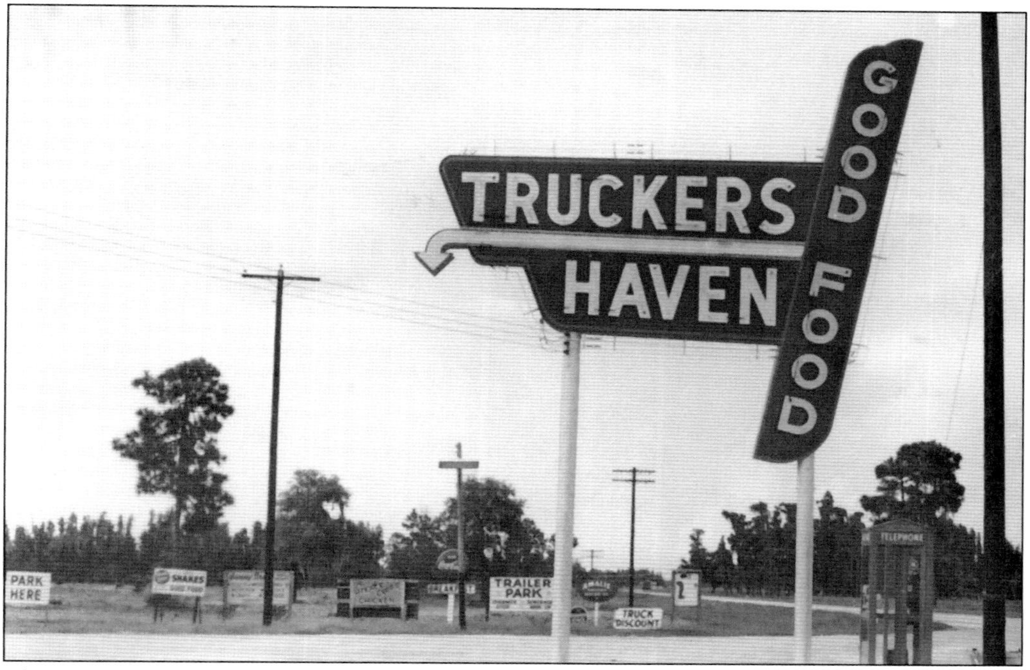

This sign is quite typical of highway signage of the 1950s that attracted drivers (in this case truck drivers) along busy highways into nearby restaurants. Notice the 1950s style of advertising "Good Food." Another vintage symbol in this photograph is the telephone booth right next to the highway. This 1957 scene is along U.S. Highway 41 north of Tampa.

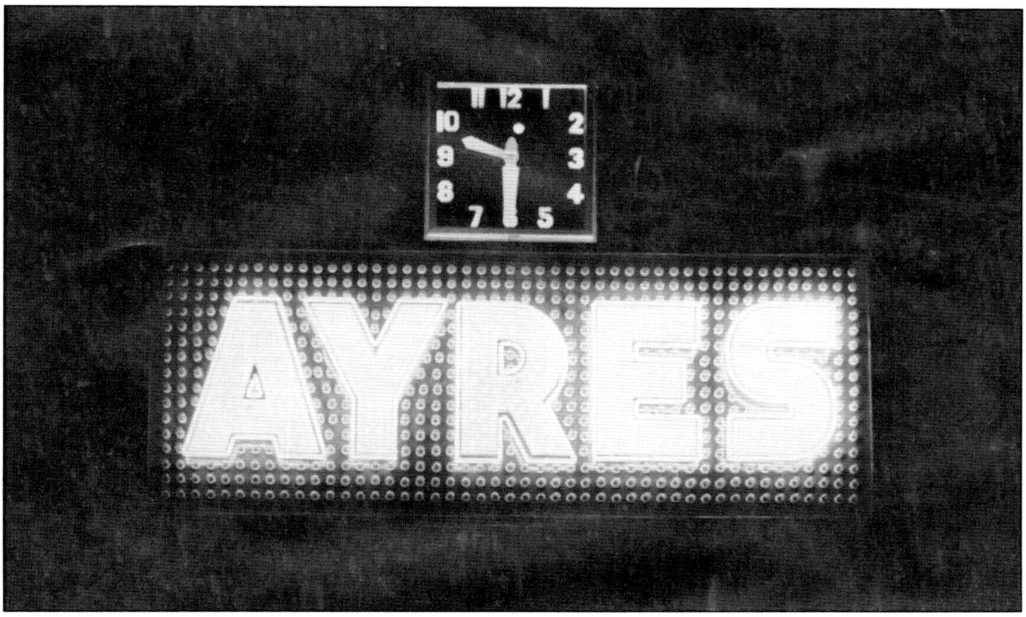

This diner is located on North Florida Avenue in Seminole Heights and is the last remaining Tampa diner of the 1950s. The diner was made famous in 1956 when Elvis Presley stopped in to have a burger after his concert at the Fort Homer Hesterly Armory. This burger palace still operates as Nicko's Diner.

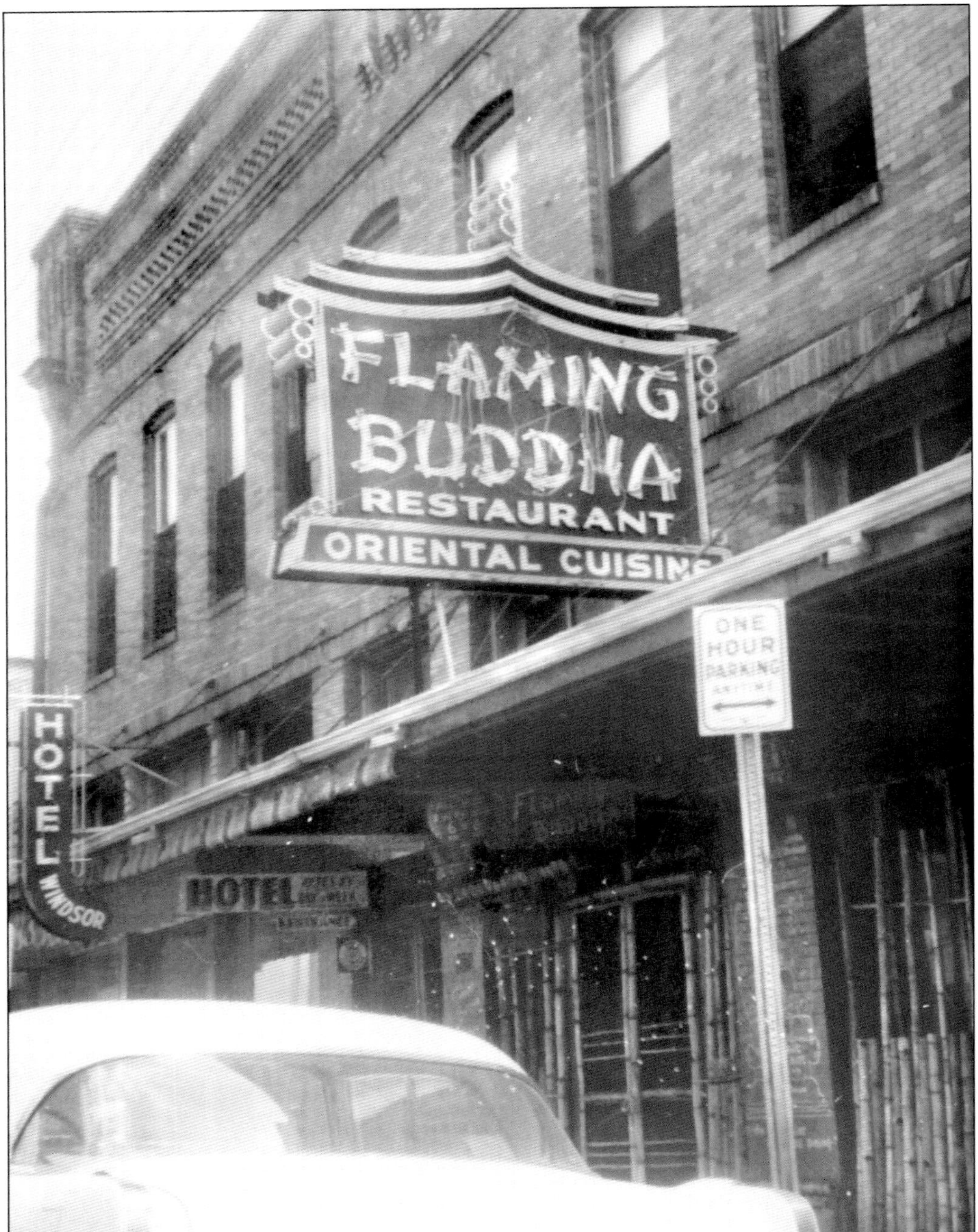

This spectacular neon sign is a work of art. Look closely to see the seated Buddha behind the lettering for the Flaming Buddha Restaurant at the Hotel Windsor on the north end of Franklin Street in 1954. Inside this restaurant, diners enjoyed their dinner in traditional form, seated on the floor by a low table. Notice the bamboo entrance to the restaurant under the canopy.

Good fortune fell on this neon beauty by Cinchett Neon Signs. This Chinese restaurant was in the Holiday House, a popular dance hall on West Hillsborough Avenue across from the Hillsboro Drive-In Theatre. Friends met here for good times with this giant neon pagoda lighting their way into an oriental haven in 1964. Notice that the design bears a striking resemblance to the neon creation made 10 years earlier, the 1954 downtown Flaming Buddha sign.

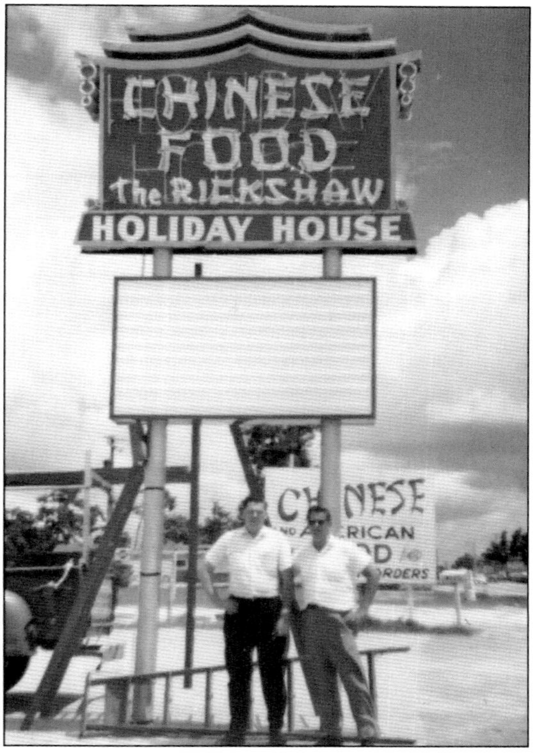

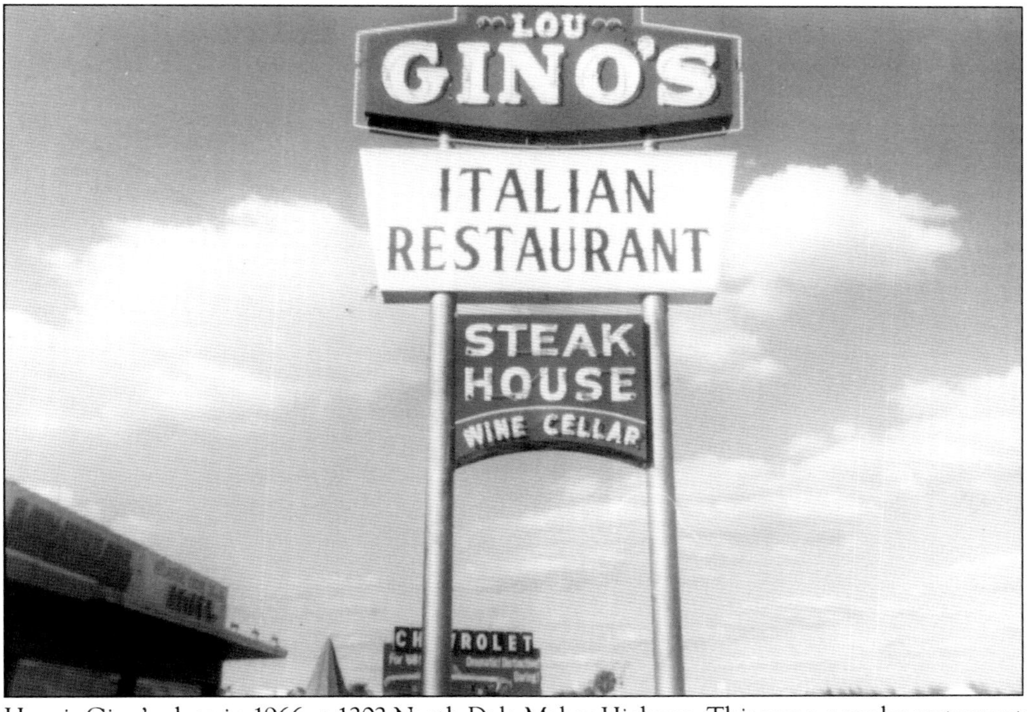

Here is Gino's place in 1966 at 1202 North Dale Mabry Highway. This was a popular restaurant in this area of the city because there were only a few Italian restaurants in Tampa at that time.

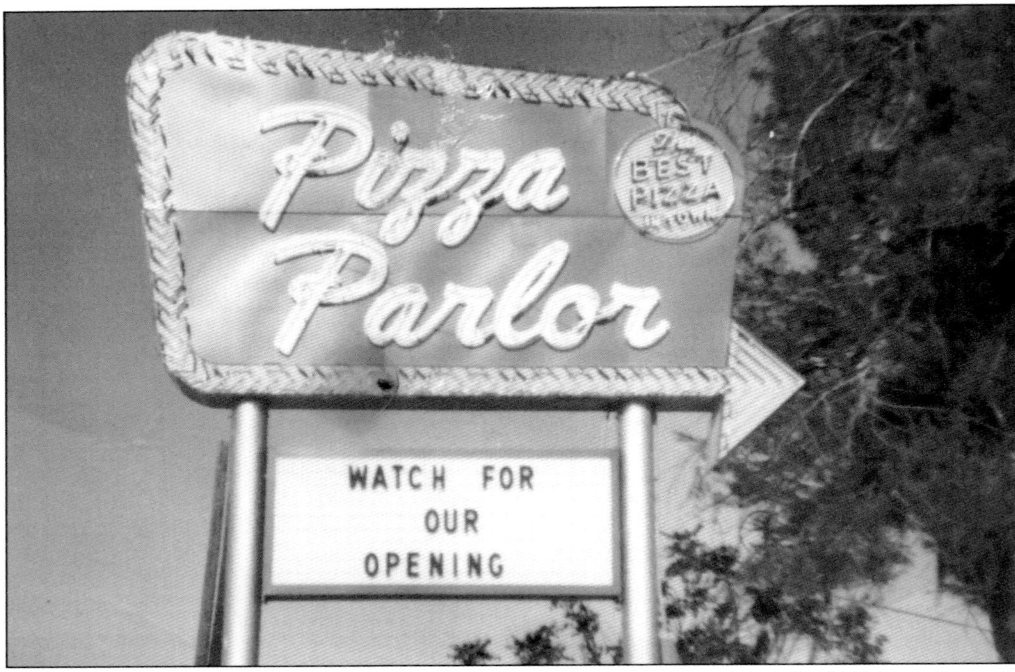

This popular pizza parlor was on East Hillsborough Avenue across from the Hillsboro Drive-In Theatre. Notice that the neon sign says "the Best Pizza in Town." This was another local hangout during the 1960s.

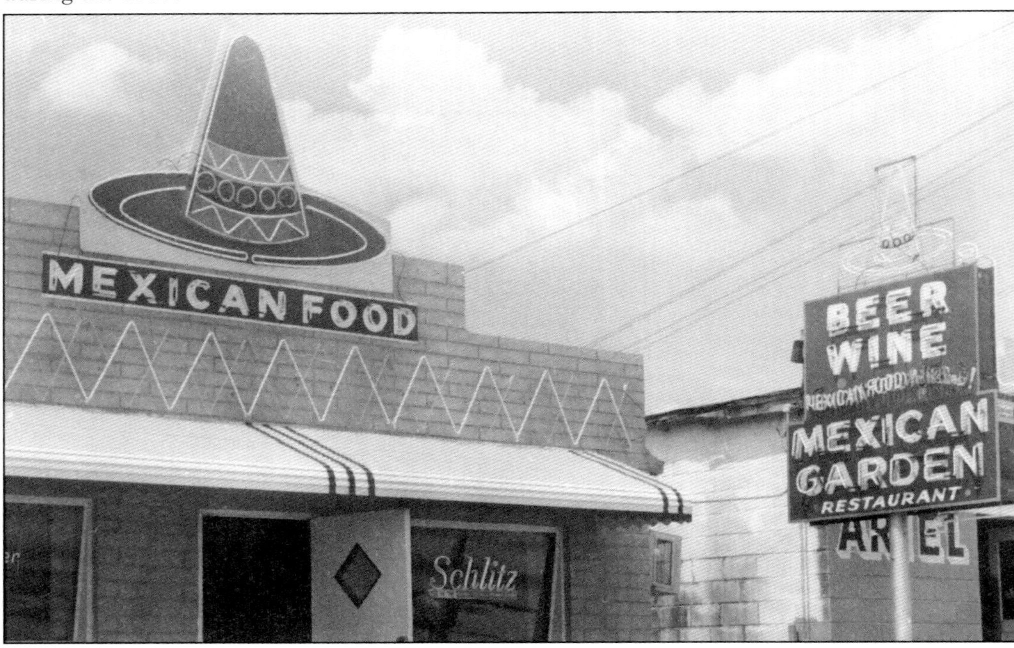

Hola amigos! This 1957 Mexican restaurant is covered in neon. The detail in this neon work is extraordinary, with a giant sombrero on top of the building and an elaborate neon pattern that spans the facade. The Collera family offered home-cooked meals here for many years, and this was among Tampa's first Mexican restaurants.

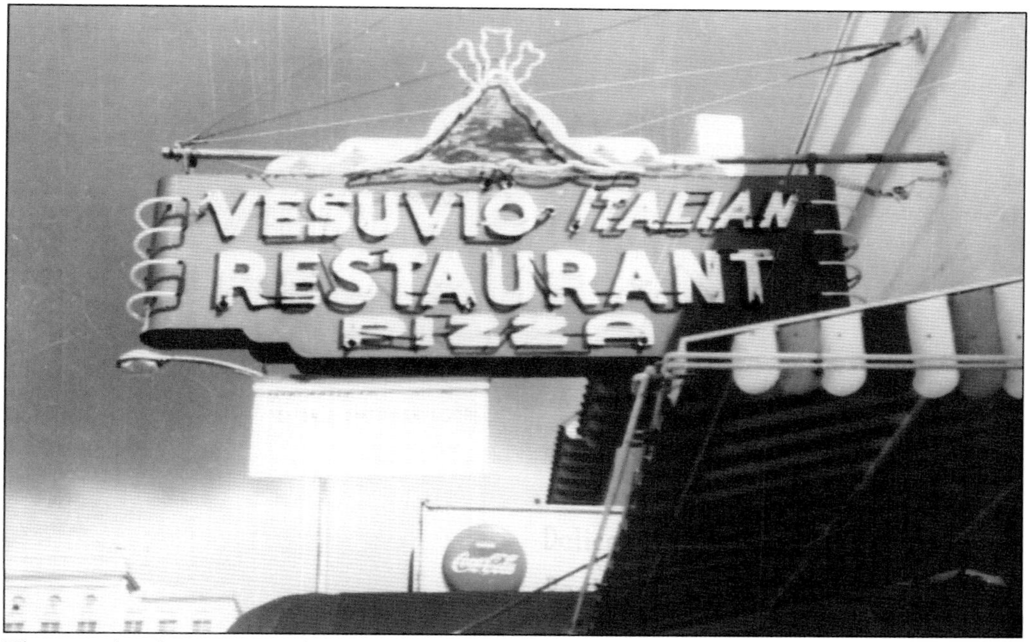

This popular downtown Italian restaurant featured a neon volcano erupting. Surely the owner meant no harm to anyone standing below but rather was paying homage to his homeland back in Italy. This was at 215 Lafayette Street (now Kennedy Boulevard) in 1958. The Tampa Terrace Hotel can be seen in the background.

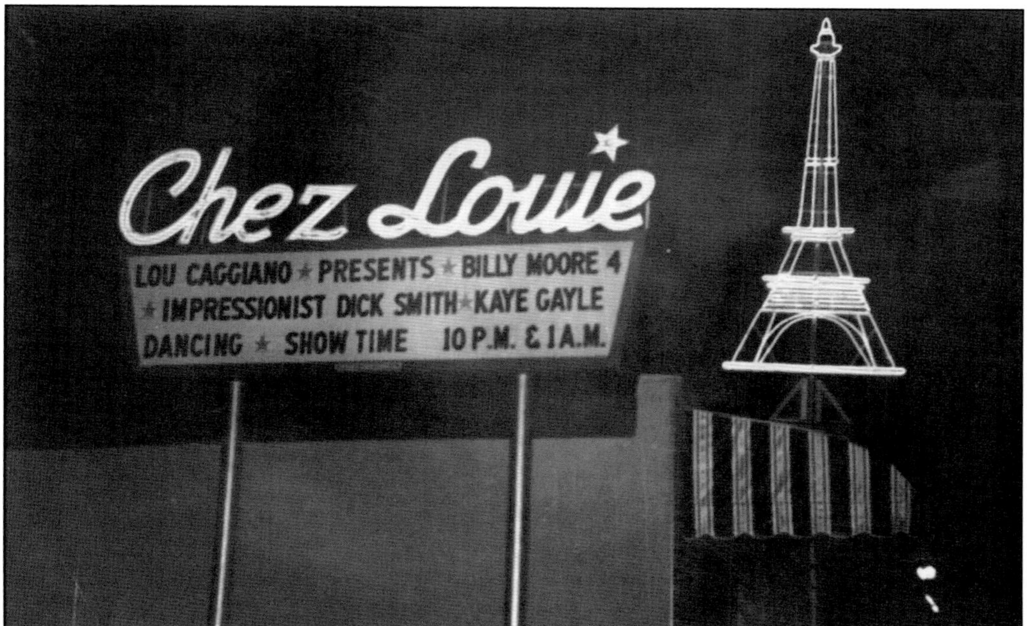

The neon sign seen here at the Chez Louie lounge was an extraordinary work of art standing nearly 15 feet tall. This elaborate recreation of the Eiffel Tower could be seen for several miles down Grand Central Avenue (now Kennedy Boulevard) as patrons approached the popular nightclub in 1960.

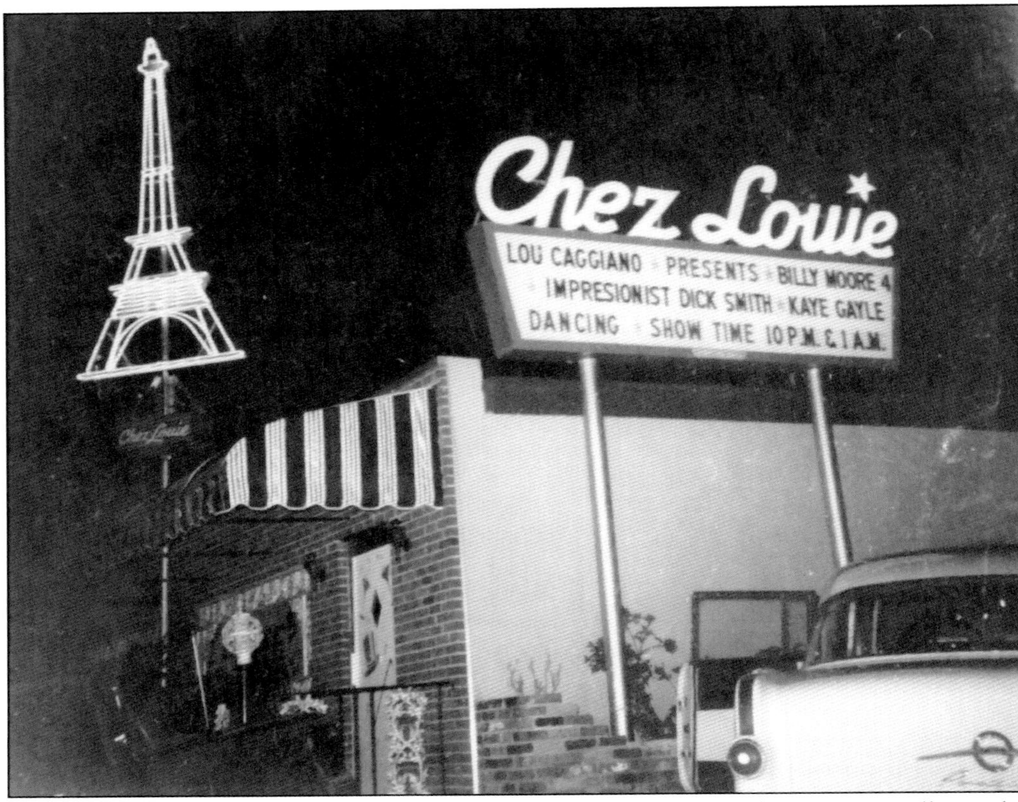

Here is another view of the giant neon Eiffel Tower at Chez Louie, and one can actually see the tower turning in this photograph from 1960. The tower was made up entirely of neon and was quite realistic in design.

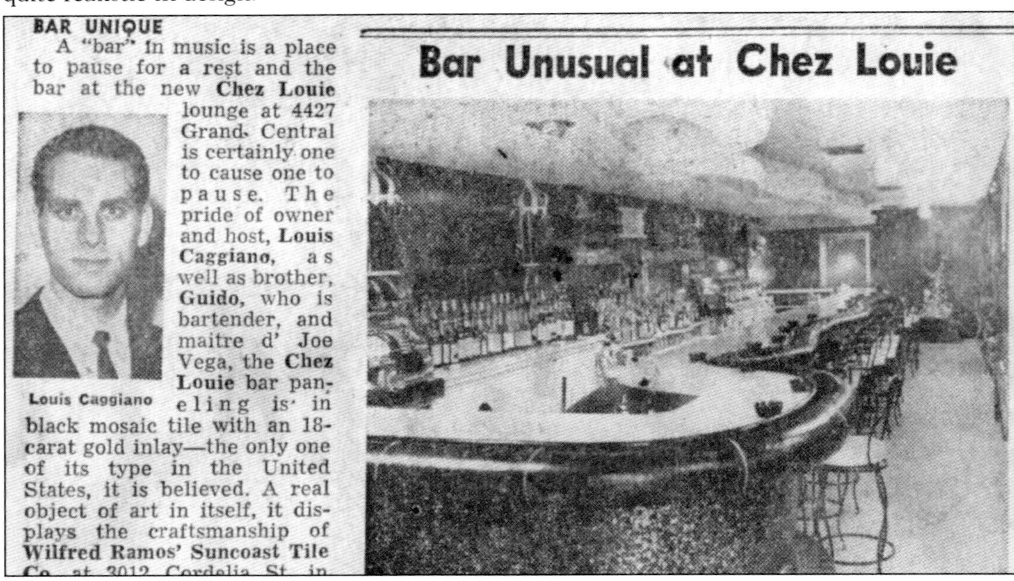

BAR UNIQUE

A "bar" in music is a place to pause for a rest and the bar at the new **Chez Louie** lounge at 4427 Grand Central is certainly one to cause one to pause. The pride of owner and host, **Louis Caggiano**, as well as brother, **Guido**, who is bartender, and maitre d' Joe Vega, the **Chez Louie** bar paneling is in black mosaic tile with an 18-carat gold inlay—the only one of its type in the United States, it is believed. A real object of art in itself, it displays the craftsmanship of **Wilfred Ramos' Suncoast Tile Co.** at 3012 Cordelia St. in

Louis Caggiano

Bar Unusual at Chez Louie

This 1960 *Tampa Tribune* article features an interior view of the new Chez Louie lounge pictured above. The article describes this new venue as being decorated in "Modern French" style.

Welcome to Grandma's for a warm home-cooked meal . . . and a cocktail. It looks like granny was trying to attract hungry travelers on this Tampa highway into her 1950s restaurant and bar next door with a bright neon martini glass topping off her flashy sign.

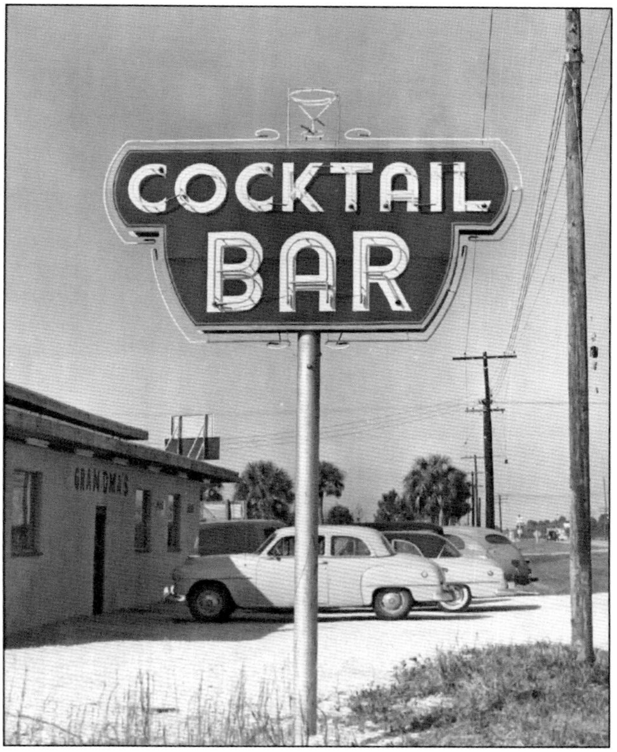

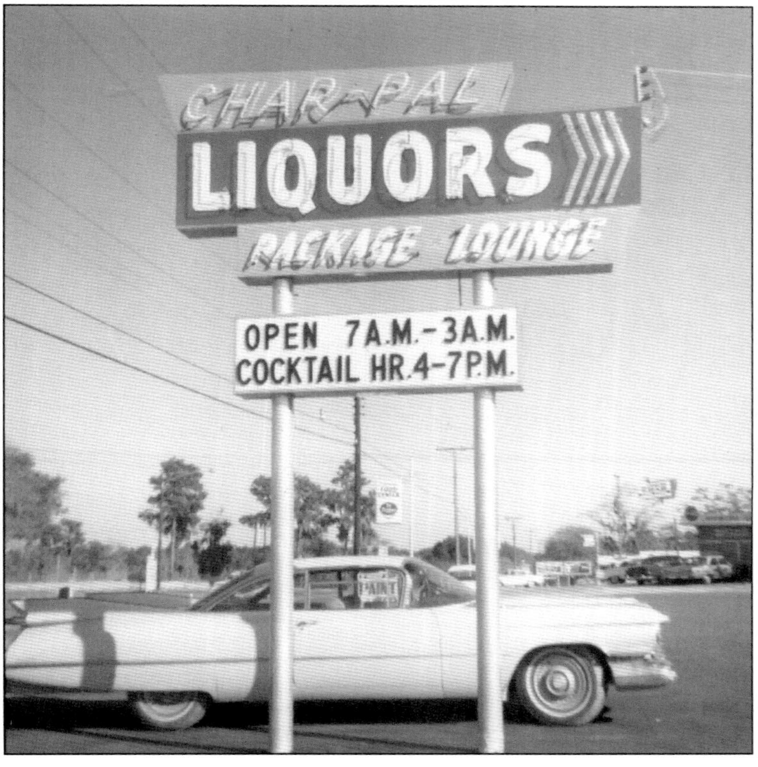

This is the Char-Pal Lounge at 3711 Temple Terrace Highway (now called Busch Boulevard) across from the property that would become Busch Gardens. In this 1964 photograph, much of the land had not yet been developed by the park designers.

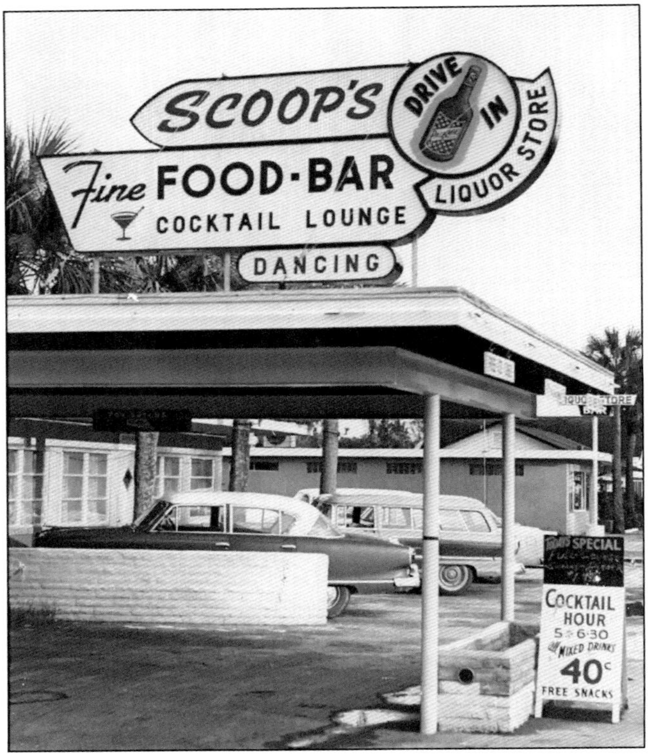

How about this deal: drinks for 40¢ at Scoops Drive-In Liquor Store, another popular 1950s cocktail lounge in Tampa. Today's special is a full-course Sunday dinner for $1.49.

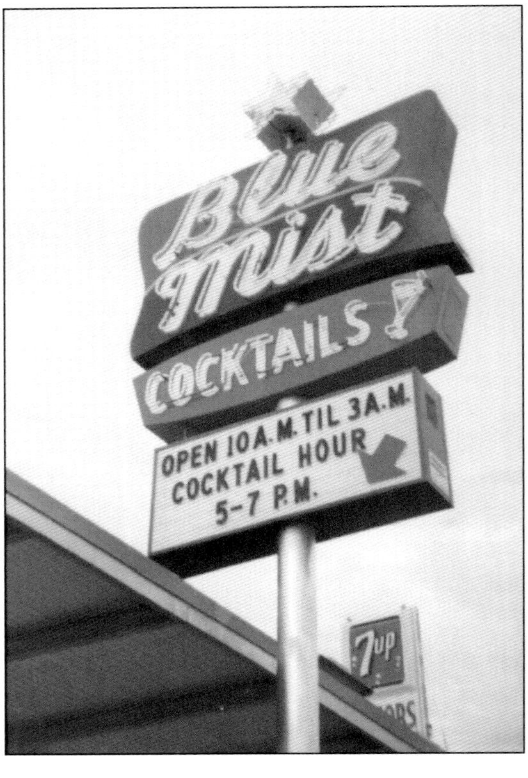

Welcome to the Blue Mist Lounge on North Dale Mabry Highway in 1964. This beautiful neon sign, with its bright yellow neon star and neon martini glass, cannot be missed.

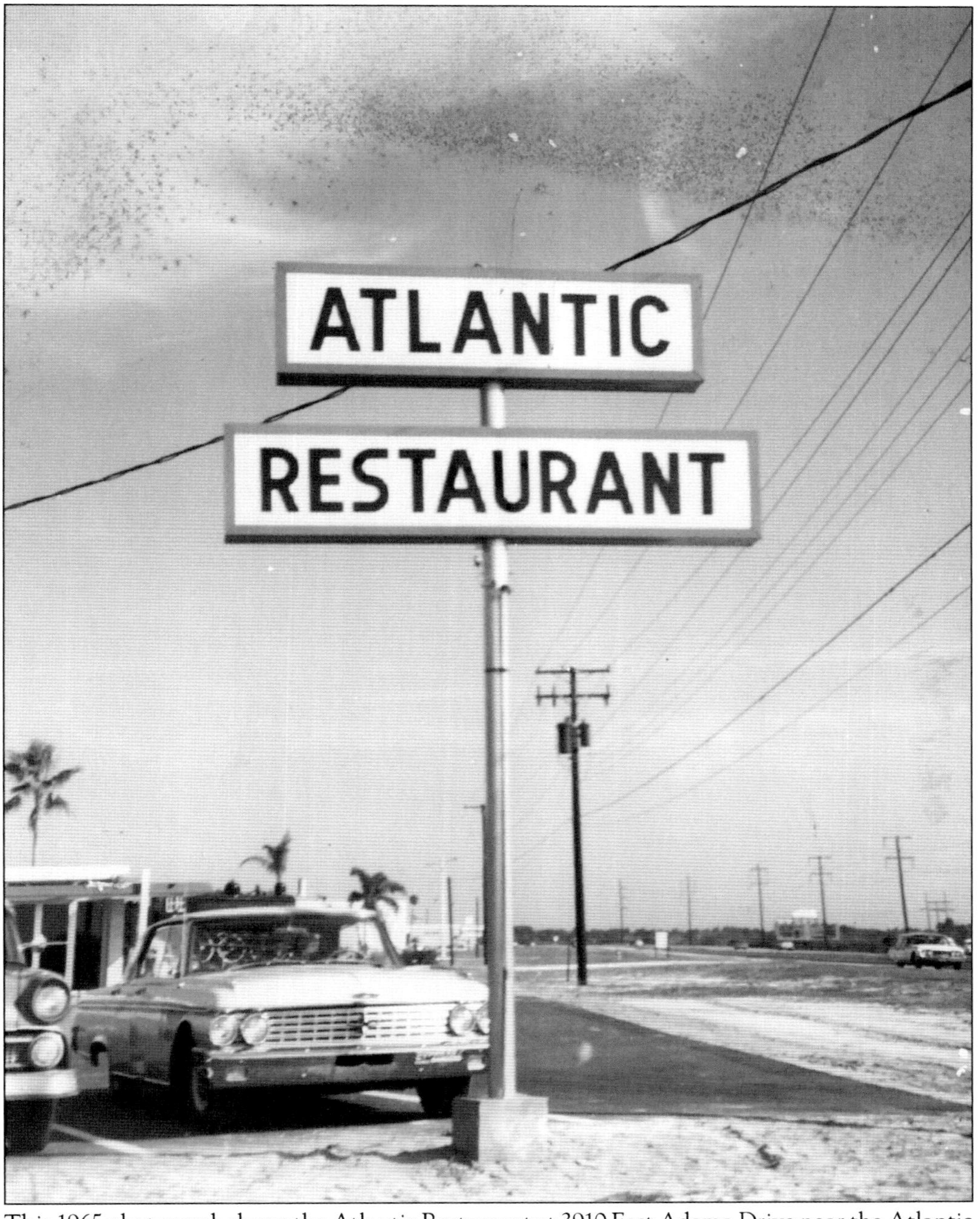

This 1965 photograph shows the Atlantic Restaurant at 3910 East Adamo Drive near the Atlantic Coastline Railroad Building. Looking closely, one can see the vintage locomotive parked on the highway just past the restaurant. This was near the entrance for the railroad offices on Adamo Drive/Highway 60, and many Atlantic employees enjoyed hot meals here for lunch.

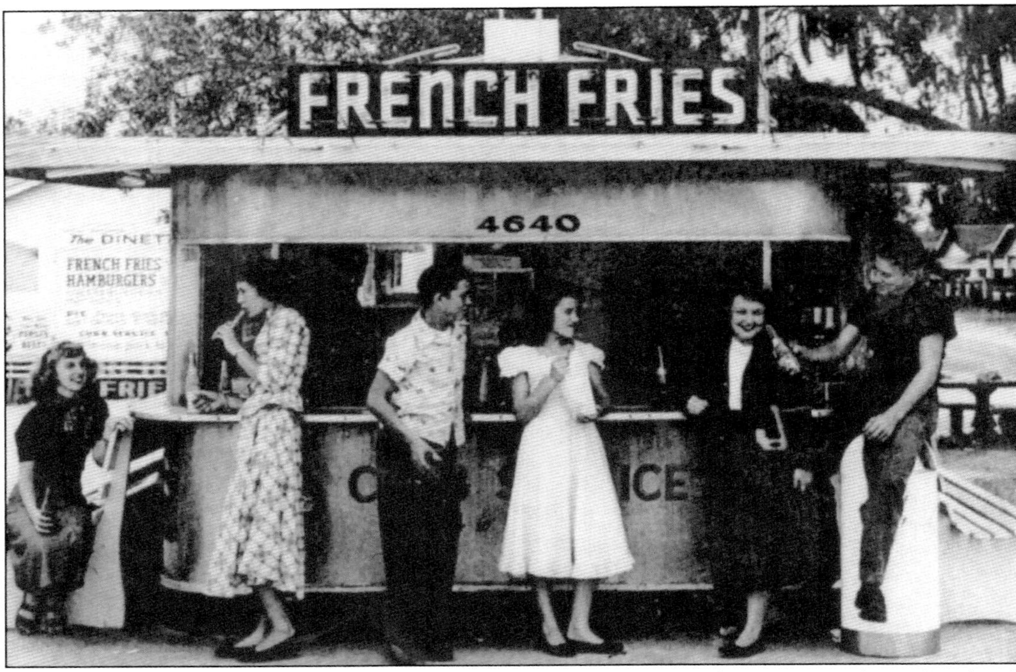

This neat burger stand, popular with high school kids and pictured in 1950, predates Cinchett's 1948 shop appearance, but in 1951, young sign-man John Cinchett not only repaired the neon, but also grilled burgers part-time at the dinette, which was right across the street from the sign shop on Florida Avenue.

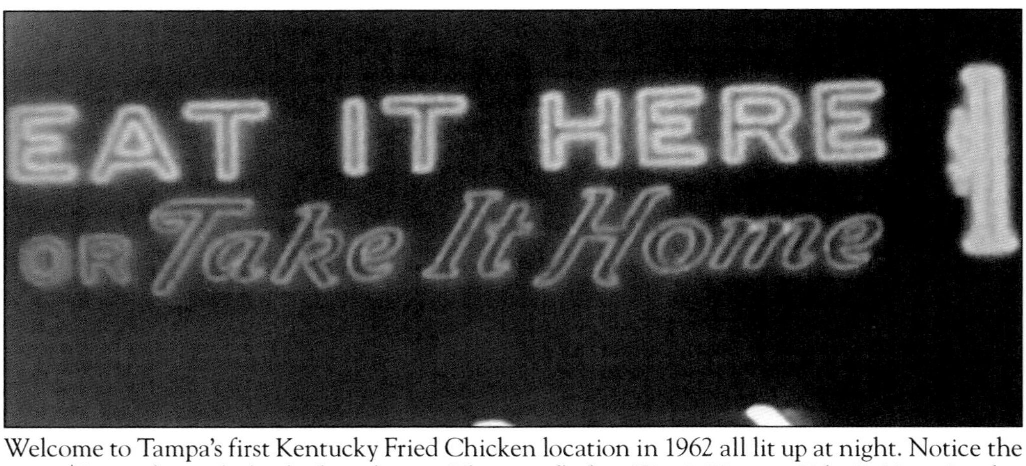

Welcome to Tampa's first Kentucky Fried Chicken location in 1962 all lit up at night. Notice the giant $1 sign for a whole chicken dinner. The sign flashes "Eat It Here or Take It Home"—this was a new concept for chicken dinners, which normally were served in traditional form at the table in the restaurant.

Three

NEON MADE IT A NEIGHBORHOOD FAVORITE

These nostalgic scenes may bring back fond memories of quick trips to the corner drugstore, neighborhood bakery, or favorite record shop. Many of the places pictured here became favorite gathering spots for neighbors who enjoyed a cup of coffee at the lunch counter on their shopping trips and catching up on family happenings with friends.

The 1950s introduced a new concept for Tampa shoppers—the shopping center. Before these giant complexes made their way along Tampa's highways, the destination for shopping was downtown. As Tampa's neighborhoods expanded, so did the need for local shopping venues. By 1956, Tampa was ready for the two largest shopping centers the city had ever seen, Britton Plaza in South Tampa and Northgate in North Tampa. These shopper's paradises offered something that downtown could not: all the free parking customers wanted for all the stores they needed to visit. Tampa's residents fell in love with these shopping mazes, and the city would never be the same again.

Many of the neon signs captured in these amazing photographs became local favorites, serving as brightly colored beacons to guide folks into their favorite neighborhood destination. The 1950s was a time for fountain luncheonettes and soda shops where friends often gathered to make plans for the upcoming dance or a trip to the theater. Television was making its way into living rooms for the first time in many homes, and it was a big affair to buy that new television, especially if one was the first in the neighborhood to have one. Tampa music shops were busy too, with those fabulous 1950s bands hitting the airwaves and schoolgirls meeting friends at the record store to pick out their favorite tunes.

Be sure to take note of the many fine details that paint a picture of this simpler time in history. The style of dress seen among shoppers, store window advertisements, and the clever designs of these glorious neon signs all bring together a stunning portrait of Tampa's landscape in the 1950s. Enjoy this trip down memory lane and remember to look for those well-known neighborhood favorites!

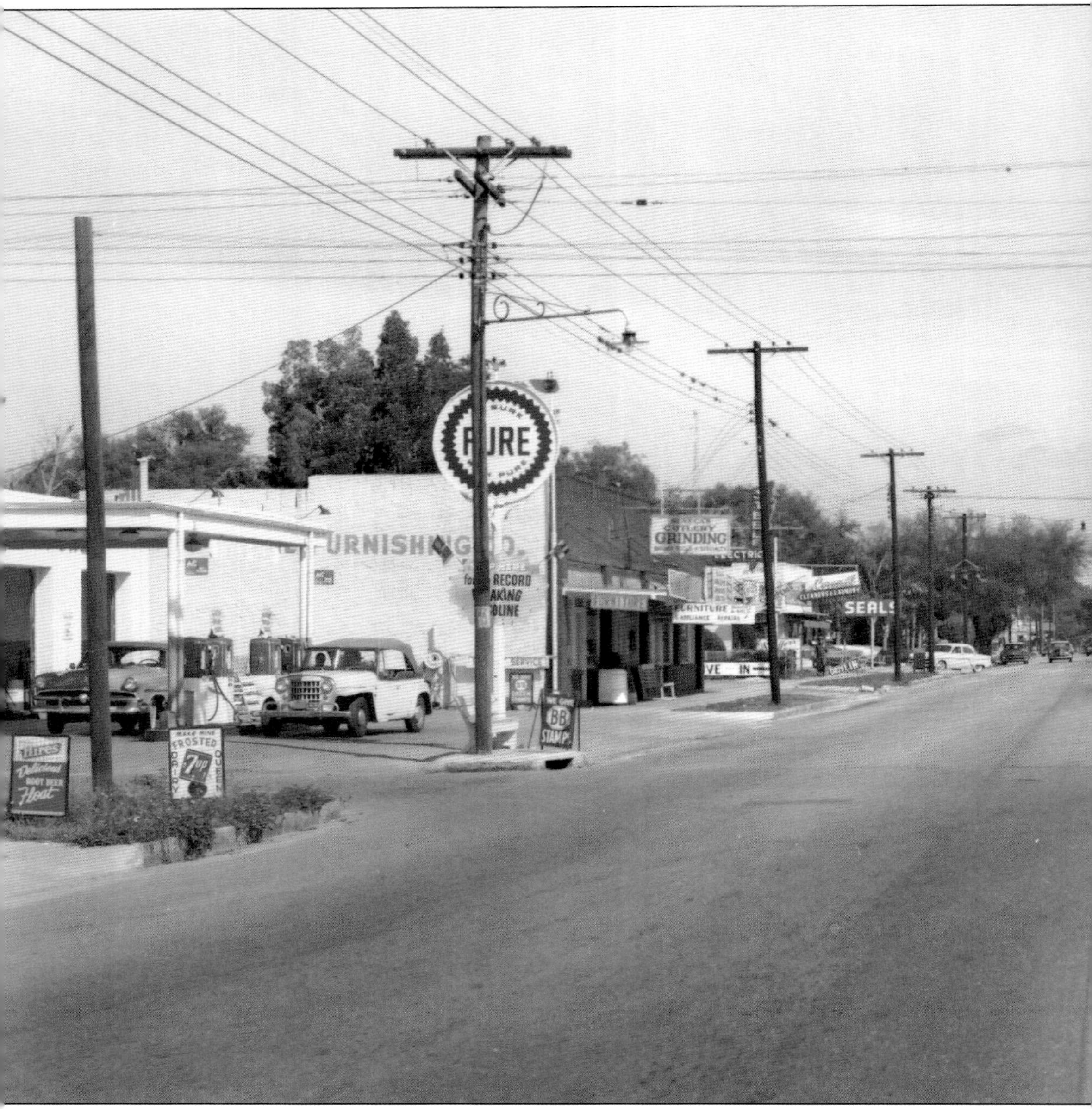

The 1950s presented many neighborhood shops and stores with a bounty of new business. In this 1956 scene along North Nebraska Avenue near Chelsea Street, several companies Cinchett Neon Signs assisted can be seen, including the Steele Electric Company and Coronet Cleaners. Some nostalgic treasures include the vintage fire-alarm call box on the right corner and those street

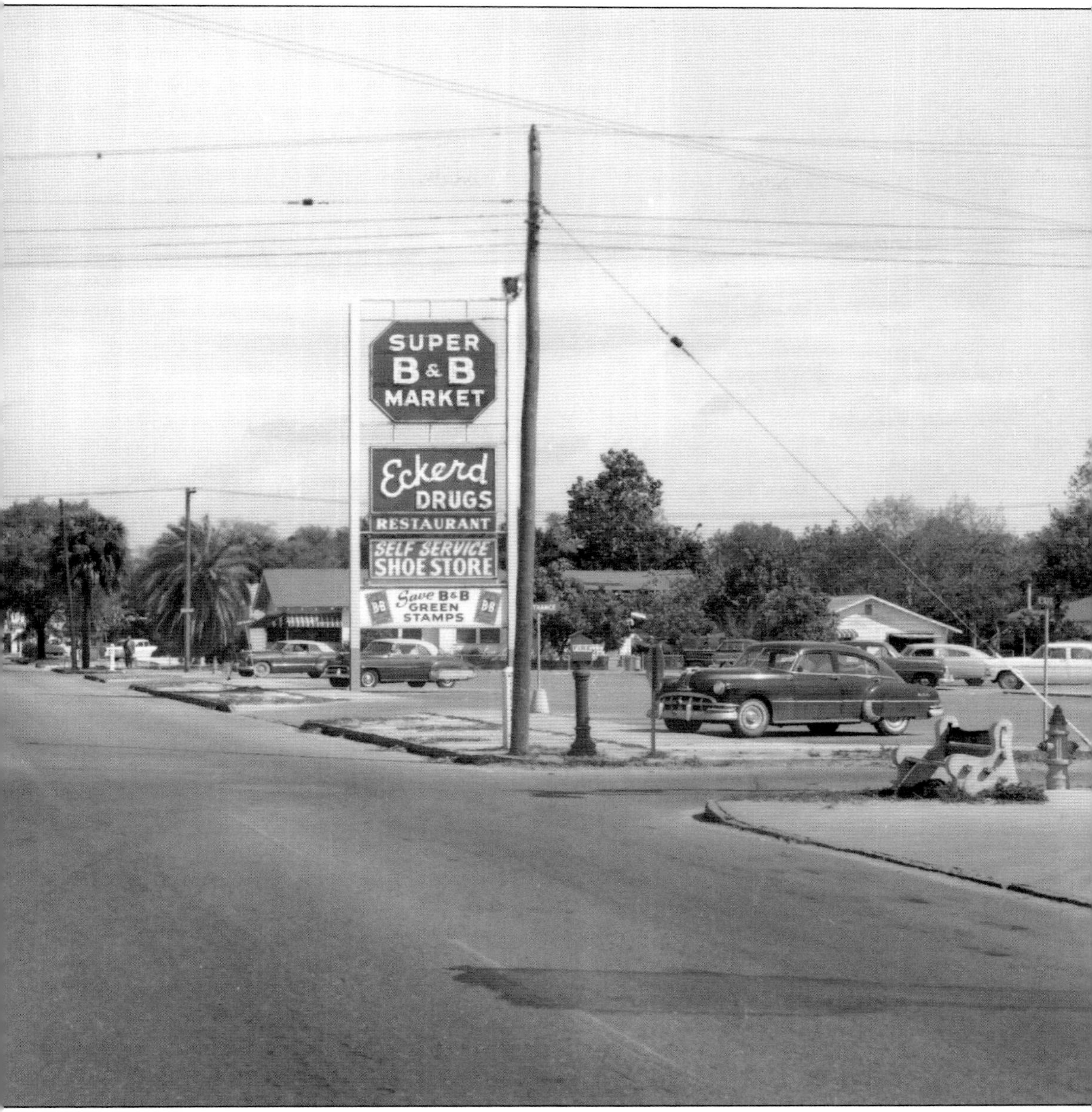

signs at the supermarket and gas station, both announcing "green stamps." Many Tampa folks will remember collecting green stamps from their neighborhood stores and gas stations to fill the booklets that could be redeemed at the local S&H Green Stamp Store. (Courtesy HCPLC.)

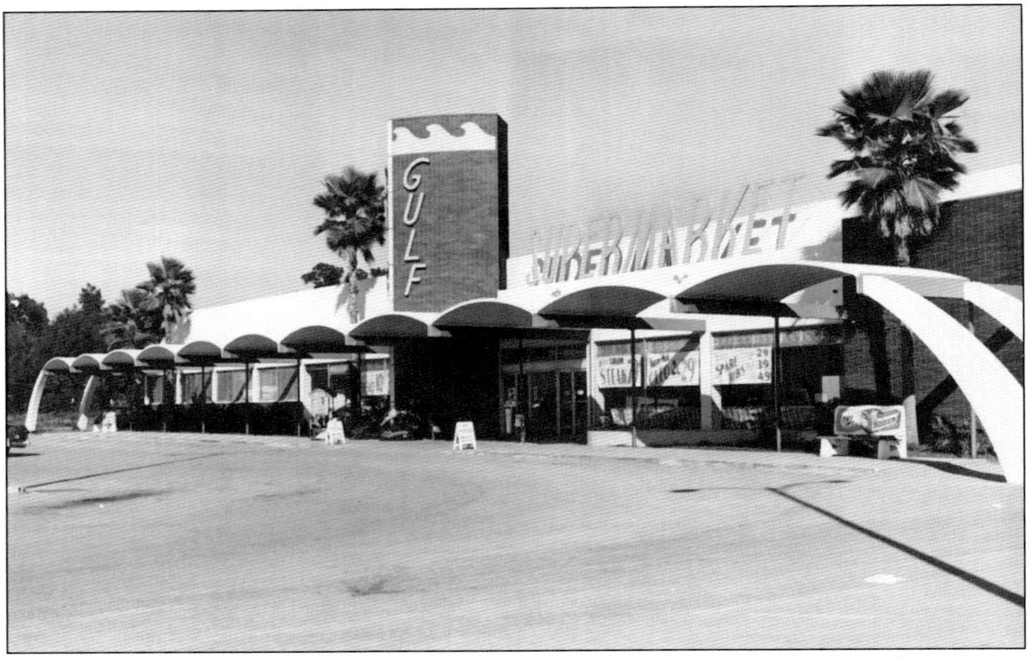

This spectacular photograph of the new Gulf Supermarket sign at 1701 North Dale Mabry Highway was taken in 1957. Notice the space-age design of this building. Check out the sale price on bread: 10¢. The photograph below shows the grand opening, and notice the price on men's shirts: 99¢.

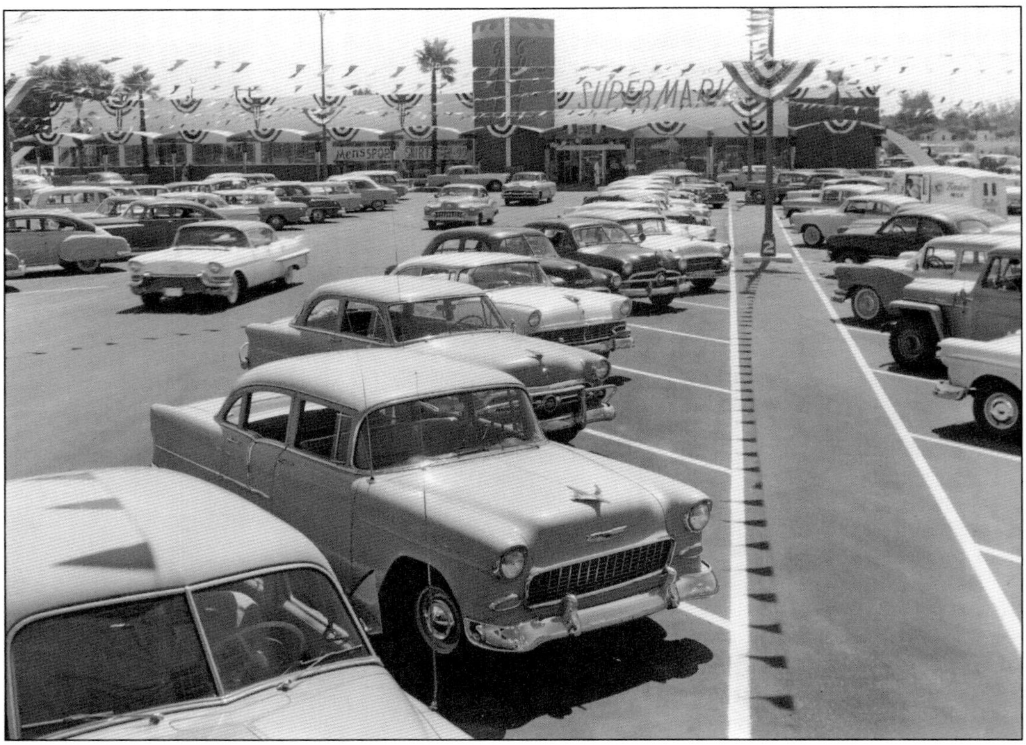

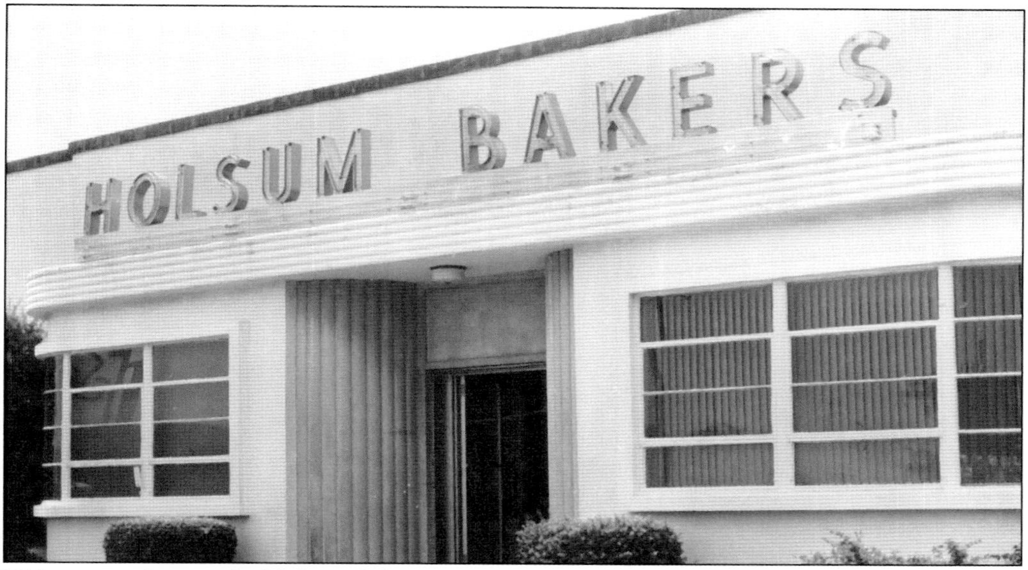

Welcome to the popular Holsum Bakery in 1949 on East Hillsborough Avenue at Twenty-second Street. This art deco–style building was accented with a backlit sign design by Cinchett Neon Signs. Below, locals packed the bakery for its annual Christmas Open House, a well-known, festive event for kids with Santa and a wonderland of decorations. Tampa folks will recall the special miniature loaf of Holsum bread that everyone received along with candy and goodies. In later years, Cinchett Neon Signs also created neon Christmas decorations for the bakery's storefront. (Below, courtesy HCPLC.)

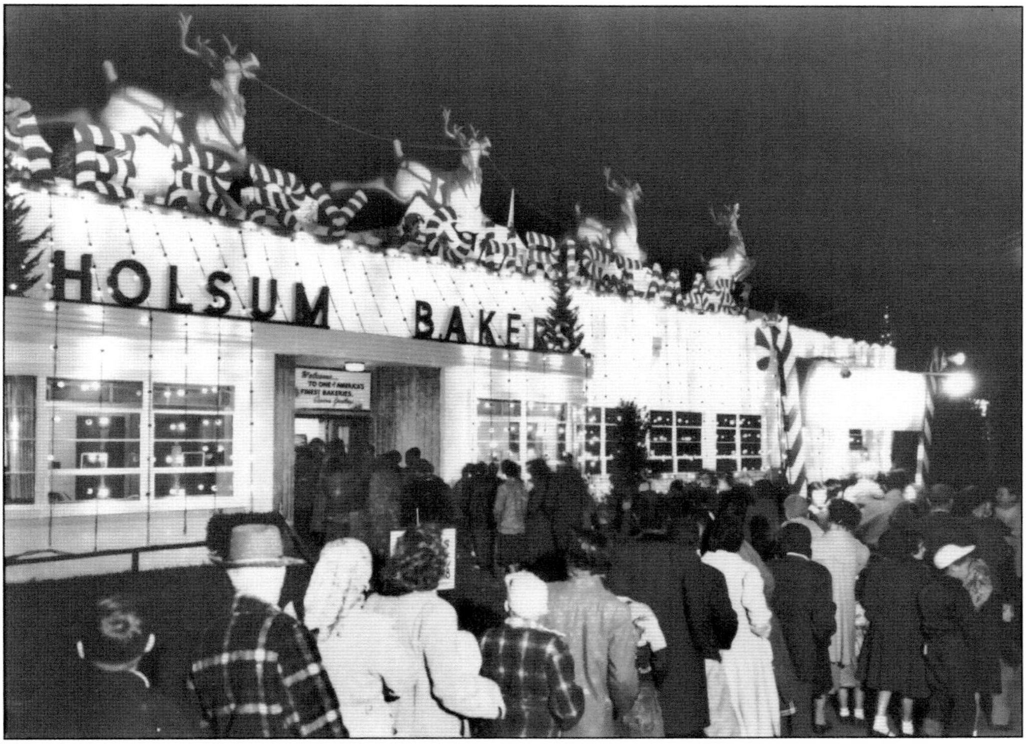

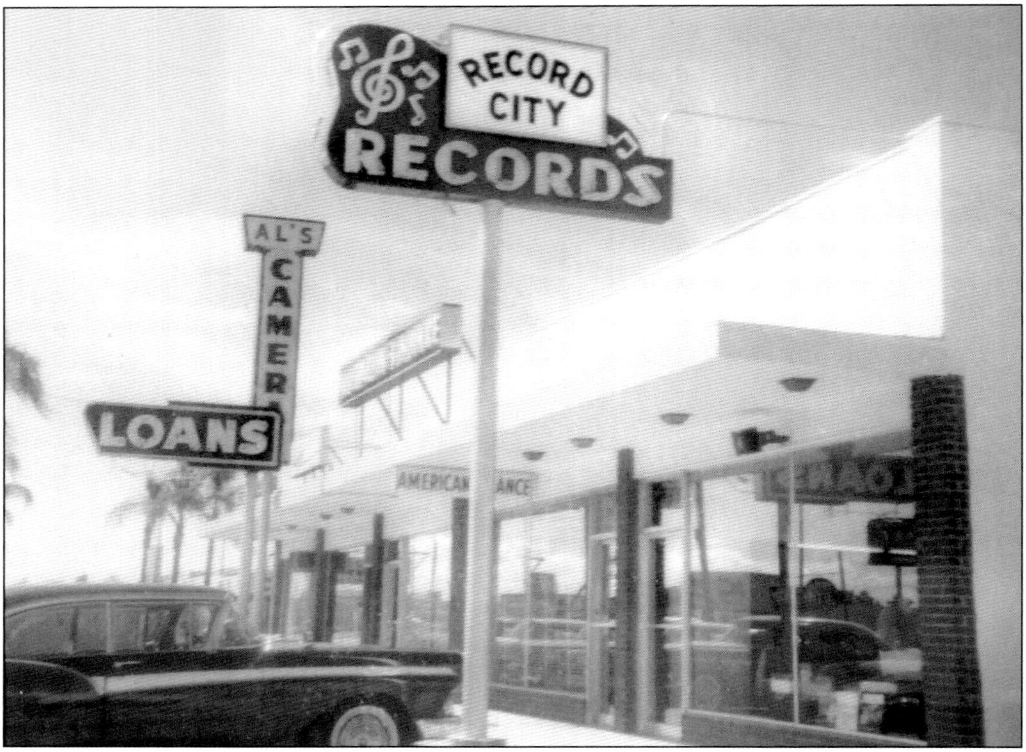

This musical neon masterpiece was made for the Record City record shop at 1531 South Dale Mabry Highway in 1959. During the 1950s, this area in South Tampa became a popular shopping destination with several small plazas between Henderson and Bay to Bay Boulevards lining both sides of the street.

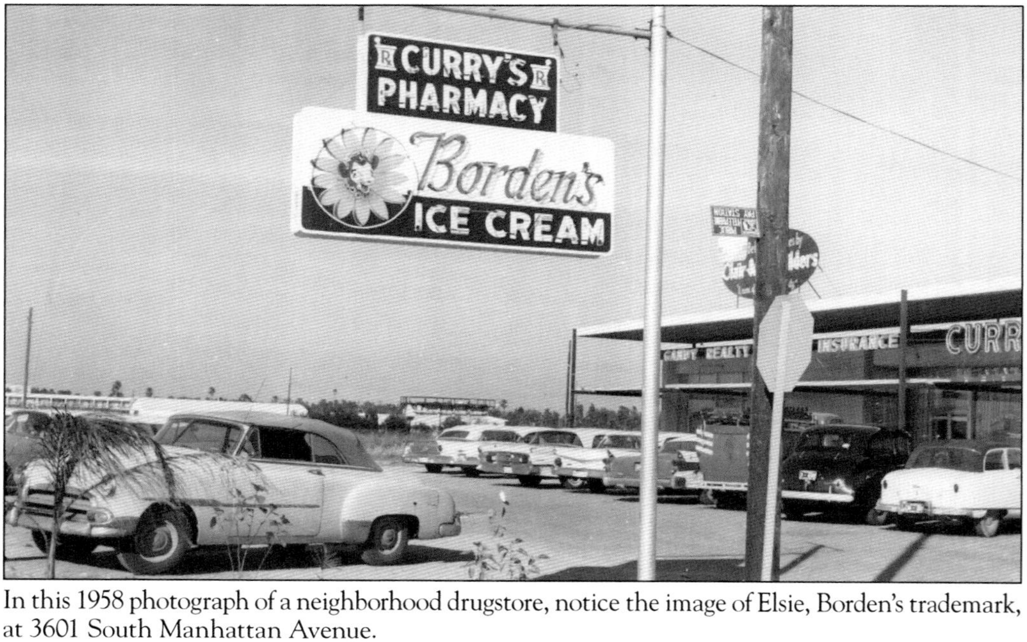

In this 1958 photograph of a neighborhood drugstore, notice the image of Elsie, Borden's trademark, at 3601 South Manhattan Avenue.

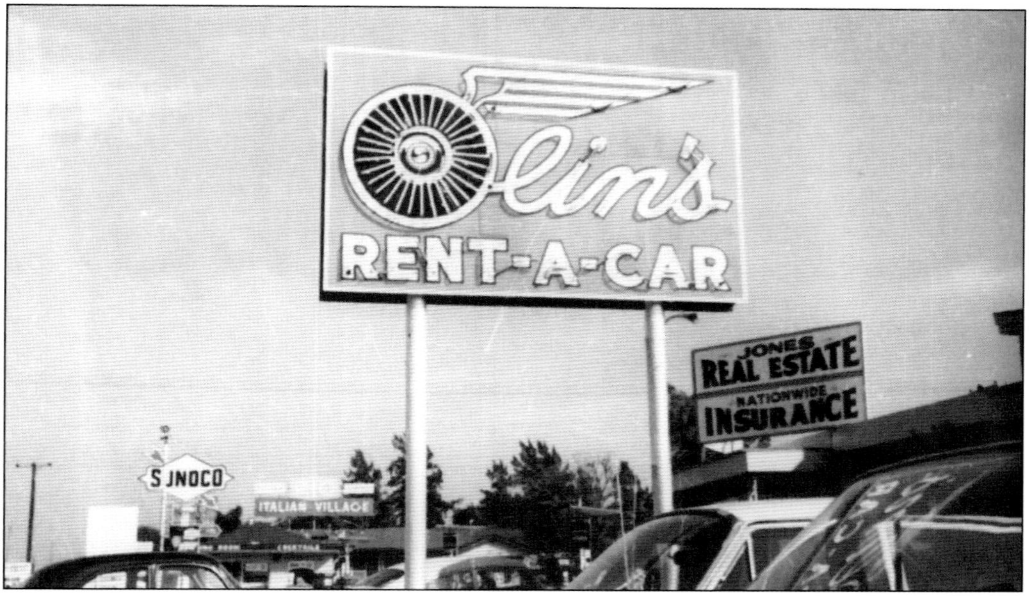

It's a bird, it's a plane, no—it's a flying hubcap with wings! This heavenly neon masterpiece for Olin's Rent-A-Car was on North Dale Mabry Highway in 1959. Across the street is the Rio Italian Village, a popular 1950s restaurant.

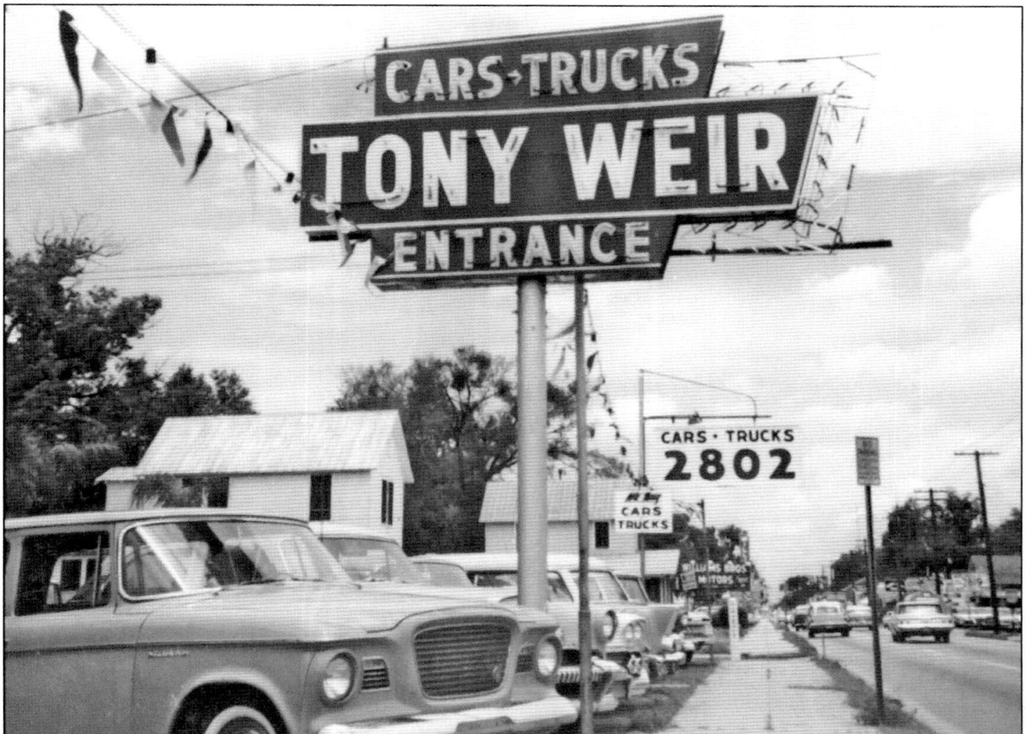

Here is another 1950s car lot at 2802 Florida Avenue with bright neon arrows to guide customers in. This 1959 photograph looks north along Florida Avenue.

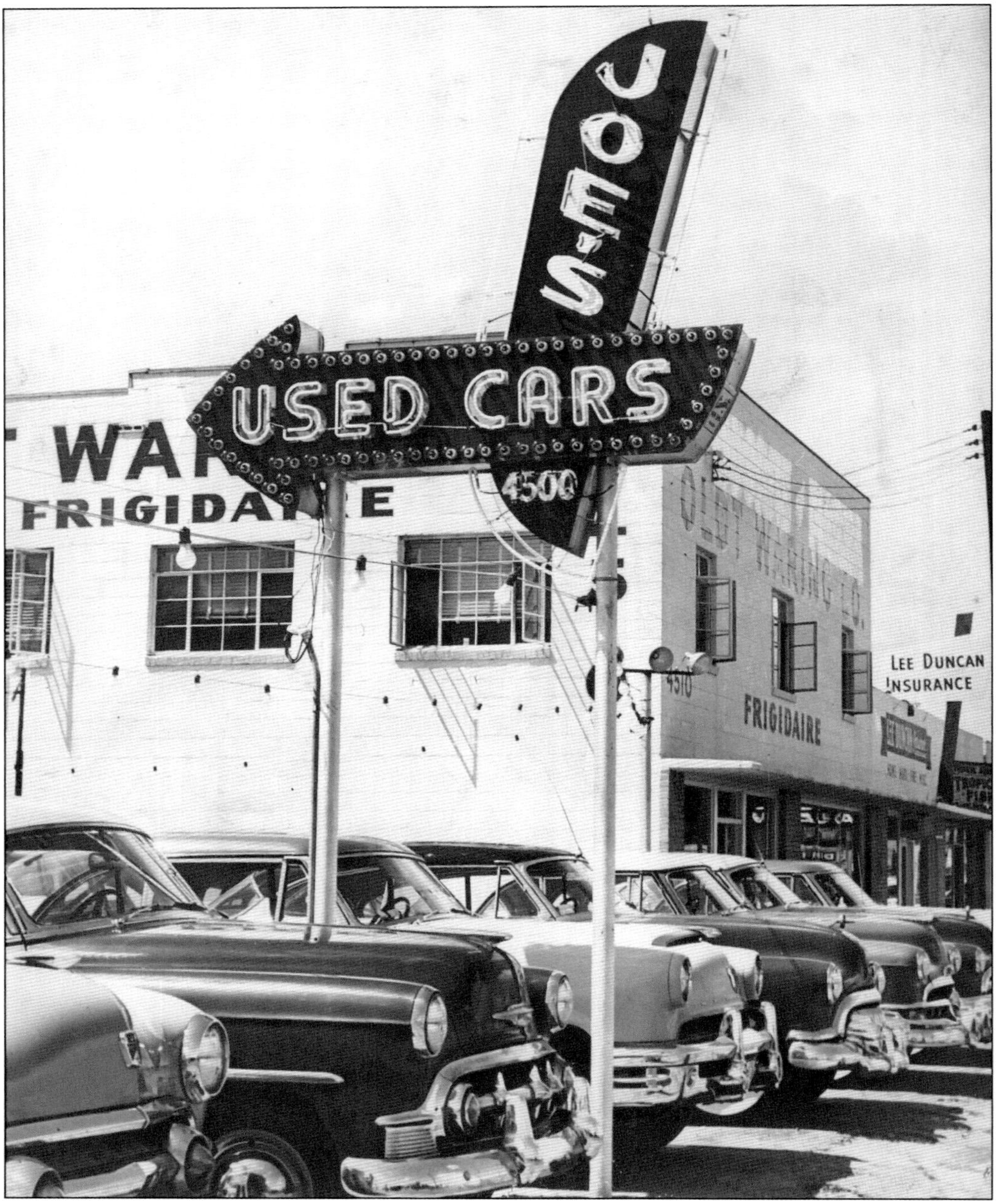

During the 1950s, Americans fell in love with their cars, and here is Joe's in 1957 at 4500 North Florida Avenue in Seminole Heights. In the building next door is the office of well-known city councilman Lee Duncan, fondly remembered for his preservation efforts in saving the historic Tampa Theatre.

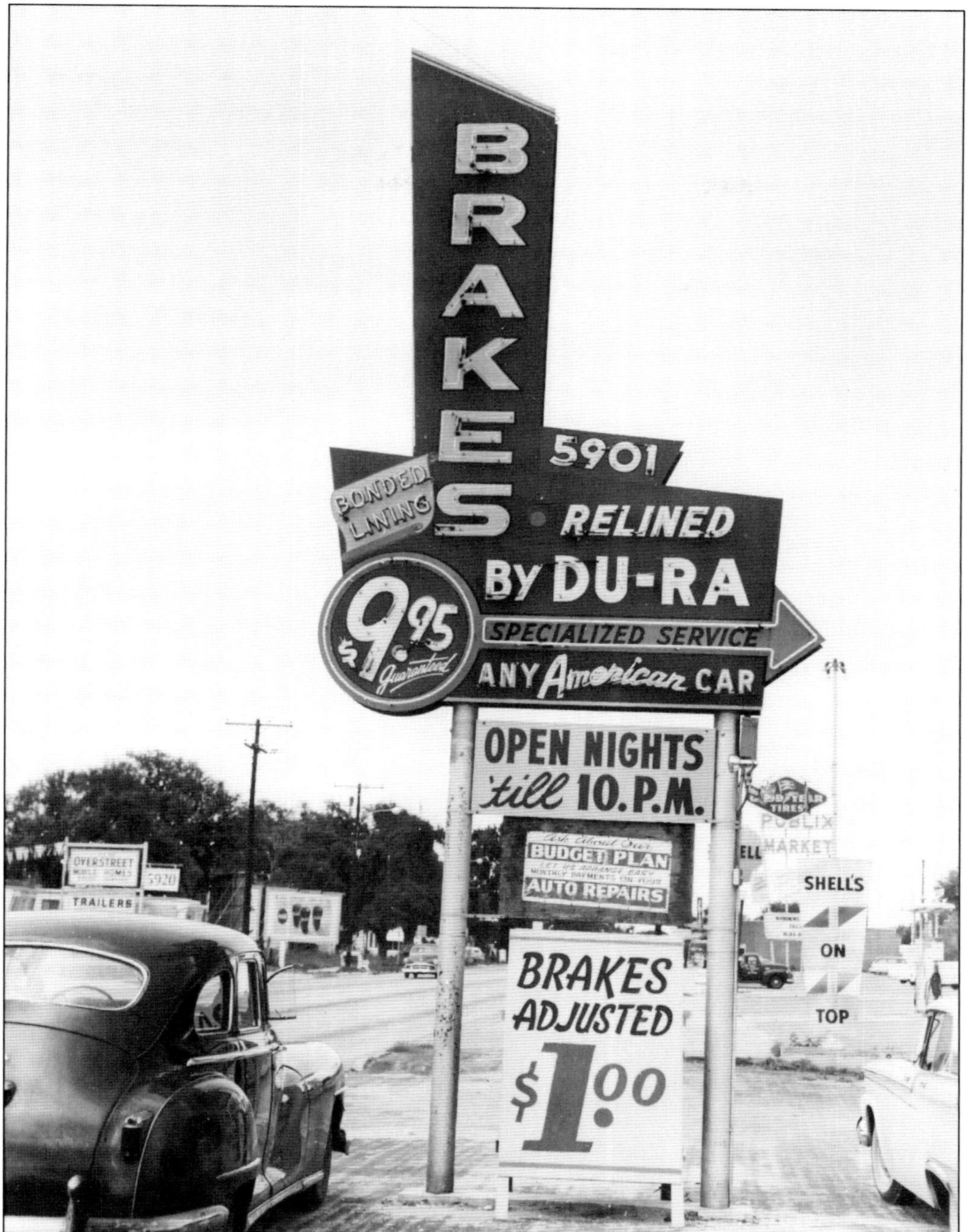

This repair shop was located on North Nebraska Avenue just south of Hanna Avenue in 1956. This photograph was taken looking north, and just beyond the repair shop sign is the Publix supermarket sign. This market is still standing and is one of Tampa's oldest. Notice the brake job advertised for $9.95 or adjusted for $1.

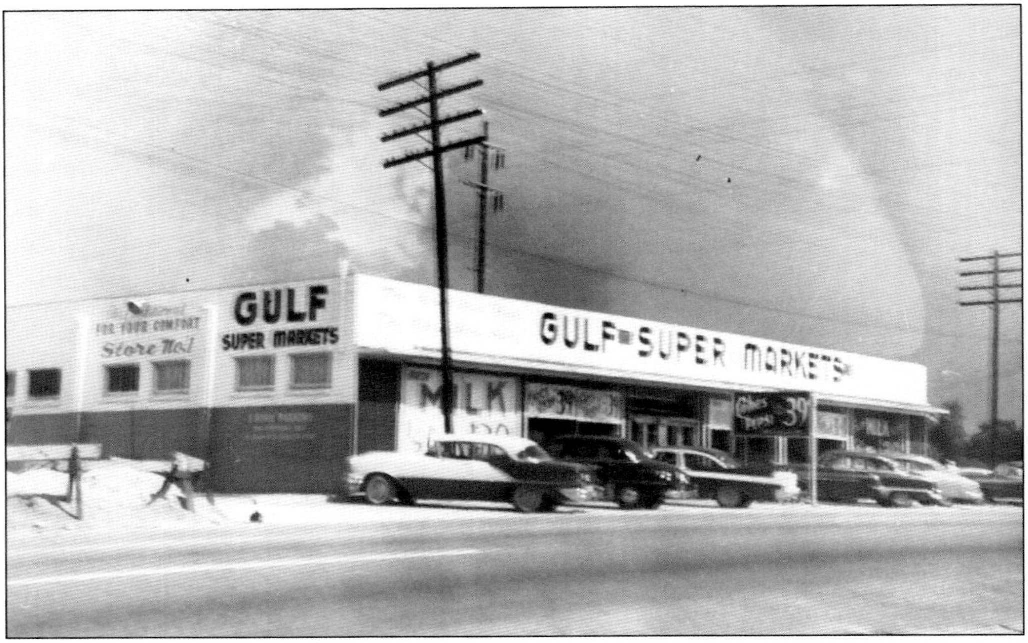

Here is another 1950s Gulf Supermarket at the corner of North Florida and Waters Avenues in Sulphur Springs. Peaches are on sale at two for 15¢, and milk is 39¢ a gallon. Notice on the side of the building is painted "Air Conditioned for your comfort"—this was a selling point to attract customers because many Tampa stores did not have air-conditioning yet in the 1950s.

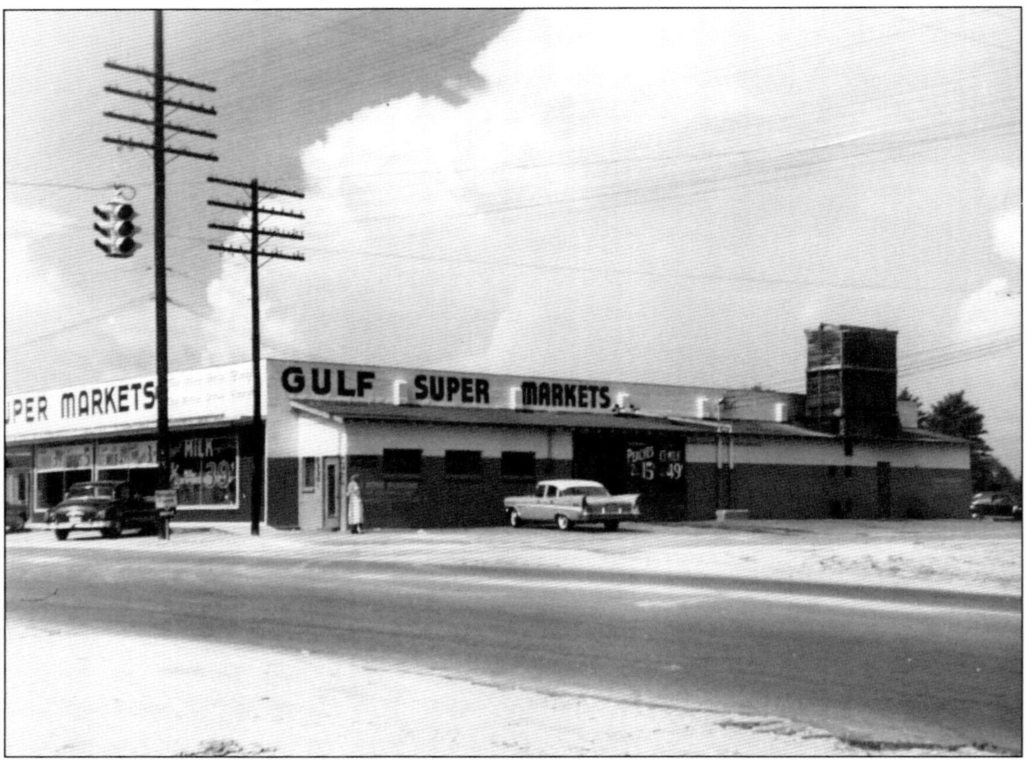

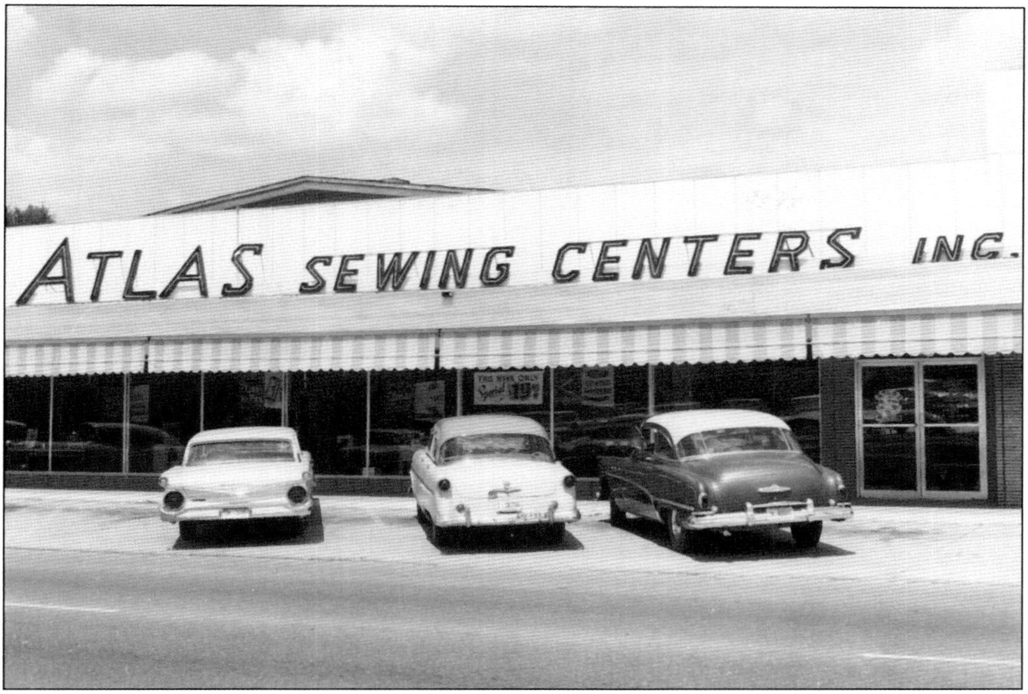

Here is the Atlas Sewing Center in Seminole Heights at 3745 North Florida Avenue in 1960. This was a popular spot for those talented girls who were too good for store-bought goods.

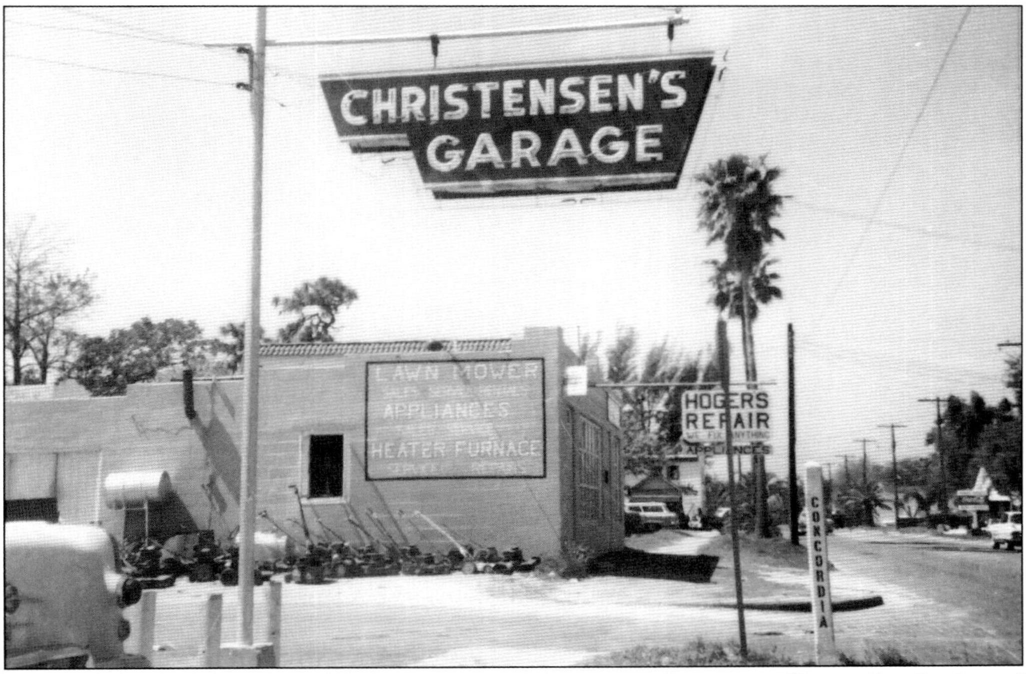

Here is a South Tampa repair shop's new neon sign in 1962 on the corner of Bay to Bay Boulevard and Concordia Avenue. This view was taken looking west along Bay to Bay Boulevard, and these two vintage buildings still stand today.

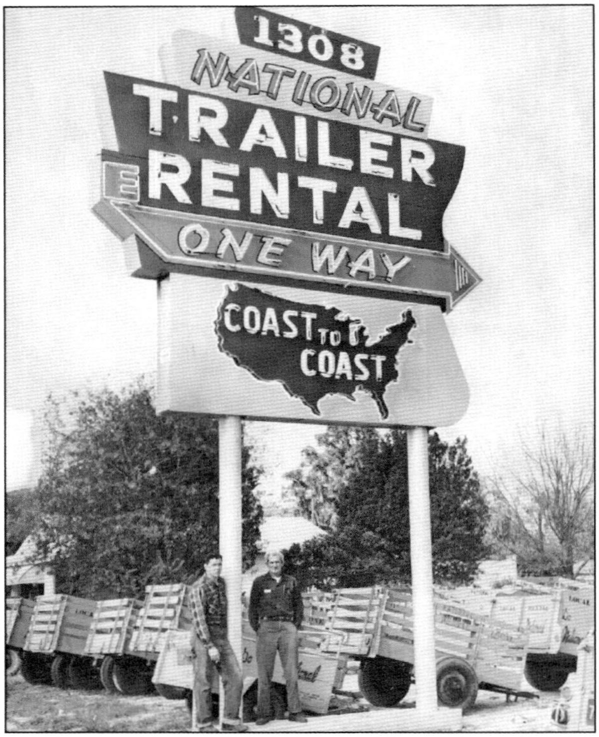

This spectacular sign featuring a giant neon U.S. map is pictured in 1952 at 1300 East Hillsborough Avenue between Nebraska Avenue and Fifteenth Street. Notice the neon "E" to assist motorists, indicating their direction as they pass the sign.

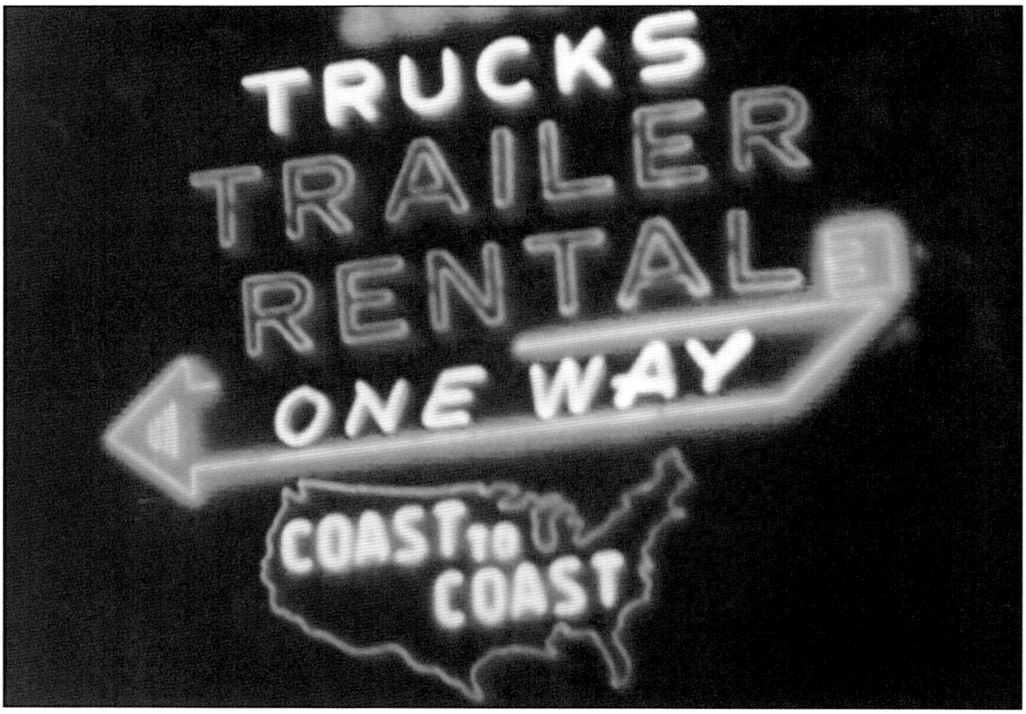

Here is a nighttime view of the National Trailer Rental sign on East Hillsborough Avenue—quite an animated work of art by Cinchett Neon Signs in 1952.

Pictured is a 1950s corner drugstore in South Tampa. Notice the vintage telephone booth next to the bench under the canopy. This was actually a revolving sign, something never seen anymore.

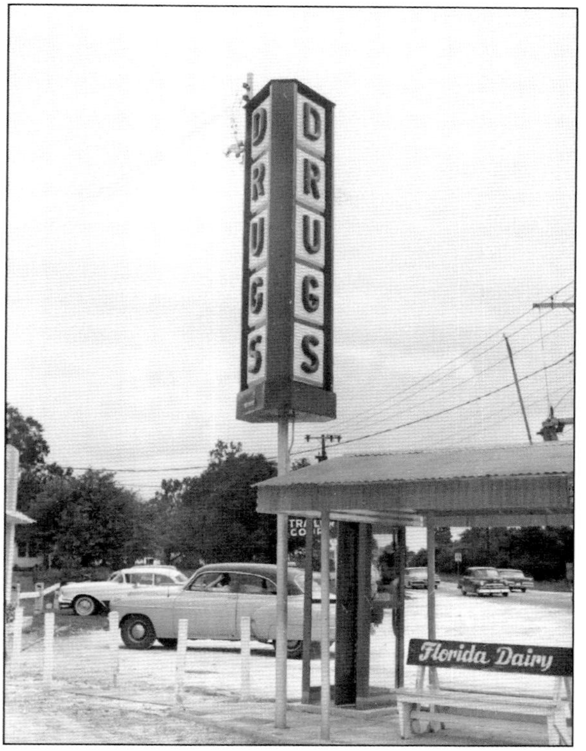

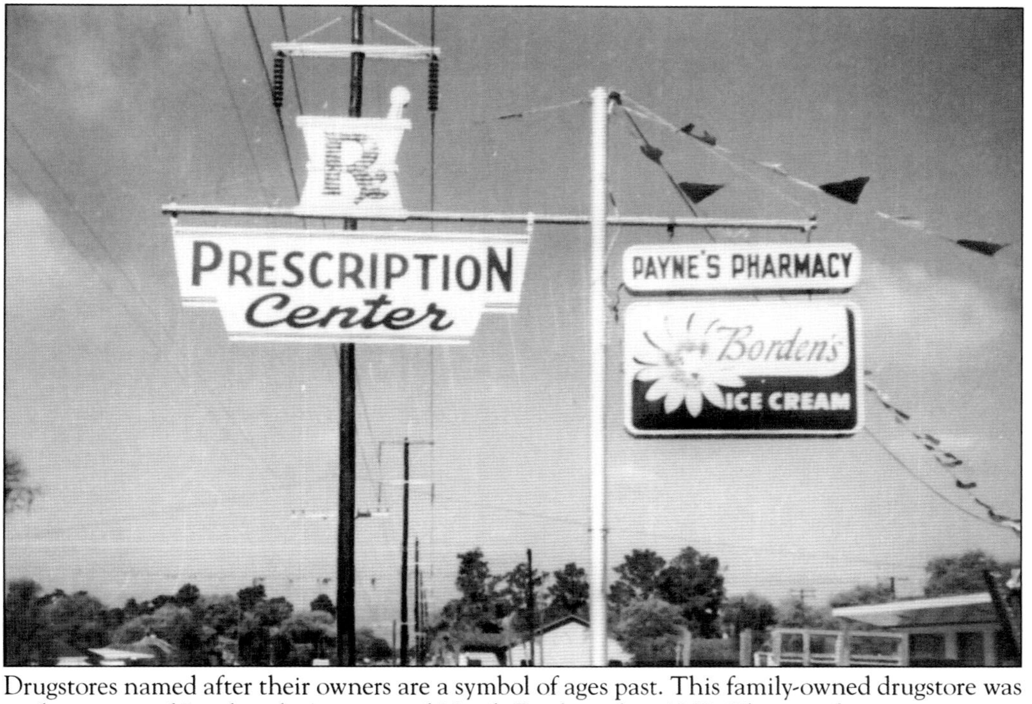

Drugstores named after their owners are a symbol of ages past. This family-owned drugstore was at the corner of Linebaugh Avenue and North Boulevard in 1960. The sign features a vintage symbol for pharmacies at the time, a neon mortar and pestle.

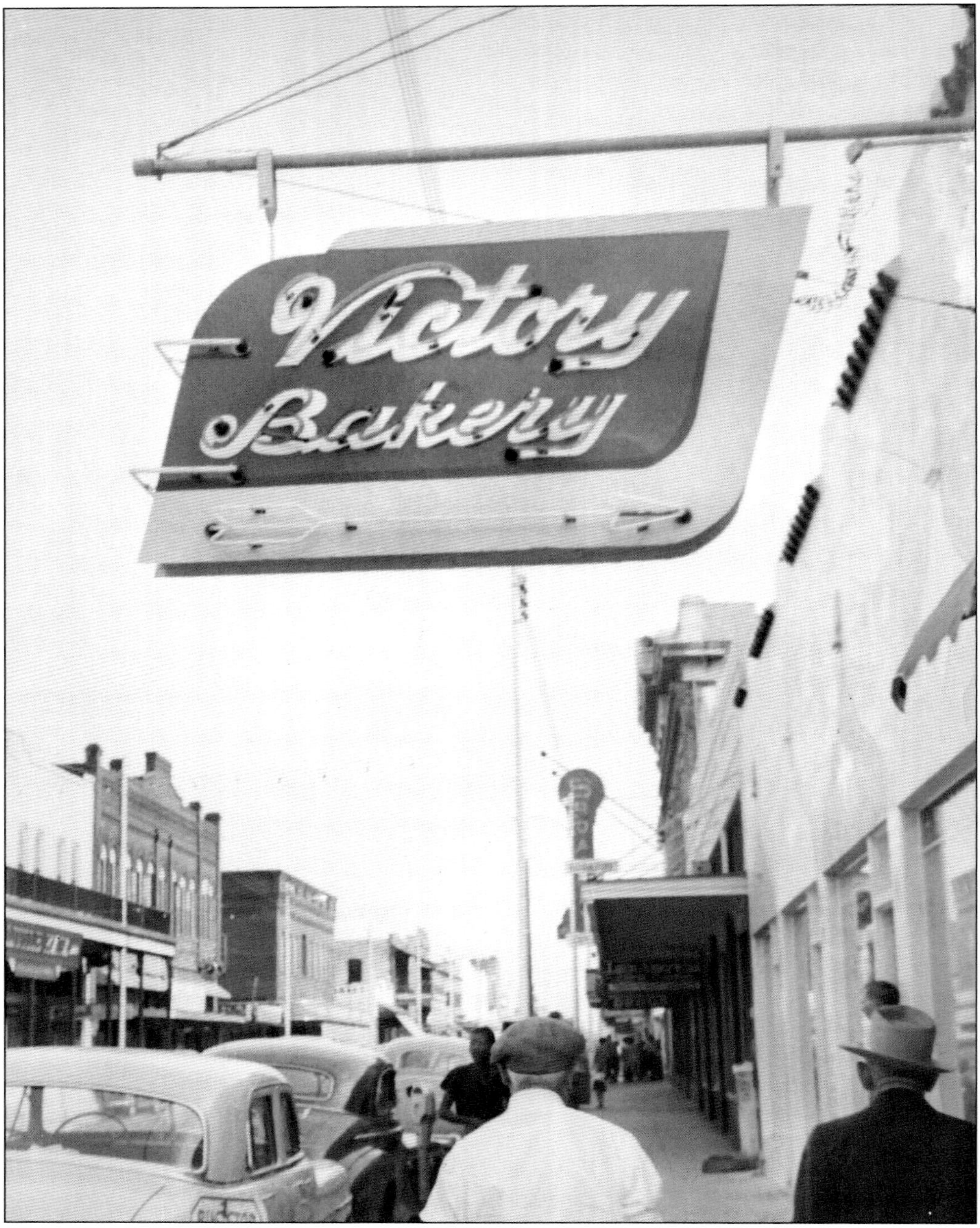

The scent of fresh baked Cuban bread calls customers to the well-known Victory Bakery on Seventh Avenue in Ybor City, pictured looking east toward Eighteenth Street. What a busy day it was for shoppers! Cinchett Neon Signs created this nifty sign in 1956.

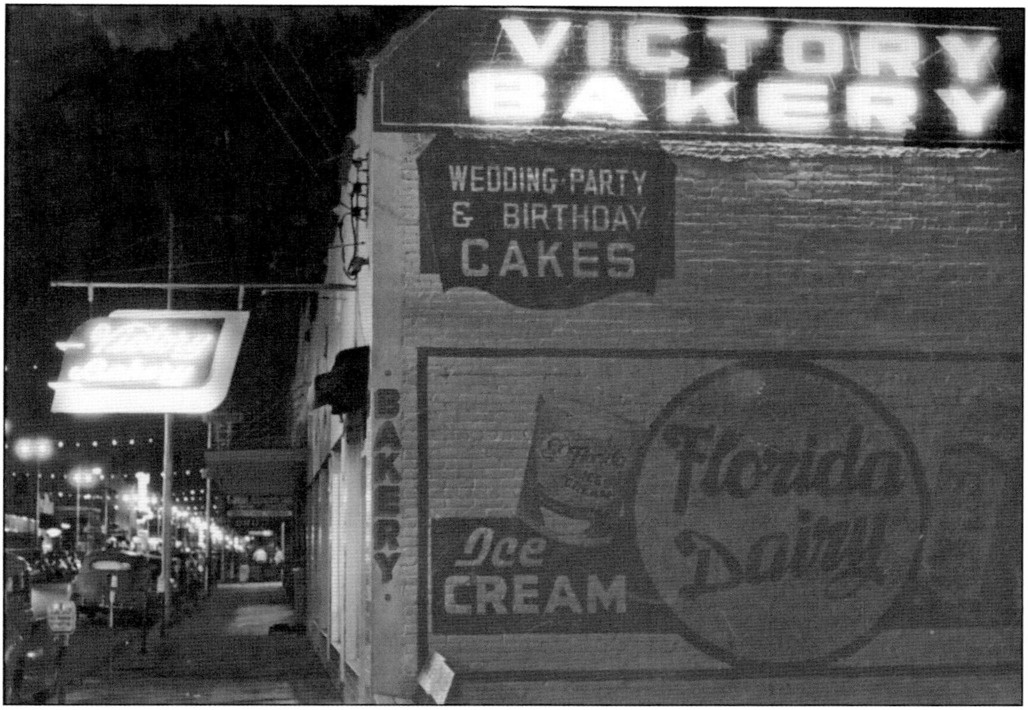

This spectacular view looks east from the Victory Bakery along bustling Seventh Avenue one evening in 1956. In the photograph below, fresh cakes and pastries wait at the bakery, and this window display is surrounded by neon, another 1950s design popular at the time. (Below, courtesy USFSCL.)

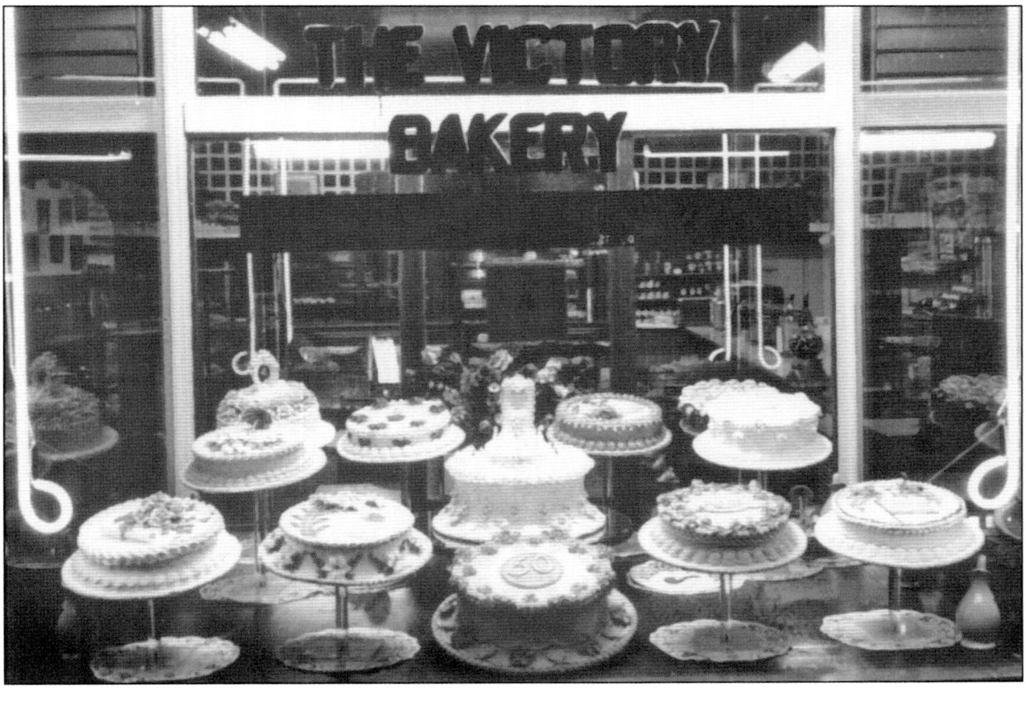

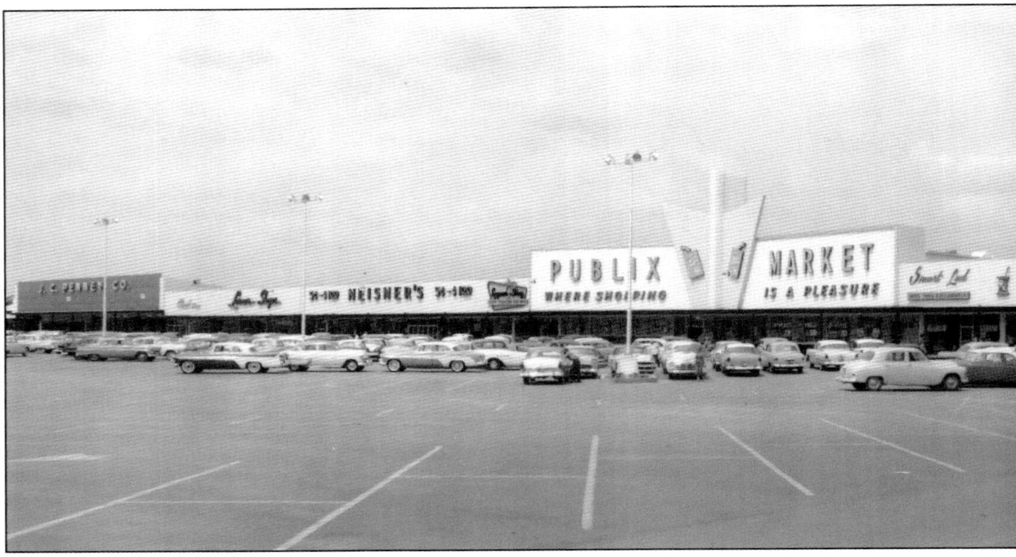

In 1956, Tampa welcomed its first major shopping centers with two massive developments. The expansive Northgate Shopping Center on North Florida Avenue took hold in what was a developing section of North Tampa and featured famous stores, including JCPenney, Grants, Rexall Drugs, and a new Publix supermarket. In South Tampa, the massive Britton Plaza offered the convenience of ample free parking and multiple stores within one plaza, something that downtown simply could not offer. Britton Plaza offered another new concept for Tampa—a movie theater in the shopping center. Many fine shops found a home at these plazas, and some of them are pictured here.

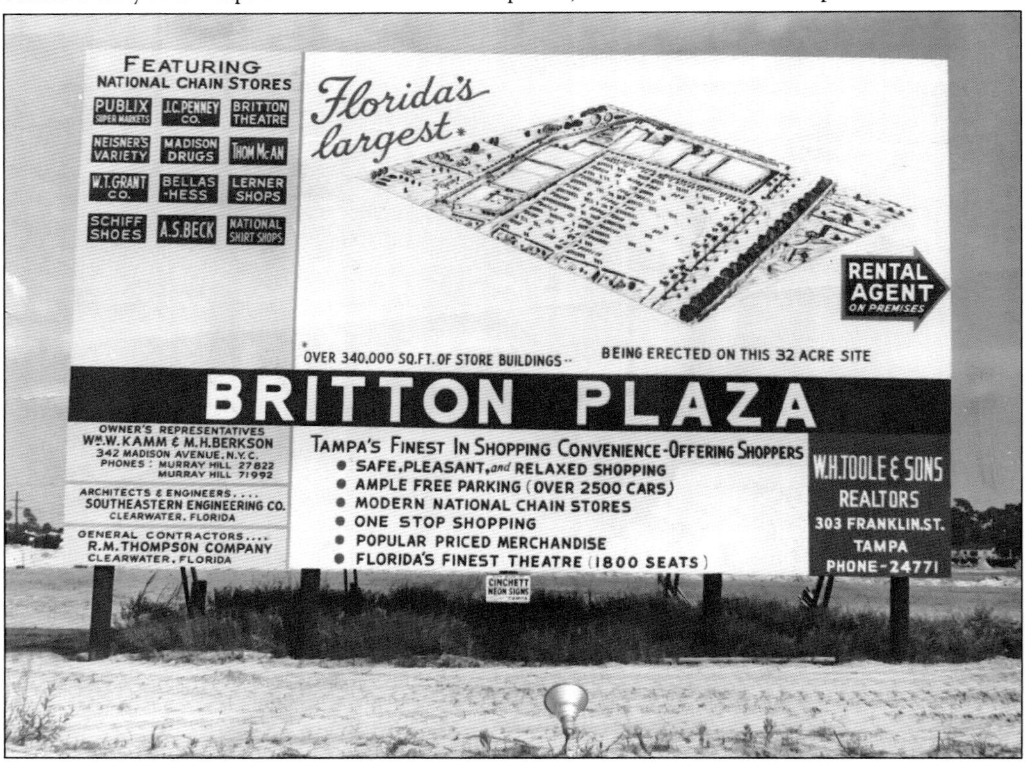

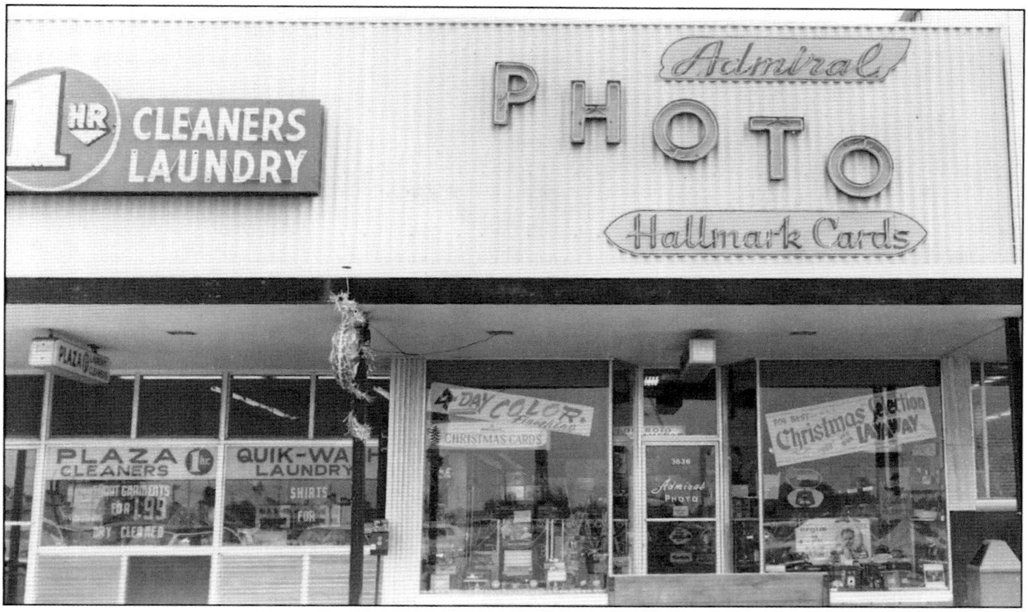

New shopping centers like Northgate, pictured among these photographs, created a new type of sign, the under-canopy sign. In this photograph, the Plaza Cleaners sign installed under the canopy overhang was lighted to direct shoppers who could not see the storefront as they walked along the plaza sidewalk. Notice the cleaners' advertised special, five shirts for 99¢. Also, the photo shop offered color prints in only four days.

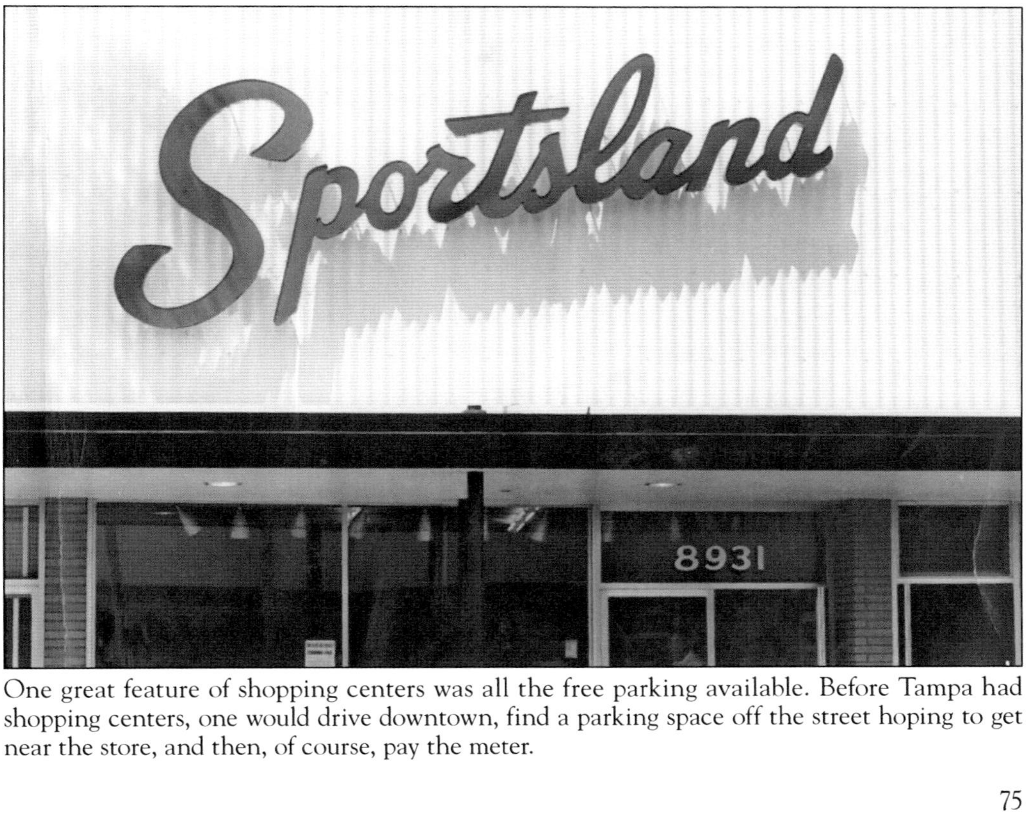

One great feature of shopping centers was all the free parking available. Before Tampa had shopping centers, one would drive downtown, find a parking space off the street hoping to get near the store, and then, of course, pay the meter.

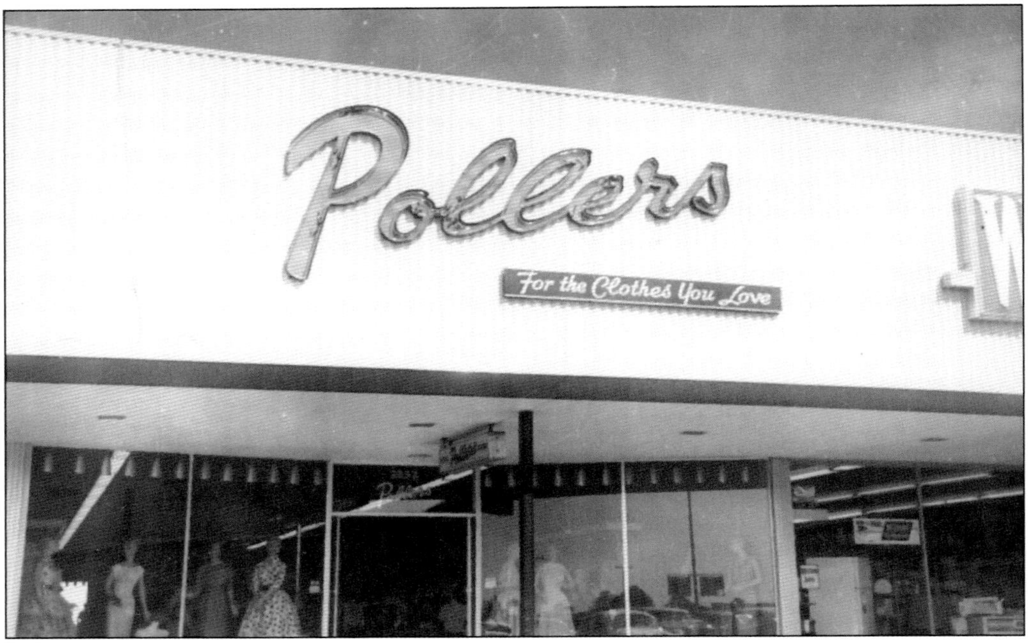

Pollers Dress Shop was one of many popular ladies stores that could be found at Northgate Shopping Center in the late 1950s. The ladies of Tampa were thrilled to have such stores nearby in plazas like Northgate to save them from planning a trip downtown. Pictured below is another popular shoe store at Northgate in 1959.

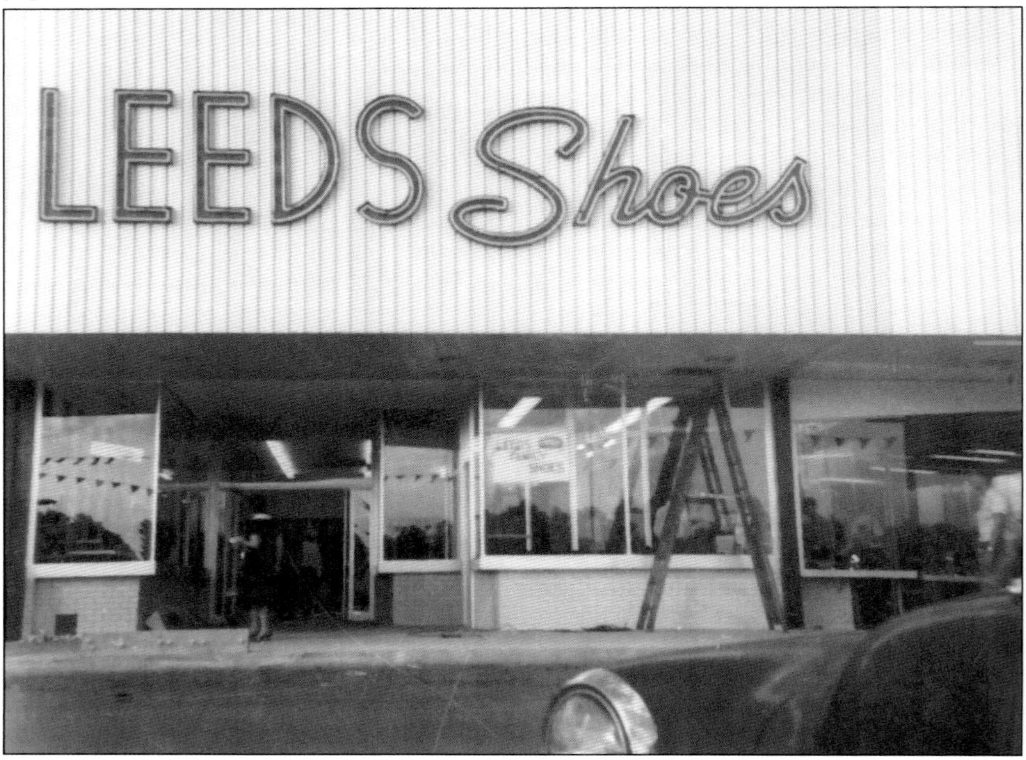

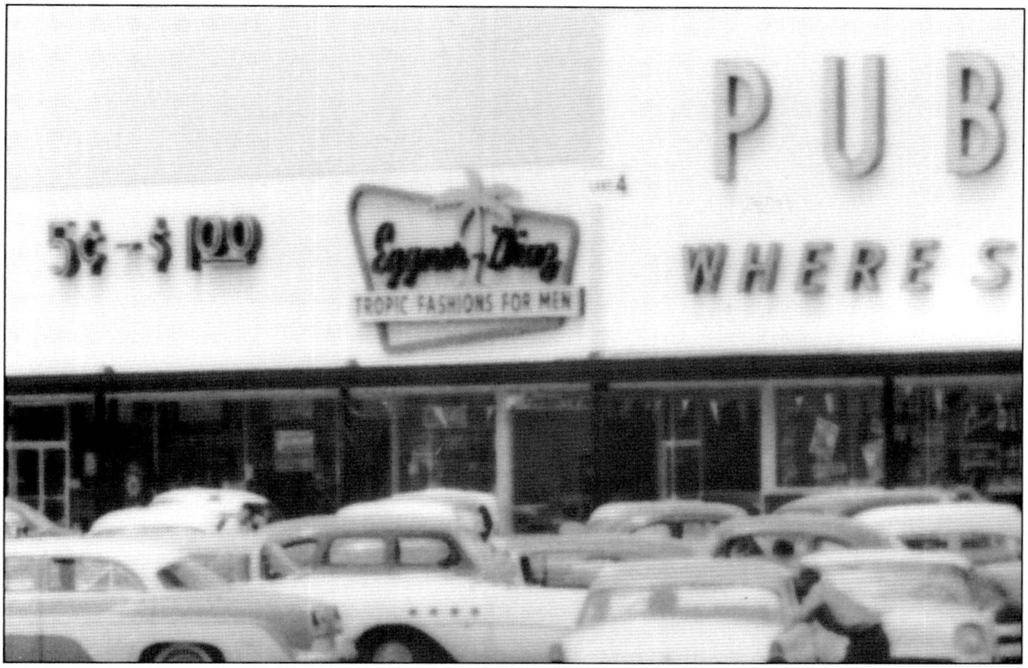

This palm tree–inspired neon sign was without a doubt the most beautiful among all those along Northgate Shopping Center. Tropic Fashions was an exclusive menswear store that was opened at Northgate in 1956 by Hollis Eggner and his business partner, a Mr. Diaz.

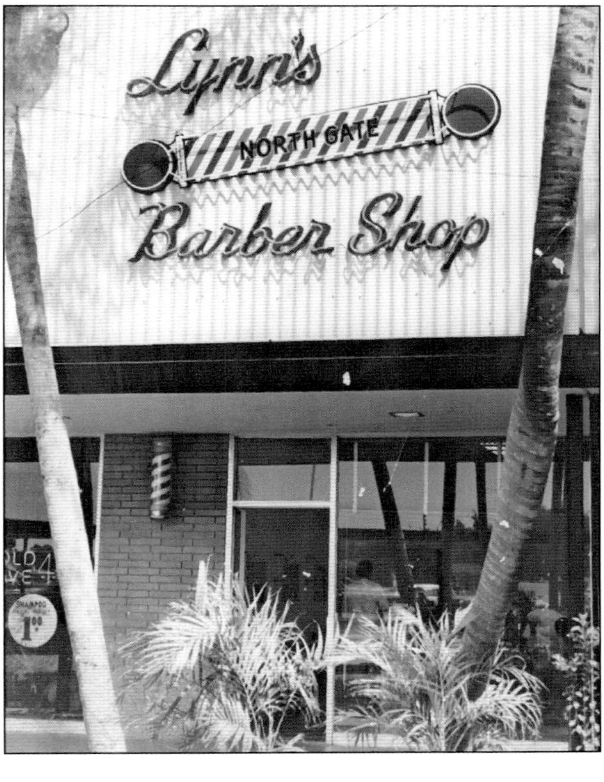

Another nice feature of shopping plazas was the one-stop shopping trip, a new concept for Tampa folks during the 1950s. One could visit the barber, shop, and drop off the dry-cleaning, all in one visit. Northgate Shopping Center became one of Tampa's most popular destinations and still stands today.

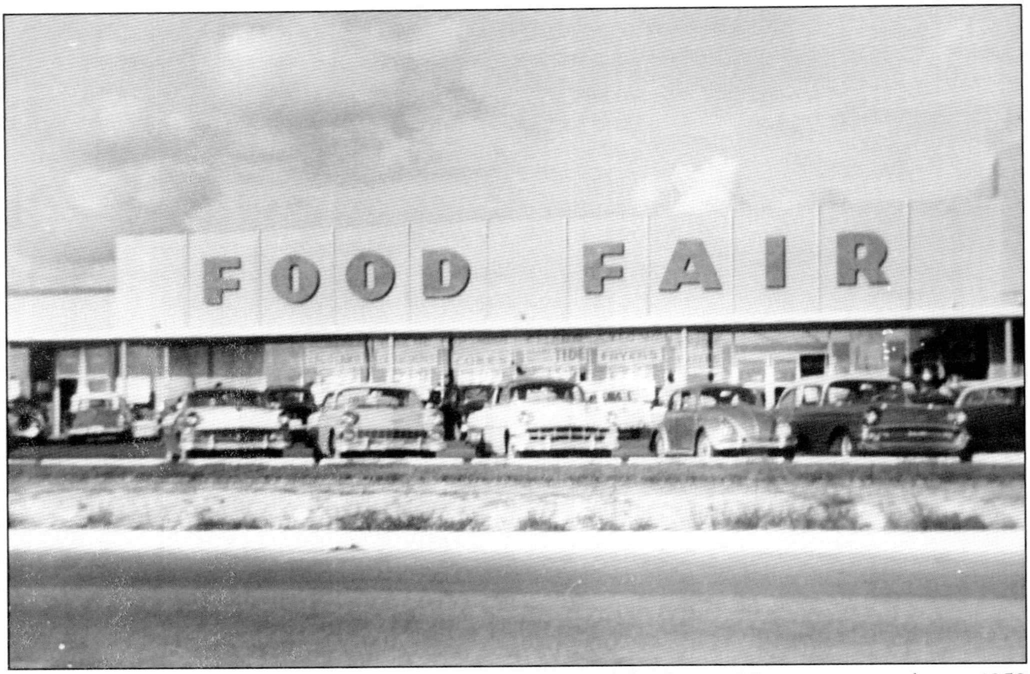

Tampa's sister city across the bay, St. Petersburg, welcomed this beautiful new supermarket in 1958 on Forty-ninth Street North near Fifty-fourth Avenue. This was a welcome sight for residents in the growing north end of town.

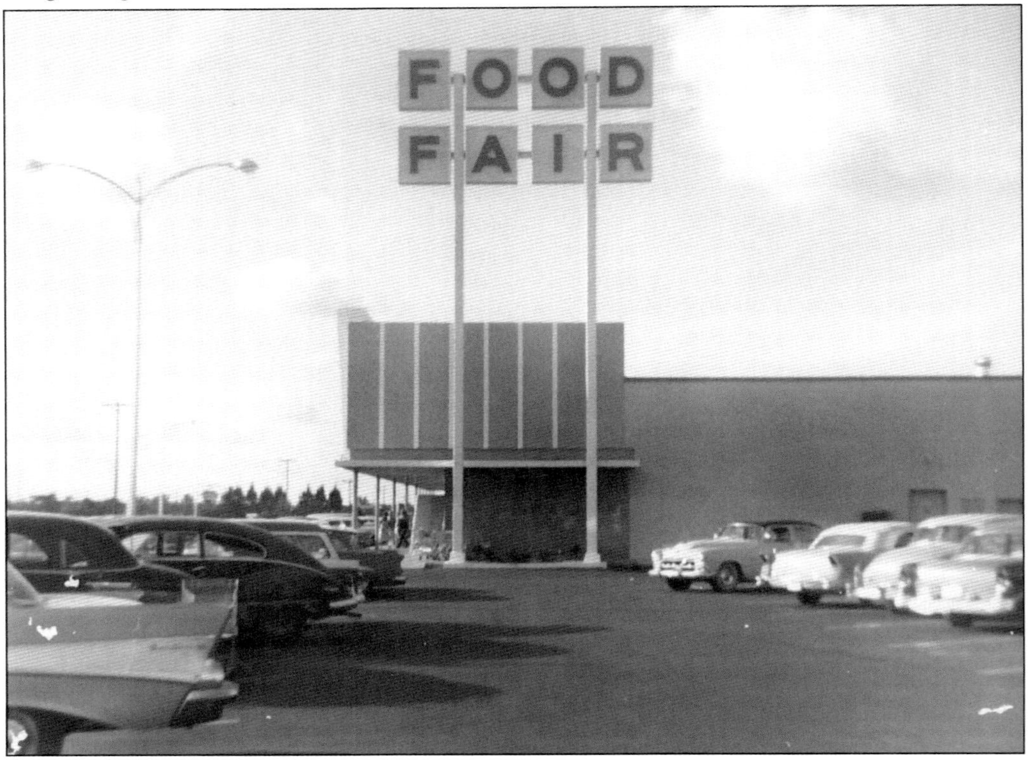

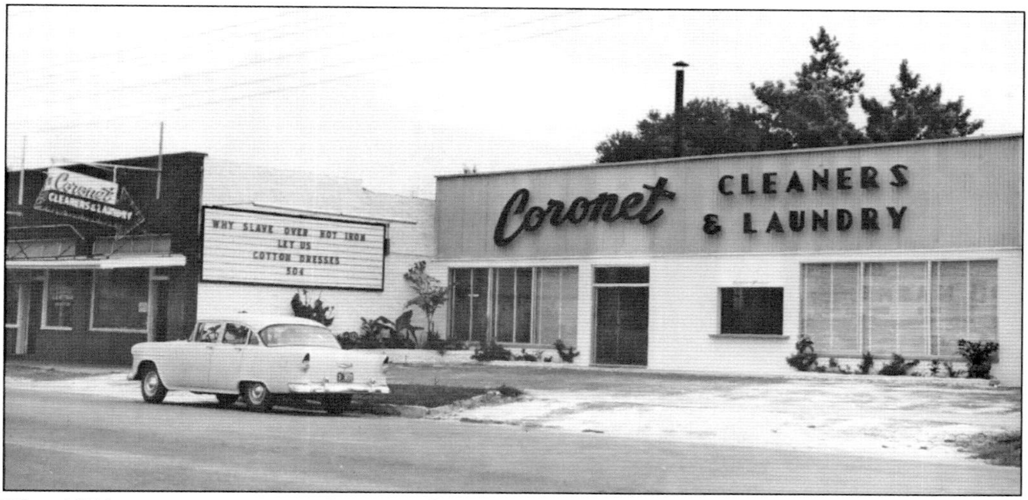

This 1956 neon assortment of signs is for Coronet Cleaners at 4410 North Nebraska Avenue in Seminole Heights. Notice the marquee message: "Why slave over hot iron—cotton dresses 50 cents."

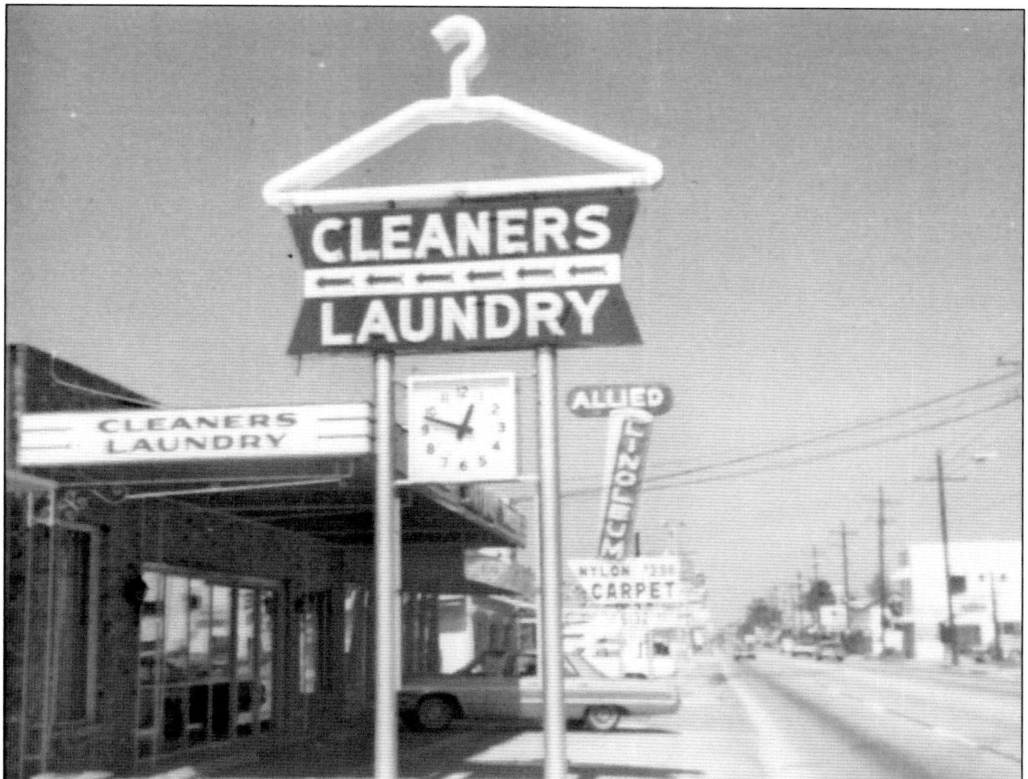

This dry-cleaner on Florida Avenue just south of Hillsborough Avenue was one of Tampa's best known, with its brightly lit neon hanger to guide customers into the store in 1963. This photograph was taken looking north on Florida Avenue. Notice the large clock under the sign—another vintage feature never seen anymore.

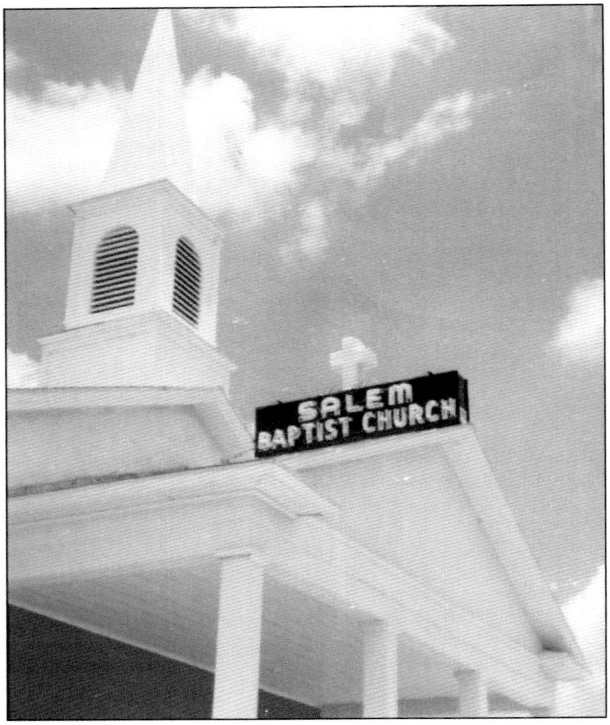

Tampa churches also needed neon signs to direct local folks to their neighborhood temple. This 1966 church sign features a lighted neon cross in front of the steeple for the good people of Salem Baptist Church on Temple Terrace Highway (now Busch Boulevard). This church was founded in 1951 and still stands today.

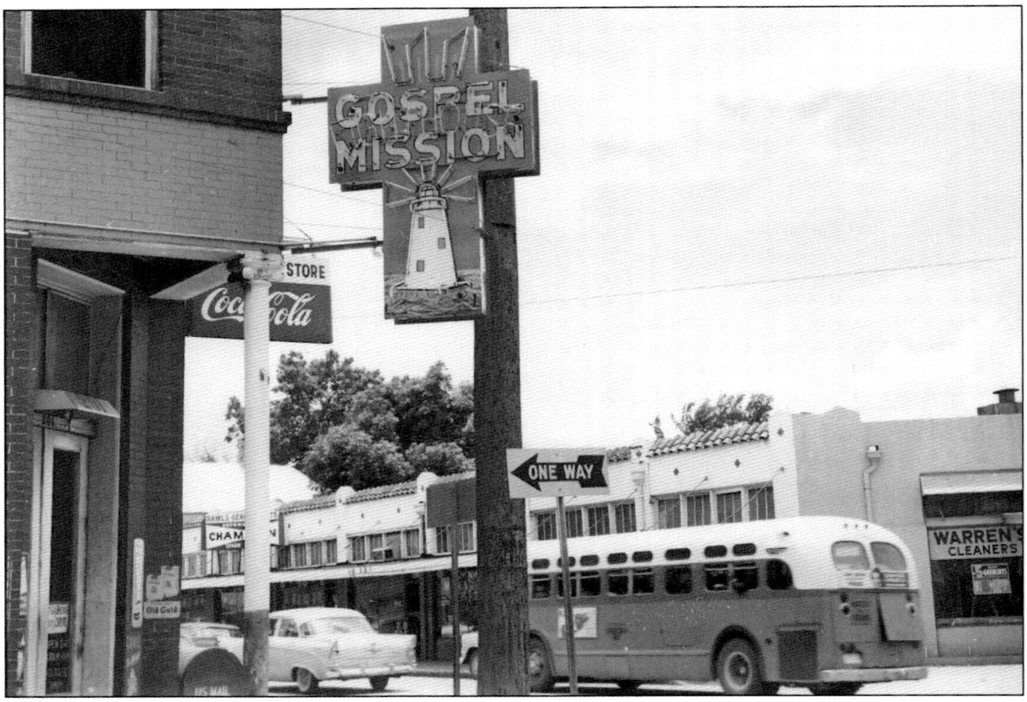

The 1957 design of this church sign at the corner of Tampa and Fortune Streets is extraordinary—a neon lighthouse with a lighted beacon and neon waves of blue water below are mounted on the cross. This was one of the most beautiful church signs designed by Cinchett Neon Signs.

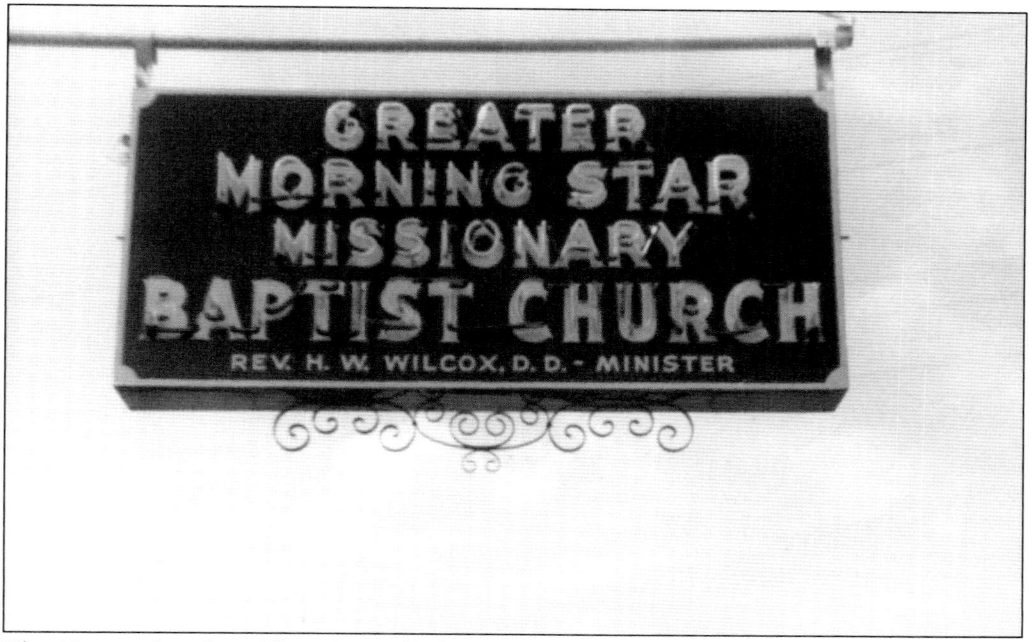

This Tampa church in Ybor City called its worshippers with a heavenly neon sign accented with ornamental iron in 1968. This was a popular feature of signs made by Cinchett Neon Signs for churches.

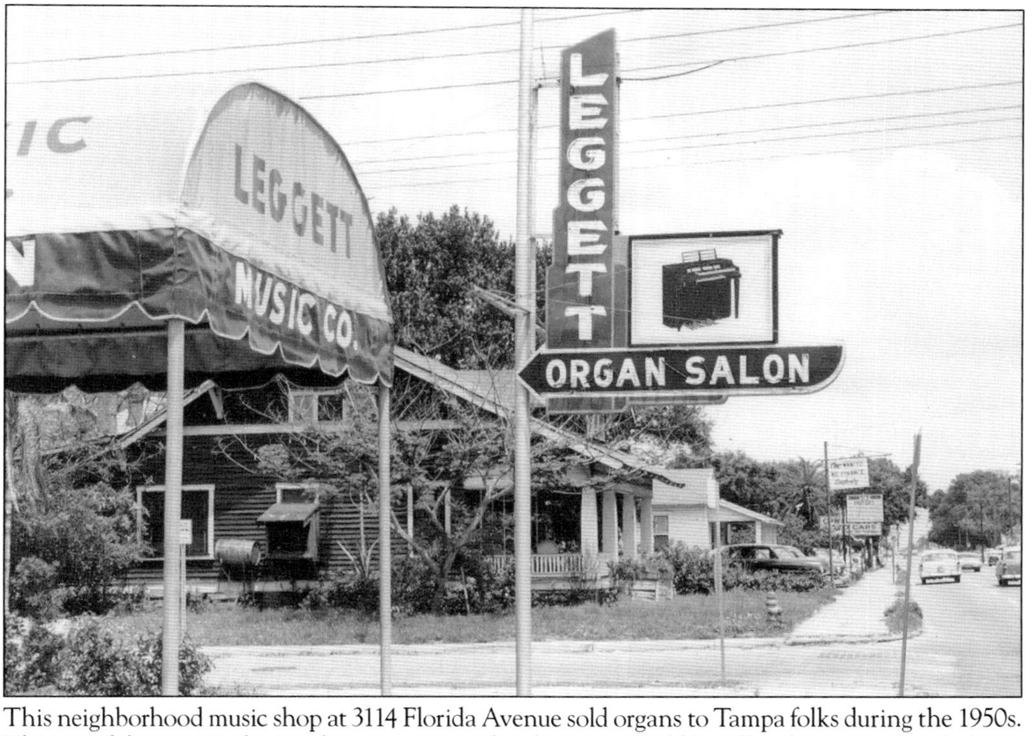

This neighborhood music shop at 3114 Florida Avenue sold organs to Tampa folks during the 1950s. The use of the term "salon" indicates a personalized service would be offered to customers, helping them select an organ suitable for their home. Notice the sign features a hand-painted organ.

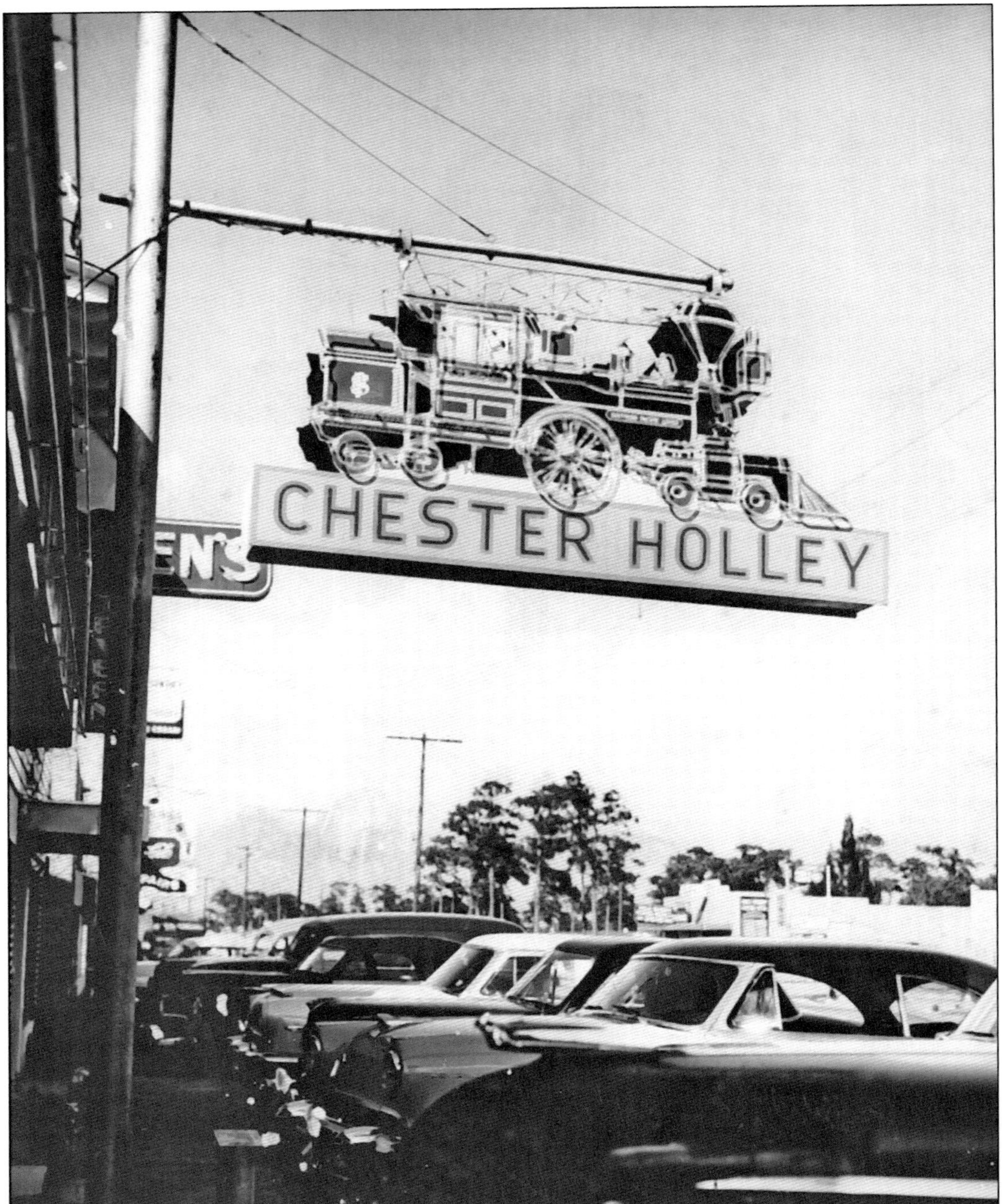

All aboard! This South Tampa toy shop featured a detailed neon train with puffs of smoke—quite a work of art by Cinchett Neon Signs. This was located at 3641 South Dale Mabry Highway in 1956.

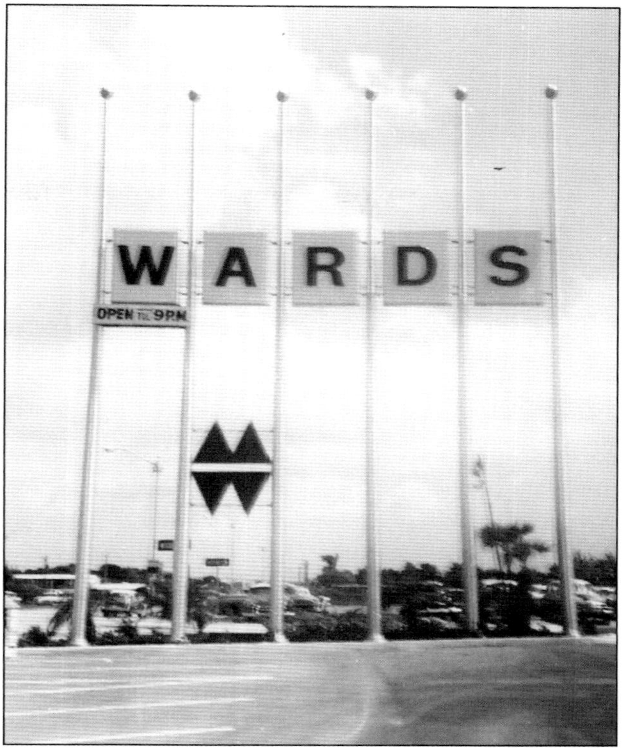

Montgomery Ward made its presence in Tampa known with this magnificent building at 1701 North Dale Mabry Highway in 1960. This multilevel department store was a popular destination for Tampa folks on the west side of the city because they did not have any large shopping centers nearby. Notice the space-age design of the building entrance.

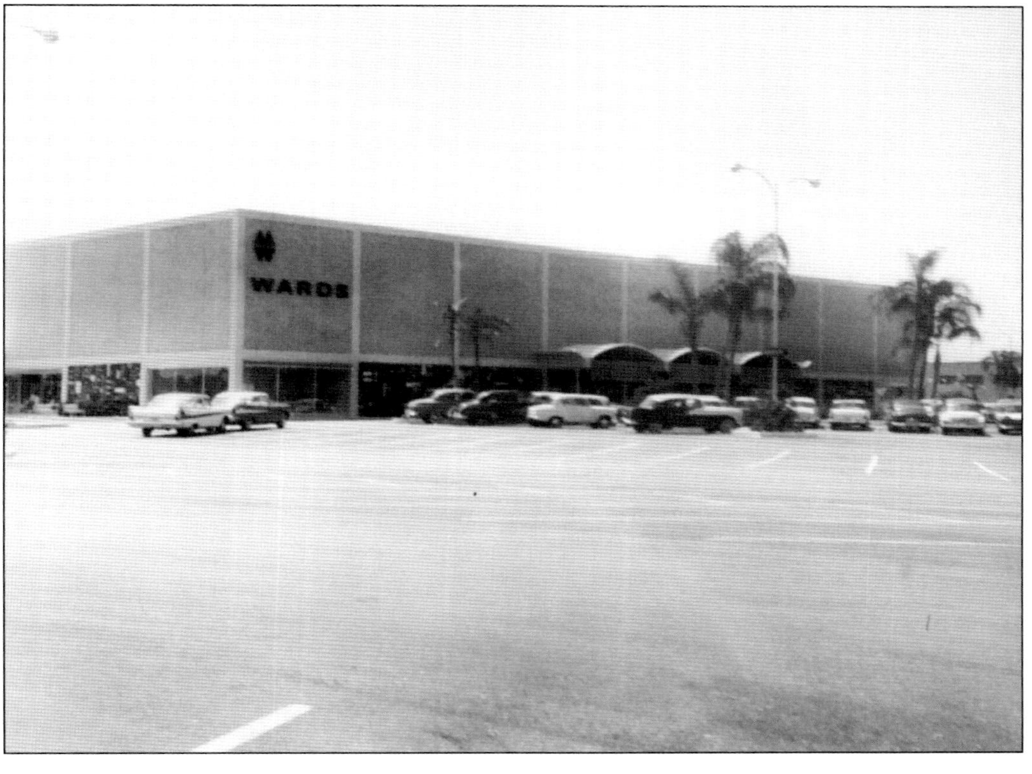

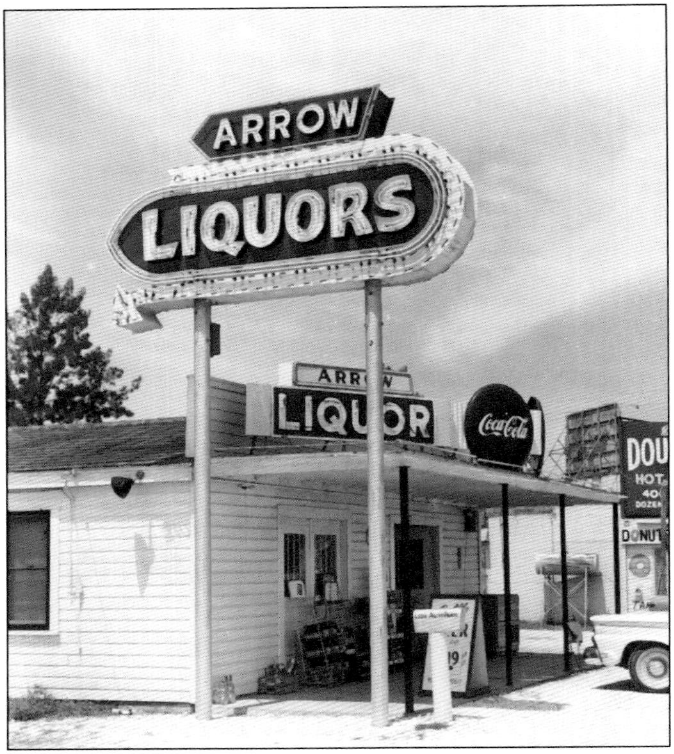

This liquor store at 3716 West Columbus Drive has a bright neon sign with flashing arrows that seems to outshine the vintage clapboard building it is attached to in this 1959 photograph.

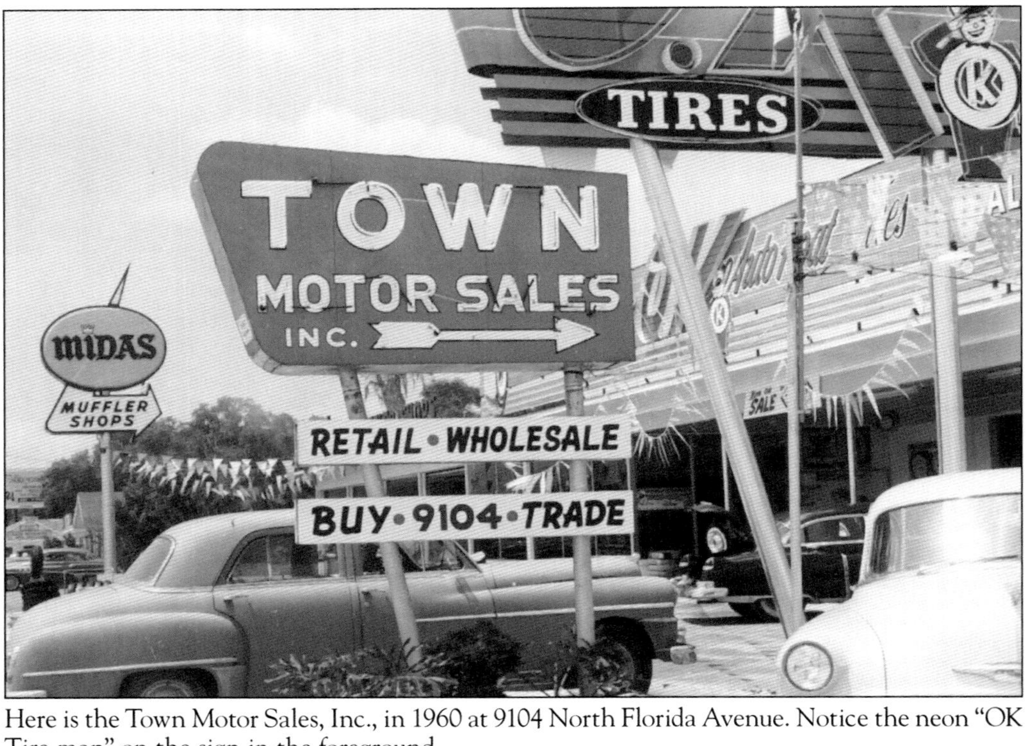

Here is the Town Motor Sales, Inc., in 1960 at 9104 North Florida Avenue. Notice the neon "OK Tire-man" on the sign in the foreground.

This giant neon wheel is surrounded by flashing arrows for the Safety Motor Company at 3700 West Columbus Drive in 1959. The picture was taken looking west toward Dale Mabry Highway. Notice that Dale Mabry Highway is a two-lane road at this time.

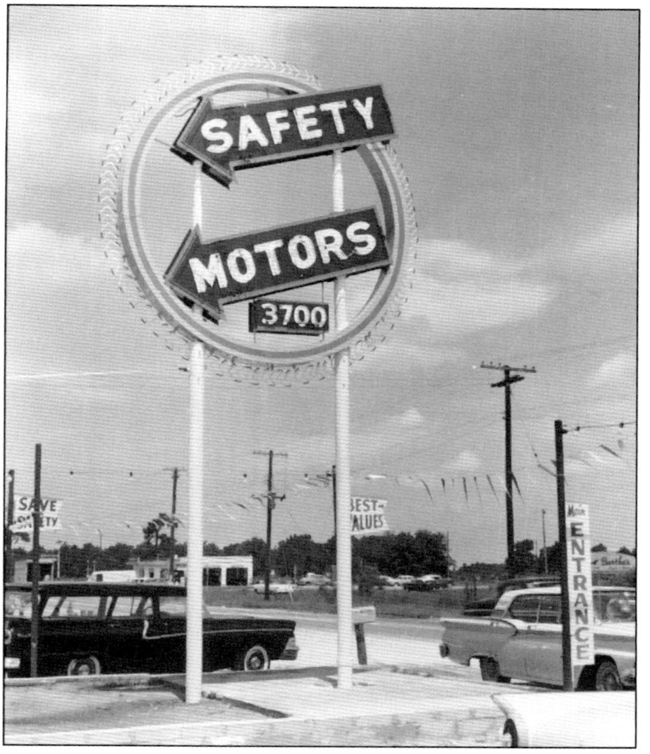

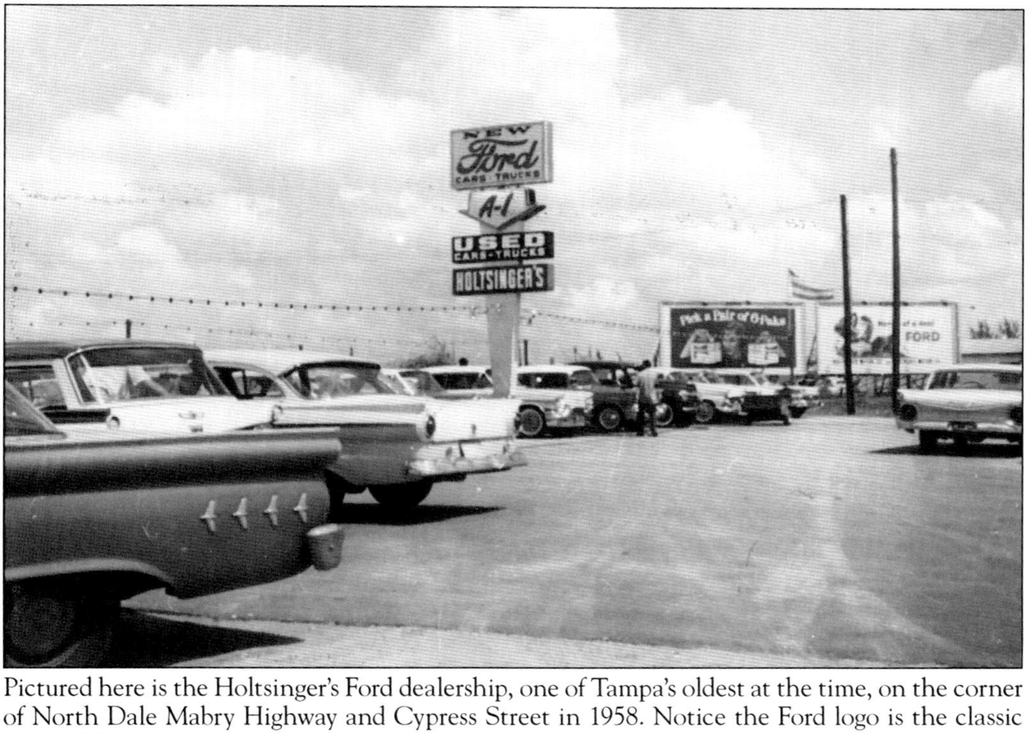

Pictured here is the Holtsinger's Ford dealership, one of Tampa's oldest at the time, on the corner of North Dale Mabry Highway and Cypress Street in 1958. Notice the Ford logo is the classic original design.

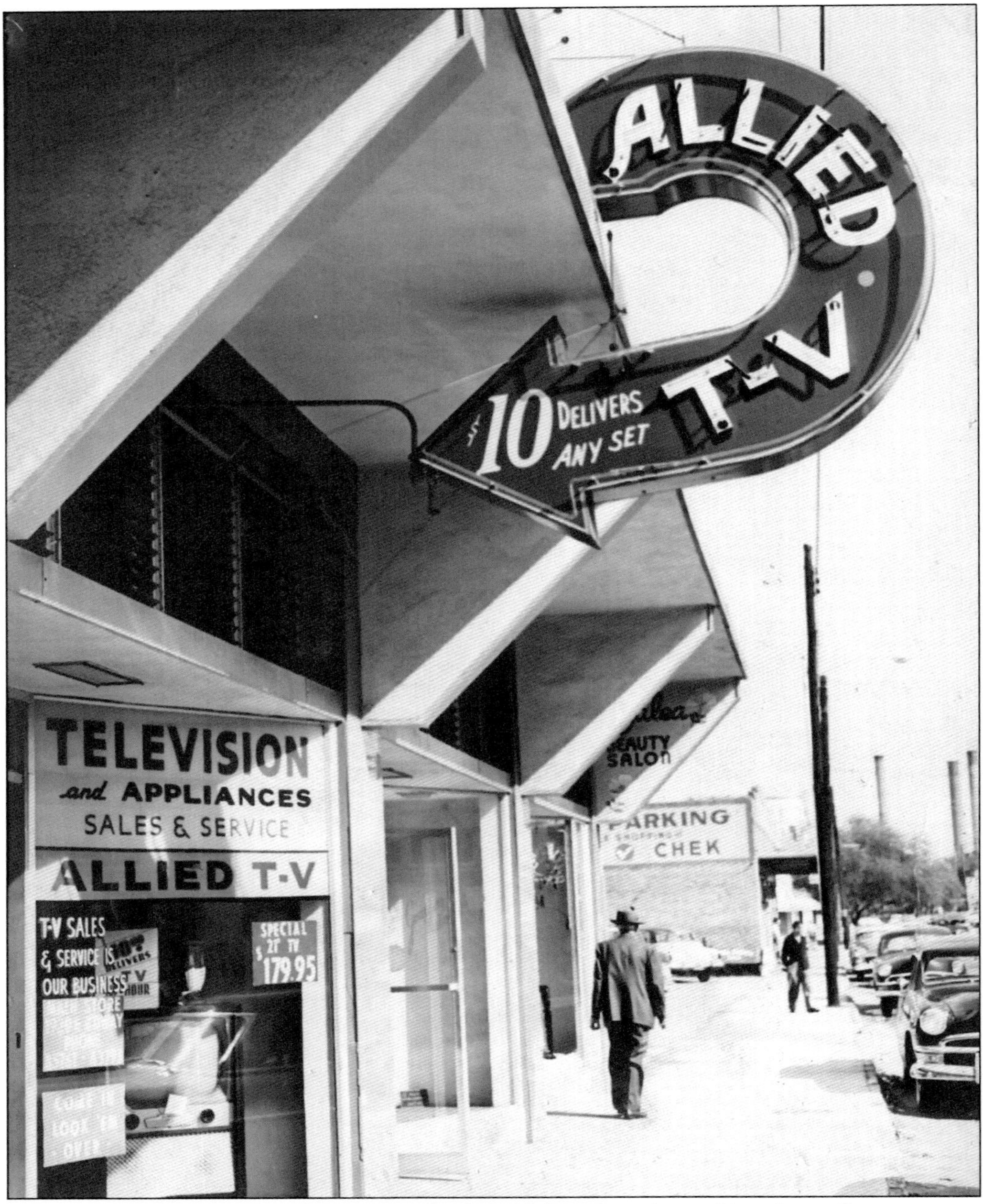

This Tampa television shop has a special—$179.95 for a brand-new 21-inch set. Buying a new television was a big event for Tampa families in 1956, when this photograph was taken for Allied TV Sales. Take notice of the older gentleman walking along with his hat and coat, typical attire for men out on an errand during this era.

Television Programs

Schedules given below are published on responsibility of the stations involved.

THIS EVENING—Saturday

Time	WFLA-TV Tampa Channel 8	WSUN-TV St. Petersburg Channel 38	WTVT Tampa Channel 13	WDBO-TV Orlando Channel 6
2:00	Humphrey	Big Picture	White Sox-Indians	White Sox-Indians
2:15	Humphrey	Big Picture	White Sox-Indians	White Sox-Indians
2:30	Humphrey	Kartoon Karnival	White Sox-Indians	White Sox-Indians
2:45	Humphrey	Kartoon Karnival	White Sox-Indians	White Sox-Indians
3:00	Humphrey	Kartoon Karnival	White Sox-Indians	White Sox-Indians
3:15	Humphrey	Kartoon Karnival	White Sox-Indians	White Sox-Indians
3:30	Stars Ov. Tex.	Your Welfare	White Sox-Indians	White Sox-Indians
3:45	Stars Ov. Tex.	Your Welfare	Scoreboard	Viewer's Digest
4:00	Stars Ov. Tex.	Kartoon Karnival	Six Gun Playhouse	Viewer's Digest
4:15	Stars Ov. Tex.	Kartoon Karnival	Six Gun Playhouse	Viewer's Digest
4:30	Western	Hopalong Cassidy	Six Gun Playhouse	Big Picture
4:45	Western	Hopalong Cassidy	Six Gun Playhouse	Big Picture
5:00	Western	Hopalong Cassidy	Cisco Kid	Amos 'n' Andy
5:15	Western	Hopalong Cassidy	Cisco Kid	Amos 'n' Andy
5:30	Roy Rogers	Champ. Bowling	Amos 'n' Andy	Fla. Drifters
5:45	Roy Rogers	Champ. Bowling	Amos 'n' Andy	Fla. Drifters
6:00	C. of C. Report	Champ. Bowling	Country Frolics	Country Frolics
6:15	C. of C. Report	Scoreboard	Country Frolics	Country Frolics
6:30	Down You Go	Ozark Jubilee	Beat the Clock	Fla. Showcase
6:45	Down You Go	Ozark Jubilee	Beat the Clock	Fla. Showcase
7:00	T. Bennett (c)	Ozark Jubilee	Jackie Gleason	Jackie Gleason
7:15	Tony Bennett	Ozark Jubilee	Jackie Gleason	Jackie Gleason
7:30	Tony Bennett	Ozark Jubilee	Stage Show	Badge 714
7:45	Tony Bennett	Ozark Jubilee	Stage Show	Badge 714
8:00	People Funny	Lawrence Welk	Two for Money	People's Choice
8:15	People Funny	Lawrence Welk	Two for Money	People's Choice
8:30	Fest. of Stars	Lawrence Welk	Hey, Jeannie	Hey, Jeannie
8:45	Fest. of Stars	Lawrence Welk	Hey, Jeannie	Hey, Jeannie
9:00	Encore Theater	Masquerade Party	Gunsmoke	Gunsmoke
9:15	Encore Theater	Masquerade Party	Gunsmoke	Gunsmoke
9:30	Hit Parade	Miss America	High Finance	Science Fic. Thtr.
9:45	Hit Parade	Miss America	High Finance	Science Fic. Thtr.
10:00	Gr. Ole Opry	Miss America	Big Town	Bob Cummings
10:15	Gr. Ole Opry	Miss America	Big Town	Bob Cummings
10:30	Marion Hendry	Miss America	All Star Theater	The Vise
10:45	North of Nome	Miss America	All Star Theater	The Vise
11:00	North of Nome	News-Theater	Outpost in Morocco	TBA
11:15	North of Nome	Mr. Universe	Outpost in Morocco	TBA
11:30	North of Nome	Mr. Universe	Outpost in Morocco	TBA
11:45	North of Nome	Mr. Universe	Outpost in Morocco	TBA
12:00	Sign Off	Mr. Universe	Outpost in Morocco	Sign Off
		Sign Off	Outpost in Morocco	
			Sign Off	

Here is the Tampa television channel and program schedule for Saturday, September 8, 1956, with a total of four television stations to watch on a new set from Allied TV Sales. Some of these television shows will bring back happy memories of gathering around the television set with family and friends.

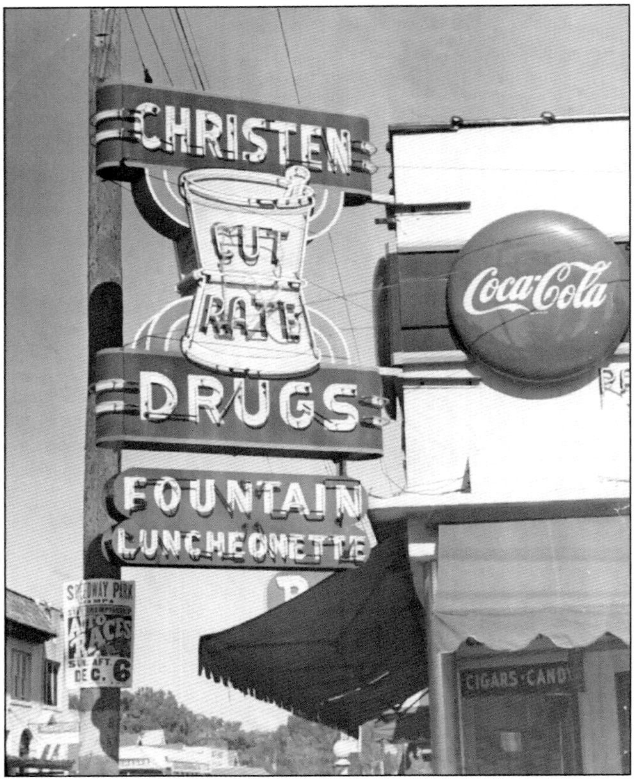

This neon sign for Christen Drugs welcomes locals (literally) to the corner drugstore and "Fountain-Luncheonette," popular during the 1950s. This was a short-order restaurant that would serve milk shakes and burgers to patrons who sat on stools at a long counter that usually stretched along one wall of the store. This drugstore was at the corner of Columbus Drive and Nebraska Avenue in 1956.

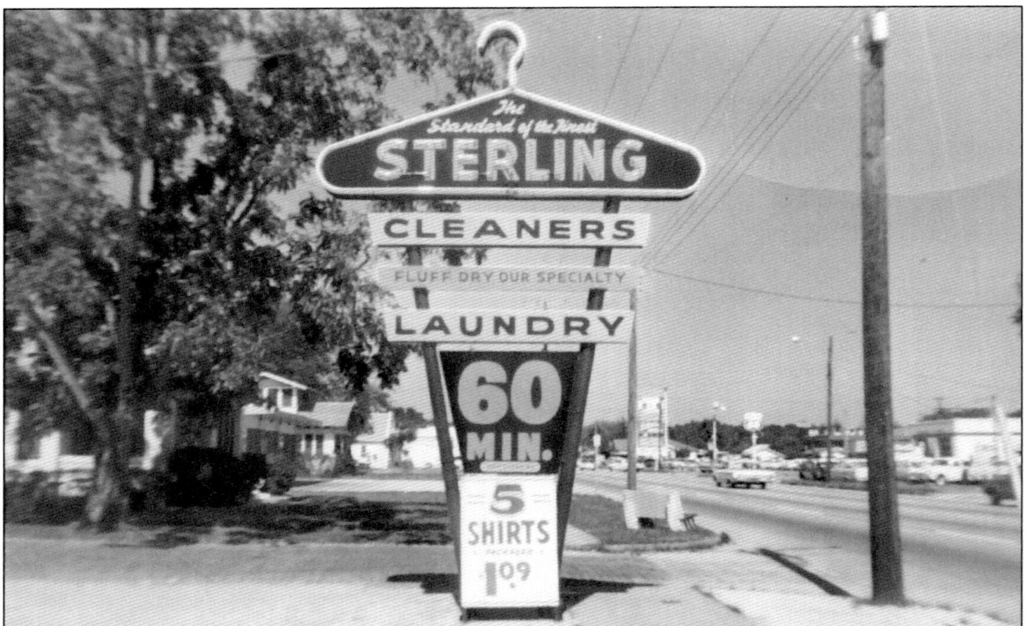

This dry-cleaning store was on Nebraska Avenue north of Buffalo Avenue (now Martin Luther King Boulevard) in 1964 and featured a neon hanger. Notice the special offered: five shirts for $1.09. This view looks north along Nebraska Avenue.

The owner's name cannot be missed with all that flashy neon at this beauty salon by Joseph's on North Florida Avenue in 1959. Notice the "cold-wave" advertised for $3.95. The sign also advertises haircuts for $1.

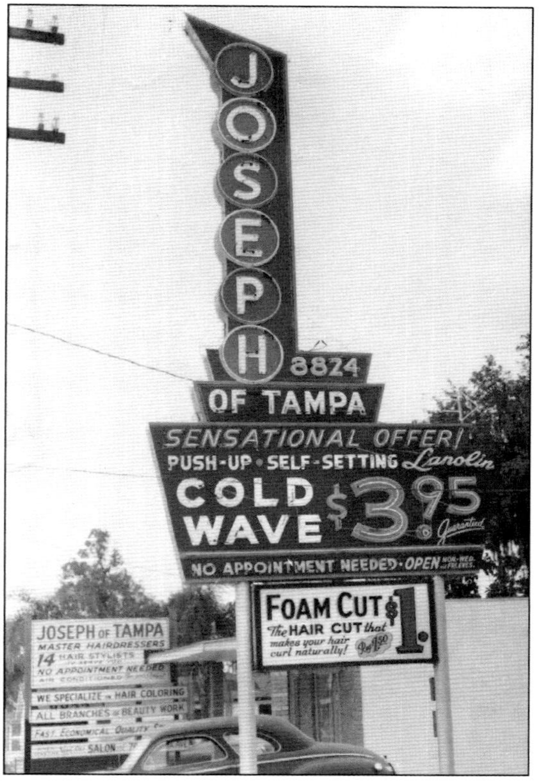

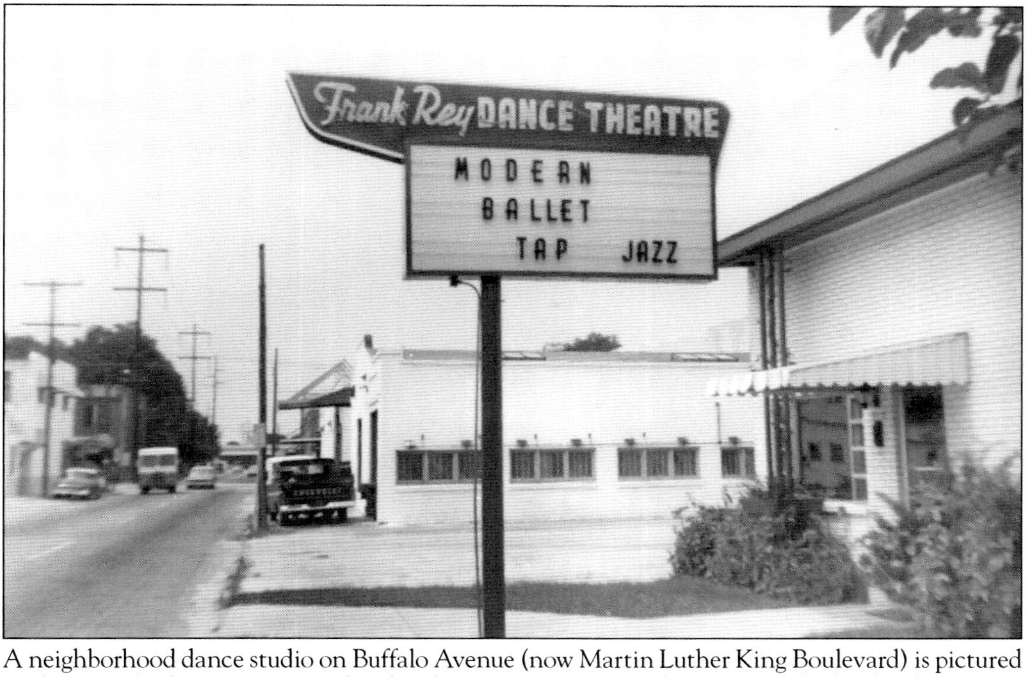

A neighborhood dance studio on Buffalo Avenue (now Martin Luther King Boulevard) is pictured in this view looking west toward Nebraska Avenue in 1959. This successful school still operates today in North Tampa.

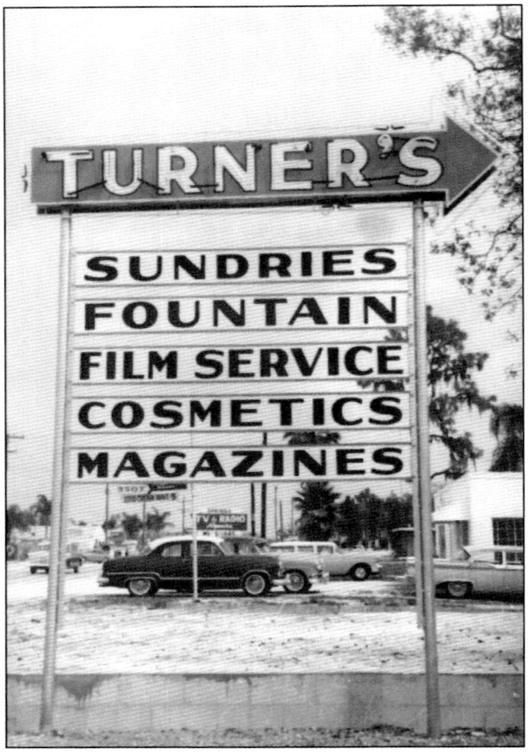

This is an example of a sign that was using the 19th-century-style term "sundries." The store advertises a fountain where customers could order ice cream sundaes at a counter inside the store. They could take a break from shopping and have a milk shake at the soda shop. This sign hearkens back to the "general store" days of small-town America and was located at 9511 Nebraska Avenue in 1962.

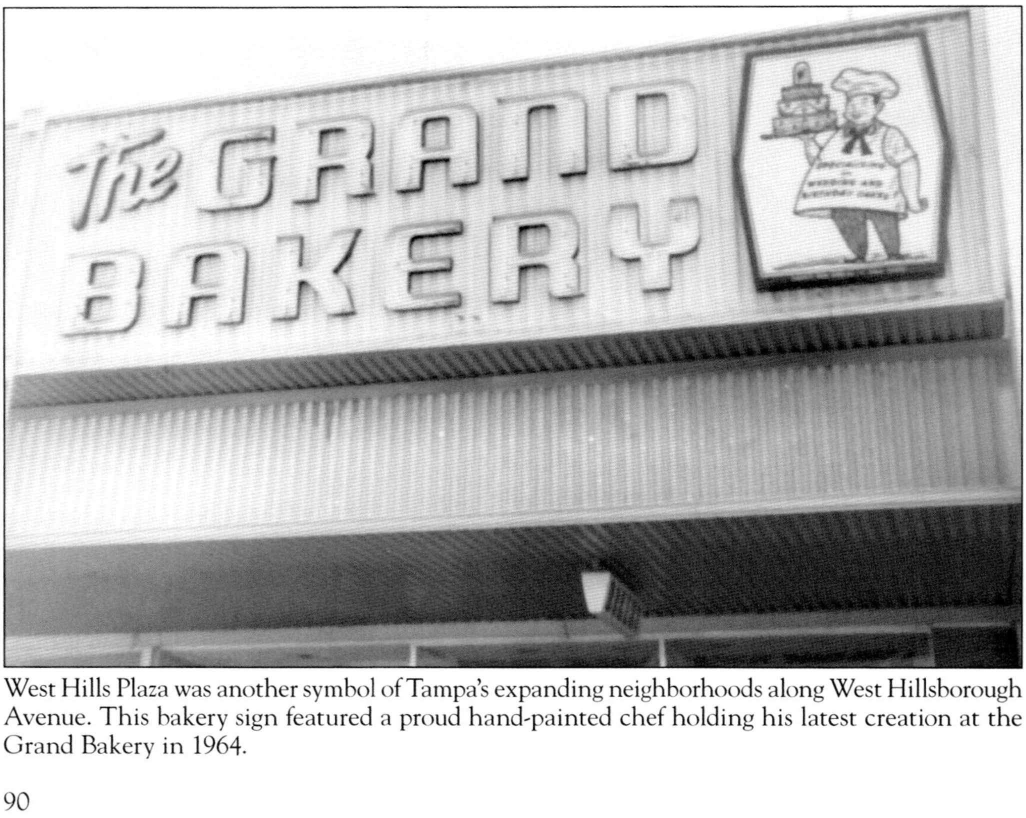

West Hills Plaza was another symbol of Tampa's expanding neighborhoods along West Hillsborough Avenue. This bakery sign featured a proud hand-painted chef holding his latest creation at the Grand Bakery in 1964.

This supermarket opened in 1950 at the corner of East Hillsborough Avenue and Fifteenth Street. Notice the sale price on melons: only 25¢ each or five for $1. This 1950 photograph was taken looking west along Hillsborough Avenue, and this store still stands today as a pawnshop.

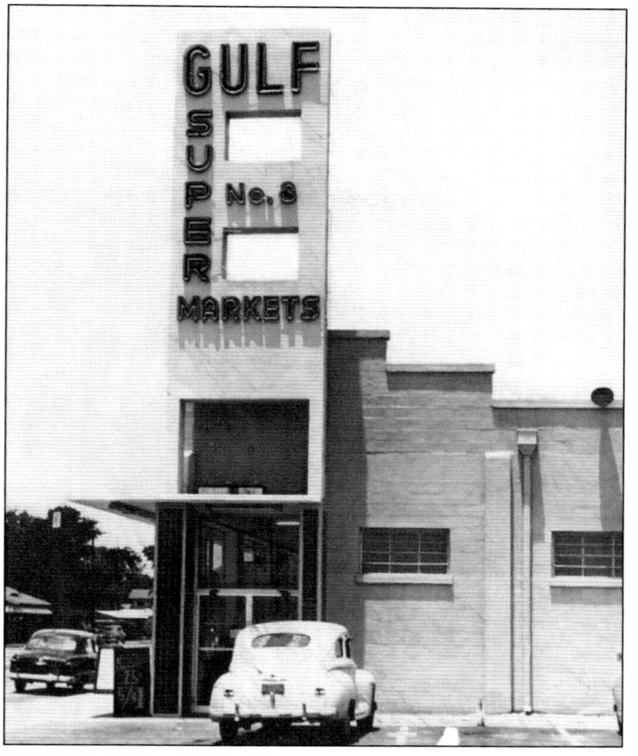

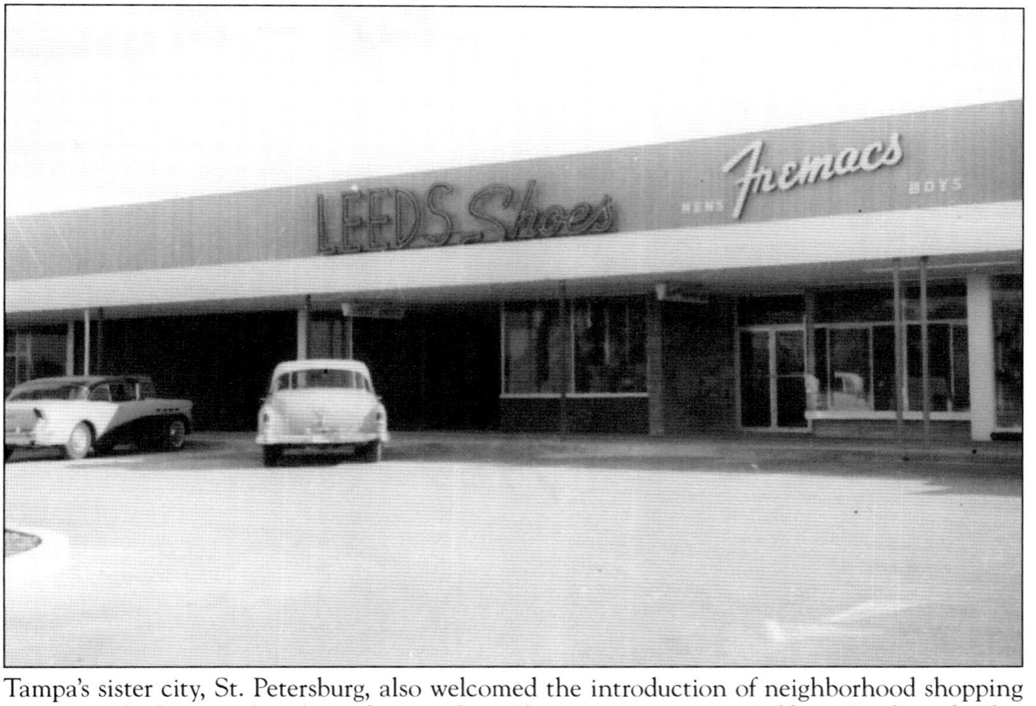

Tampa's sister city, St. Petersburg, also welcomed the introduction of neighborhood shopping centers with this popular plaza, the Pasadena Shopping Center on Gulfport Boulevard. This photograph was taken in 1959 for Leeds Shoes, and this plaza still stands today.

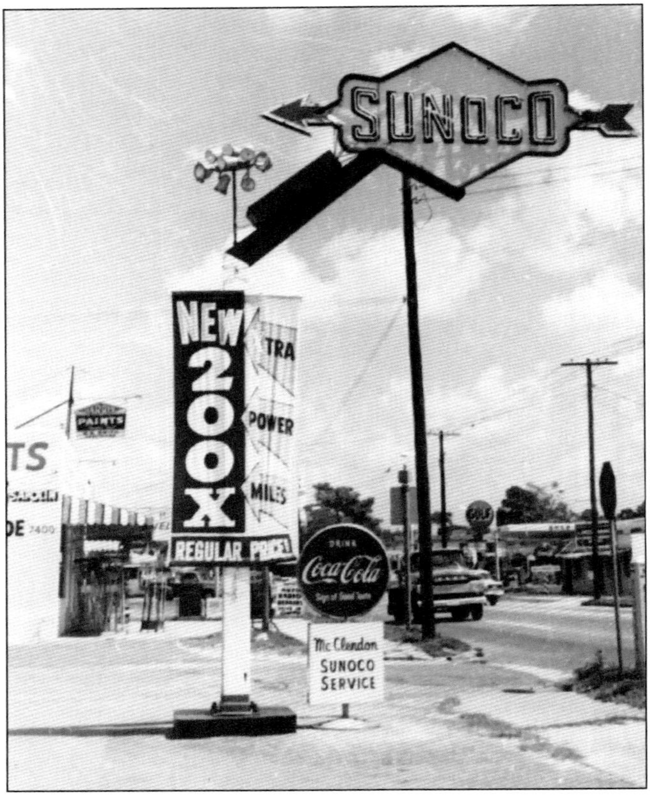

The busy Sunoco station is seen in this 1956 picture looking north on North Florida Avenue at Clinton Street in Seminole Heights. The original Gulf gas station's logo can be seen across the street. One vintage feature in this photograph is in the bottom right corner: the concrete marker that Tampa used for street signs, keeping the pedestrian in mind.

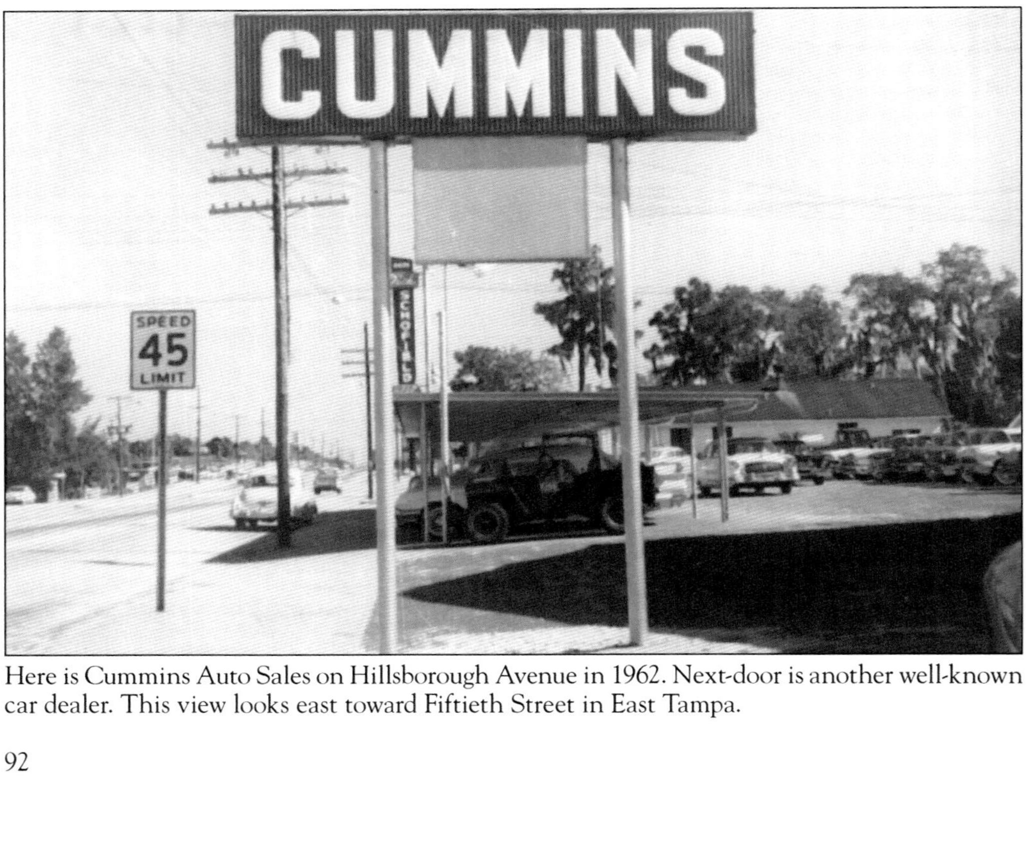

Here is Cummins Auto Sales on Hillsborough Avenue in 1962. Next-door is another well-known car dealer. This view looks east toward Fiftieth Street in East Tampa.

This beautiful sign features a giant colorful neon orange to catch the attention of shoppers. The family-owned corner drugstore was located at 2318 West Linebaugh Avenue in 1966. Notice that the store had a restaurant inside—this lunch counter is another vintage symbol of ages past. Most drugstores had these short-order restaurants inside them during the 1950s and 1960s.

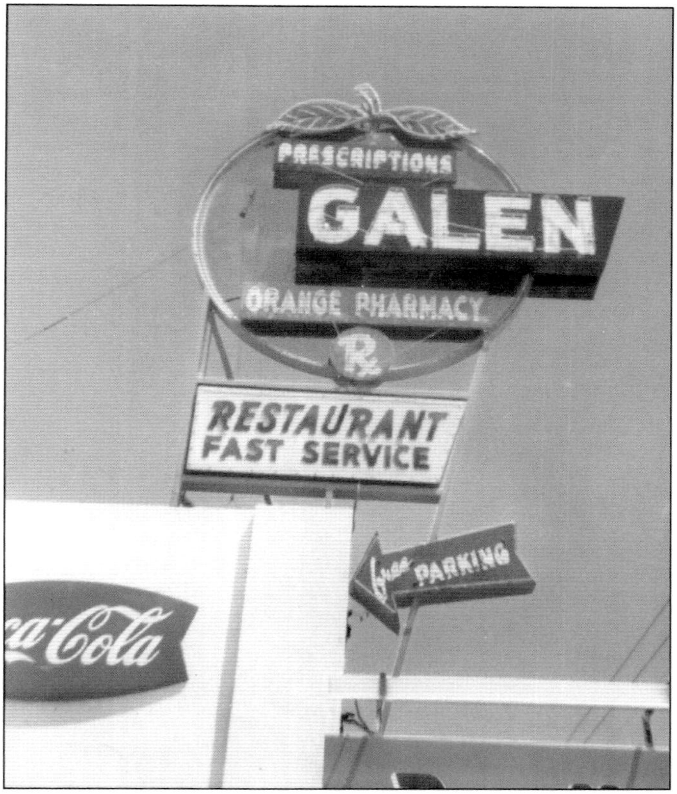

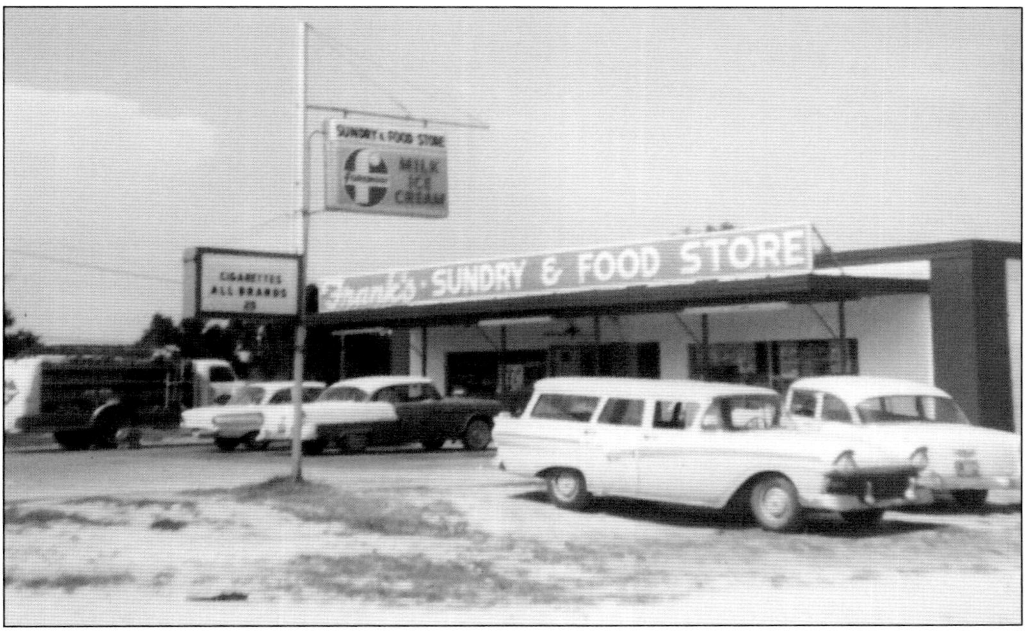

Here is another popular neighborhood market pictured in 1962. Notice the term "sundry" used in this food store's name—a 19th-century term that has been long forgotten in today's society. Notice the marquee advertising cigarettes for 25¢ per pack.

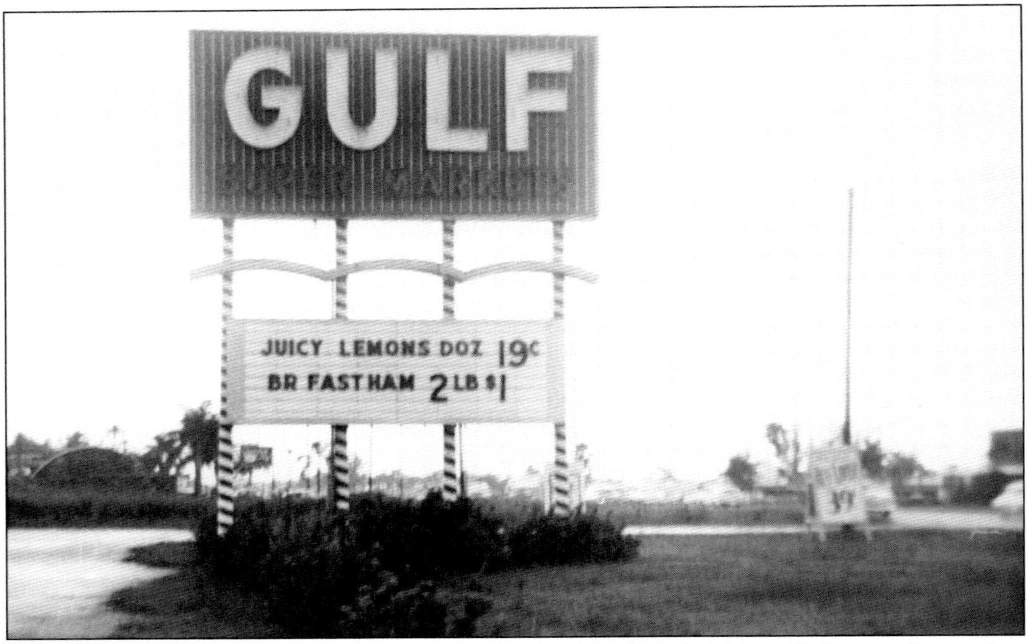

The neon sign for the new Gulf Supermarket at 1701 North Dale Mabry Highway is featured in this view looking south in 1957. Notice that the interstate has not made its way into town yet. Lemons are on sale for 19¢ a dozen, and ham is 50¢ a pound. In the scene below at the store's grand opening, shoppers have lined up their cars to pack the groceries.

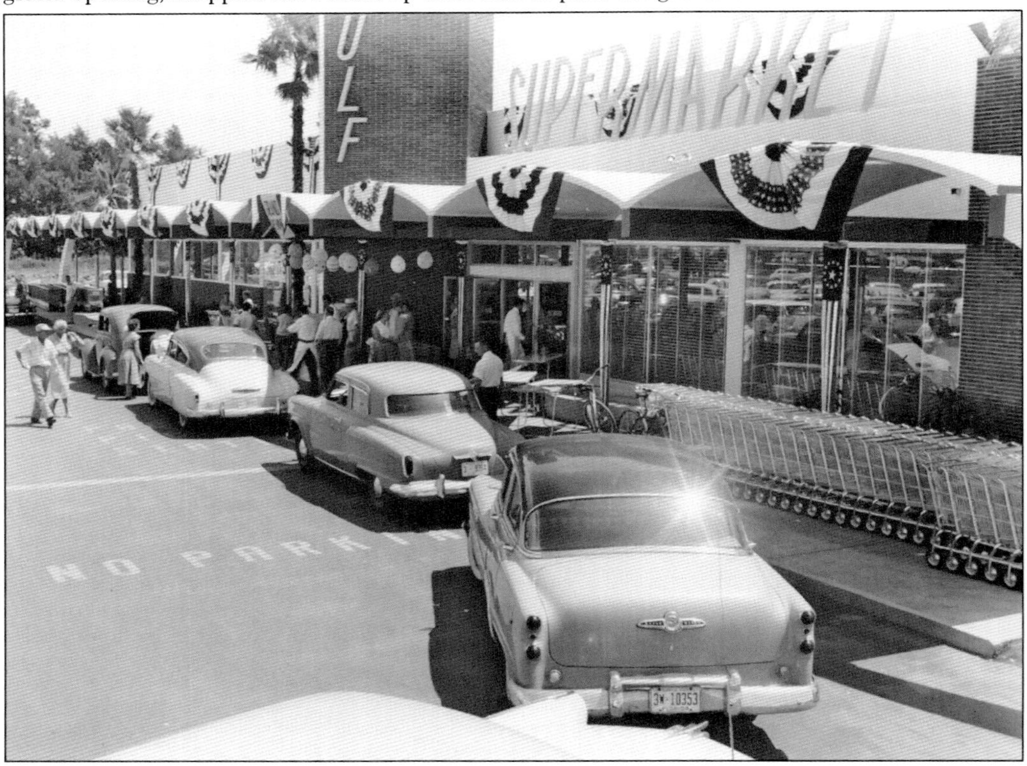

This South Tampa beauty salon was located at 3645 South Manhattan Avenue in 1960. This neighborhood in South Tampa saw major development during the 1950s with several subdivisions and small shopping centers constructed along the Manhattan Avenue and Westshore Boulevard corridors between Gandy Boulevard and Grand Central Avenue (now Kennedy Boulevard).

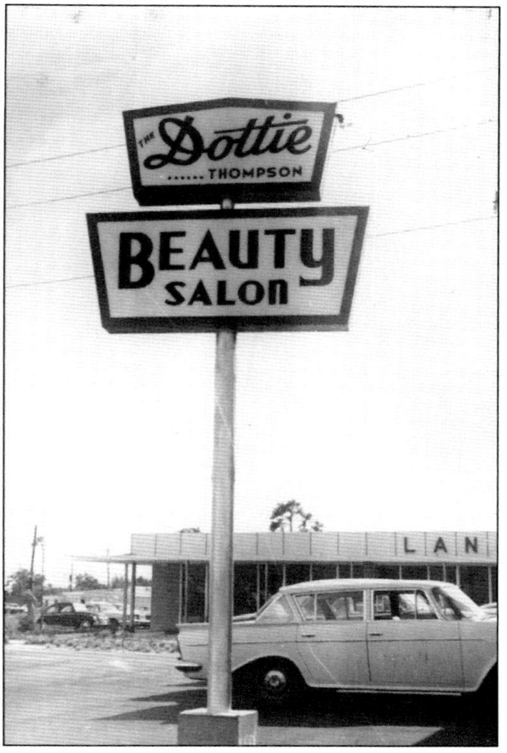

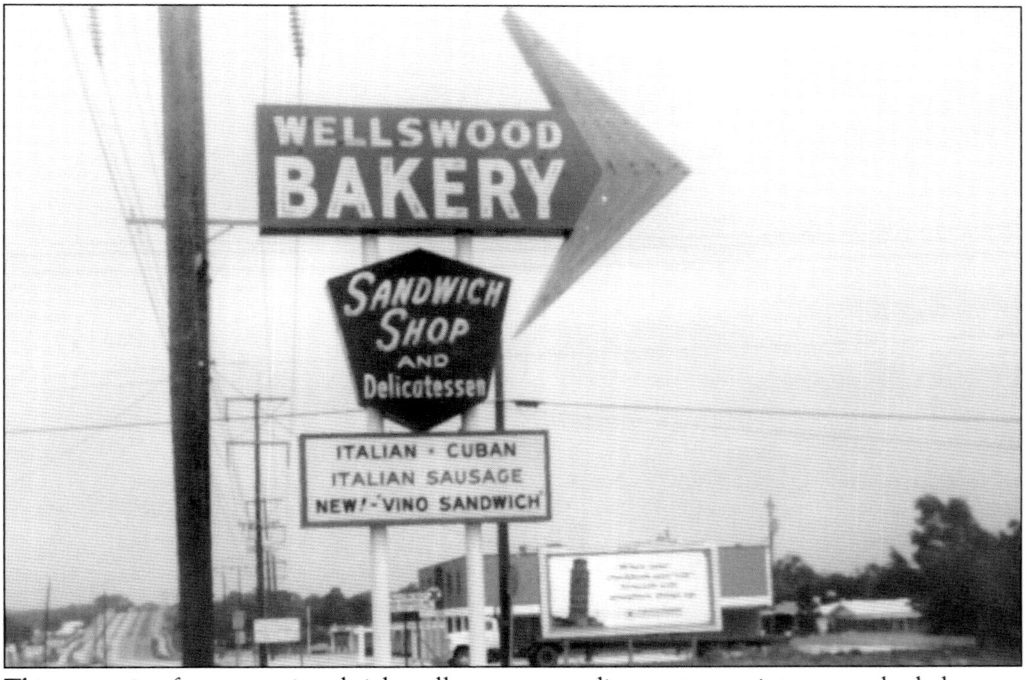

This neon sign features a giant bright yellow arrow sending customers into a popular bakery on West Buffalo Avenue (now Martin Luther King Boulevard) in 1966. The photograph was taken looking east toward the bridge.

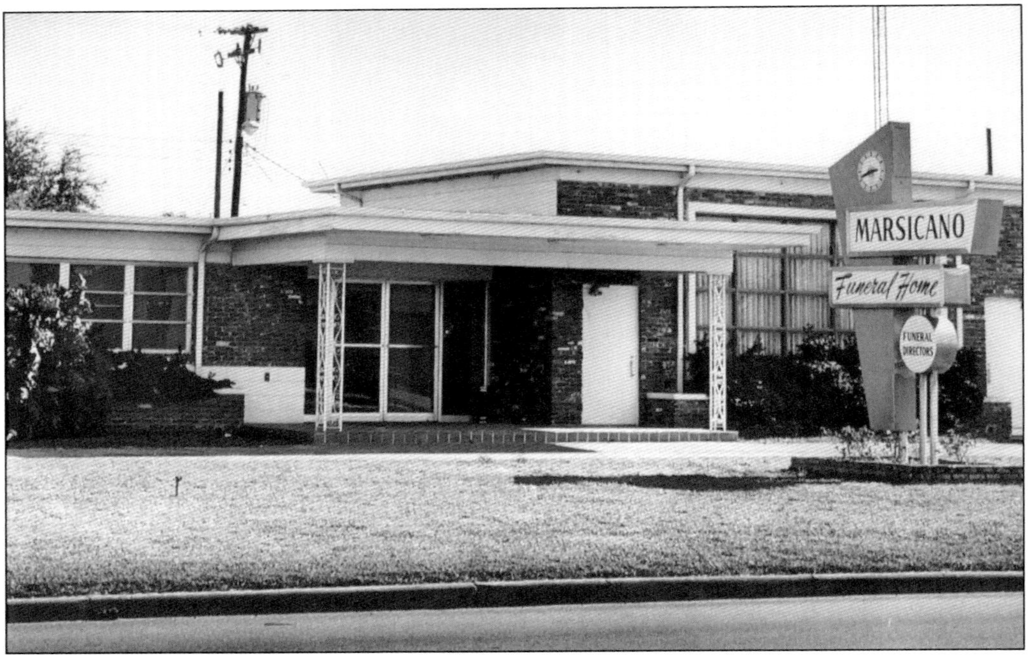

The Marsicano family established their funeral home in 1956 at 4040 Henderson Boulevard. This was another expanding South Tampa neighborhood during the 1950s. Twin brothers Ralph and Charles Marsicano created another success story for Tampa's family-owned business community that continues today with more than 50 years of dedicated service to Tampa families. In the image below, one can see the funeral home's Cadillac hearse, which was occasionally used for the ambulance service they also offered.

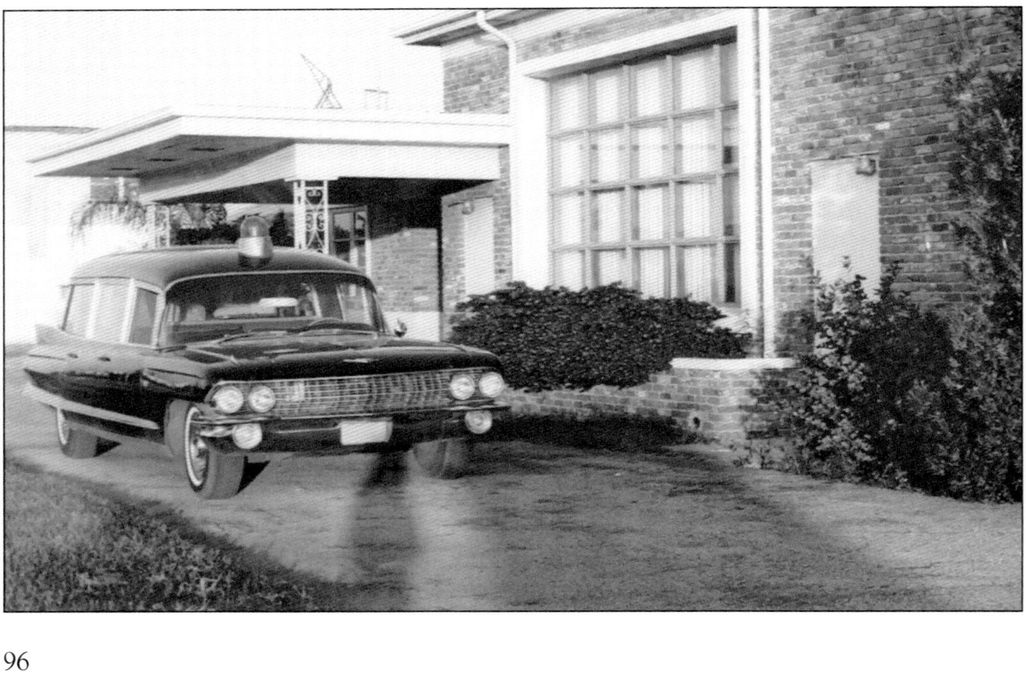

Four

Neon Lights for Recreational Sites

During the 1950s and 1960s, Tampa experienced record-setting population growth that has not been seen since. This amazing growth spurred a major expansion of the city's highways and bridges, bringing thousands into the city and creating endless possibilities for Tampa business owners, who welcomed tourists and new citizens alike into their neighborhoods. It was during this period in the city's history that two of the most popular tourist attractions in the area were developed: Busch Gardens and Lowry Park. These two city ventures offered residents a weekend oasis away from their busy work schedule to enjoy spending the day with their family.

With Tampa's roadways expanding and the interstate system making its way into town, local motels started to appear along busy thoroughfares for drivers needing a cozy room along their journey. Many hard-working Tampa families realized their dream of owning a family business in the motel industry during this era. Family-owned motels had a warm and inviting presence to them that made travelers feel comfortable asking for a room on those late-night trips. As the popularity of these highway havens increased, the neon signs created for them became icons of this glorious era. Many of the neon creations for these places were works of art that became colorful welcome signs to guide motorists into their roadside getaway.

Among the pictures in this chapter are many well-known recreational destinations for Tampa folks that were ready for an enjoyable day of fun with the family. Mom would fill up the picnic basket to start the day at one of Tampa's parks, and what an exciting adventure it was to end the day with a trip over to the drive-in movie theater. Many folks filled their weekends with plans for a day at the beach or maybe a wrestling match at the local armory. Dance halls were another popular destination for couples looking forward to an enjoyable evening with friends.

These beautiful scenes provide a stunning portrait of a 1950s Tampa continuing to expand her horizons and welcome happy tourists into that inviting Florida climate. Tampa was quickly becoming one of the jewels in Florida's treasure chest. The essence of this iconic period in Tampa's history has been captured among these scenic images. Come along now for a nostalgic journey into Tampa's past and perhaps find a happy memory among these photographic treasures.

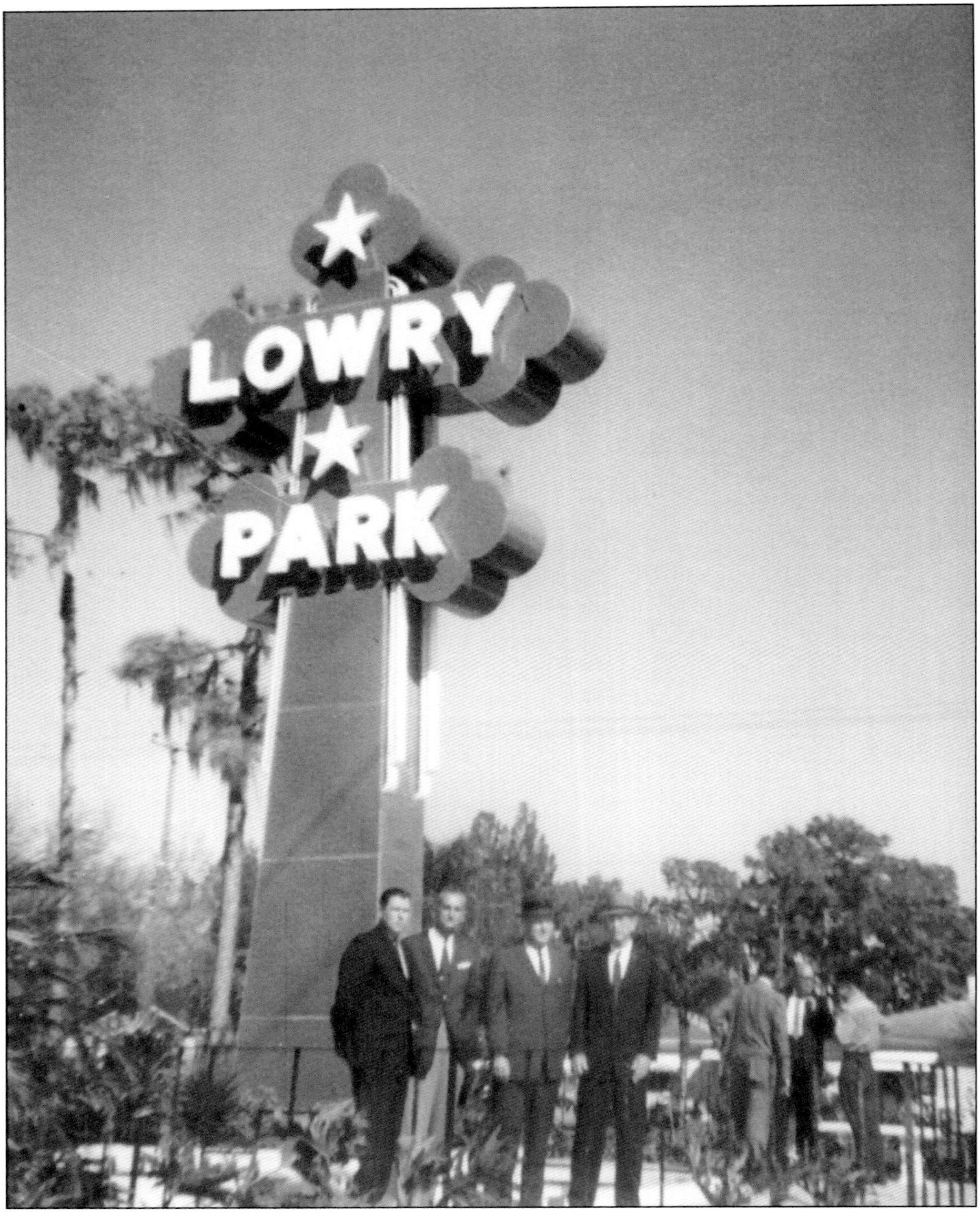

Tampa's mayor asked Cinchett Neon Signs to create the new Lowry Park zoo sign, and here is the dedication ceremony for the giant edifice at Sligh Avenue and North Boulevard in 1961. This sign was a well-known Tampa landmark for more than 30 years. Development on Lowry Park began in 1957 with the children's Fairyland amusement park. Today this park has become a popular tourist destination and world-class zoo. Pictured here are, from left to right, company president John F. Cinchett, parks director Frank Neff, Tampa mayor Julian Lane and Gen. Sumpter Lowry.

Here is Fairyland, a popular children's destination at the Lowry Park. Opening in 1957, this was a magical place for Tampa's children, with winding paths leading to a journey through an enchanted woodland village of animated fairy tales and nursery rhymes. Mayor Nick Nuccio envisioned this children's wonderland and brought it to reality. Lowry Park was also a popular spot for birthday parties at picnic tables under the grand oaks.

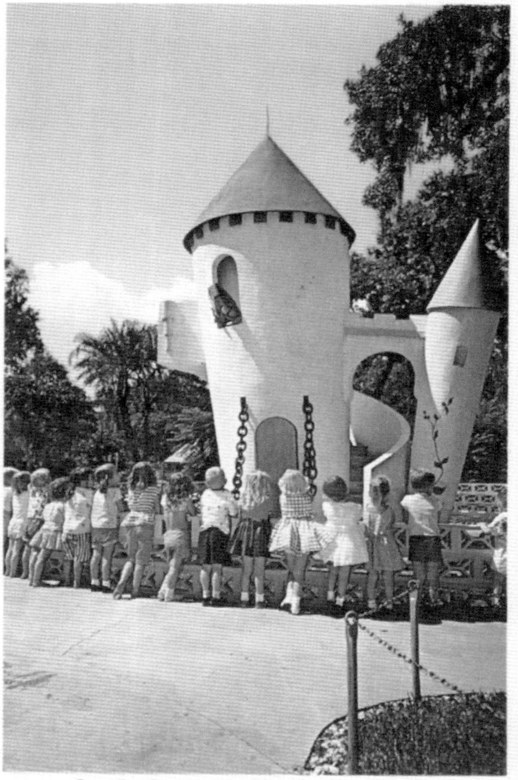

Fairyland in Lowry Park, Tampa, Florida

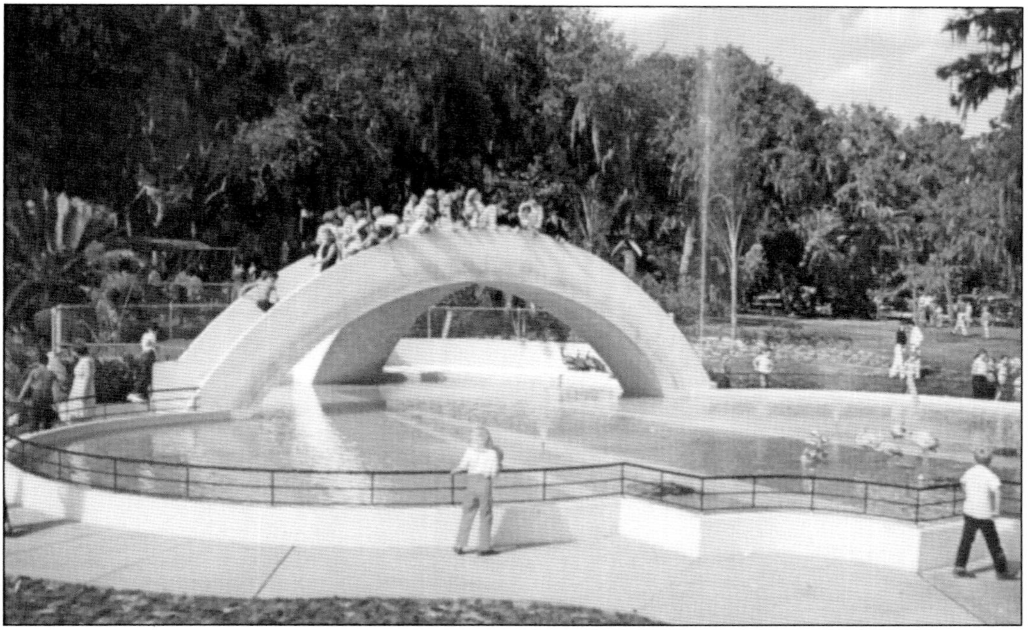

Happy memories of childhood fun are brought to mind by this beautiful scene of the Lowry Park Rainbow Bridge in 1957. This was the entrance to Fairyland, the amusement park and zoo.

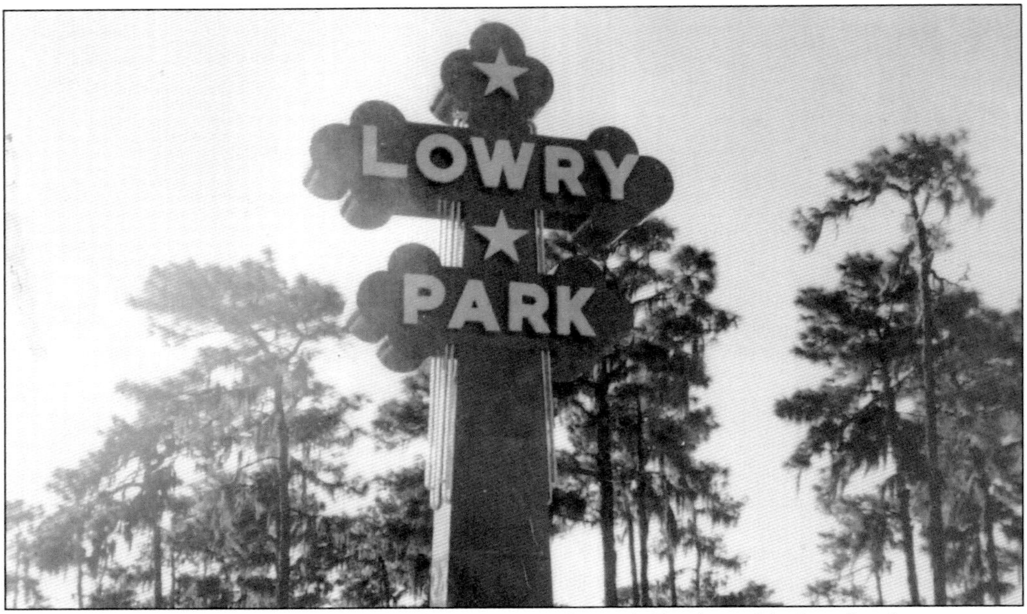

This 1961 scene shows the land on Sligh Avenue and North Boulevard before development was completed of the now-popular Lowry Park. The Lowry Park sign stood nearly 40 feet tall and was made of turquoise porcelain with white neon letters and stars. This Tampa landmark was actually a memorial cross honoring members of the Lowry family, who donated the land to the city for a park.

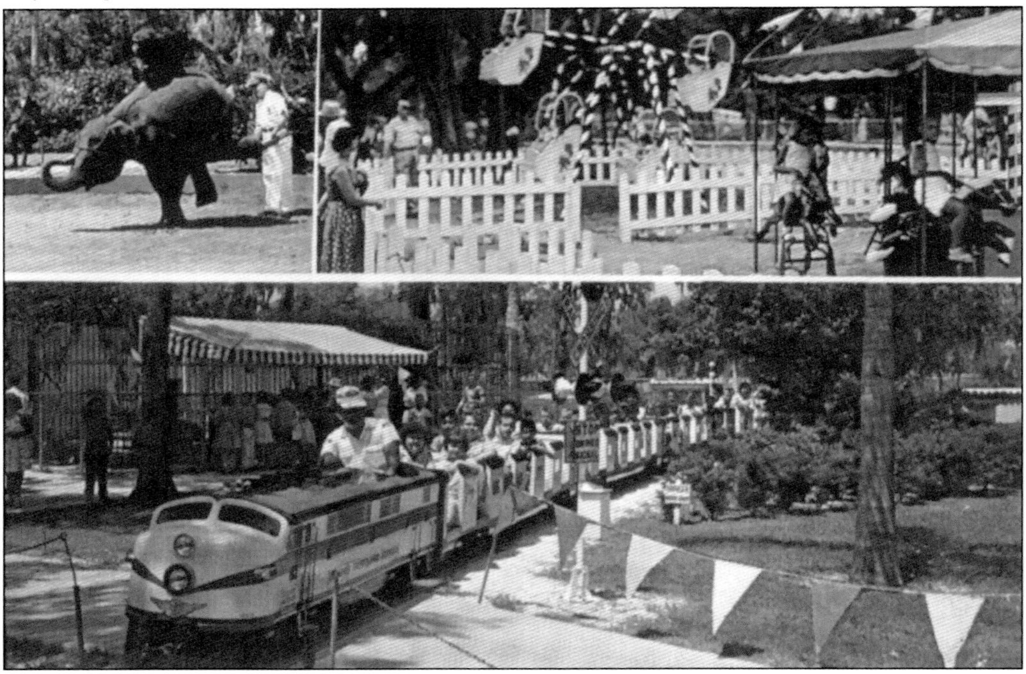

Welcome aboard the Fairyland Express train-ride at Lowry Park. This 1961 photograph will bring back fond memories of the amusement park and zoo that the train would wind through on its route. At the zoo, visitors could meet Sheena the elephant, pictured above at left, or feed the seals.

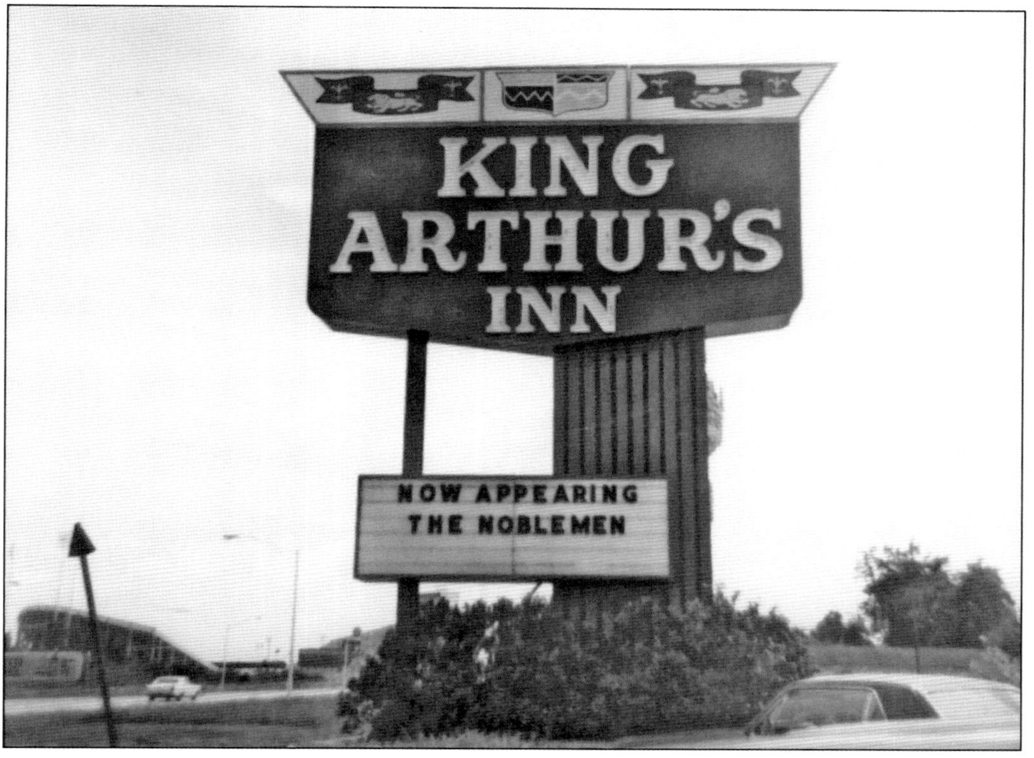

Here is one of several hotels built in the late 1960s in the Airport/Westshore area of Tampa. This majestic neon masterpiece was for the King Arthur's Inn, across the street from the brand-new Tampa Stadium on Dale Mabry Highway. In the 1968 photograph above, notice that the stadium (later nicknamed the "Sombrero") is not yet completed at the end zones. The hotel's nightclub was well known in the early 1970s for hosting major music headliners.

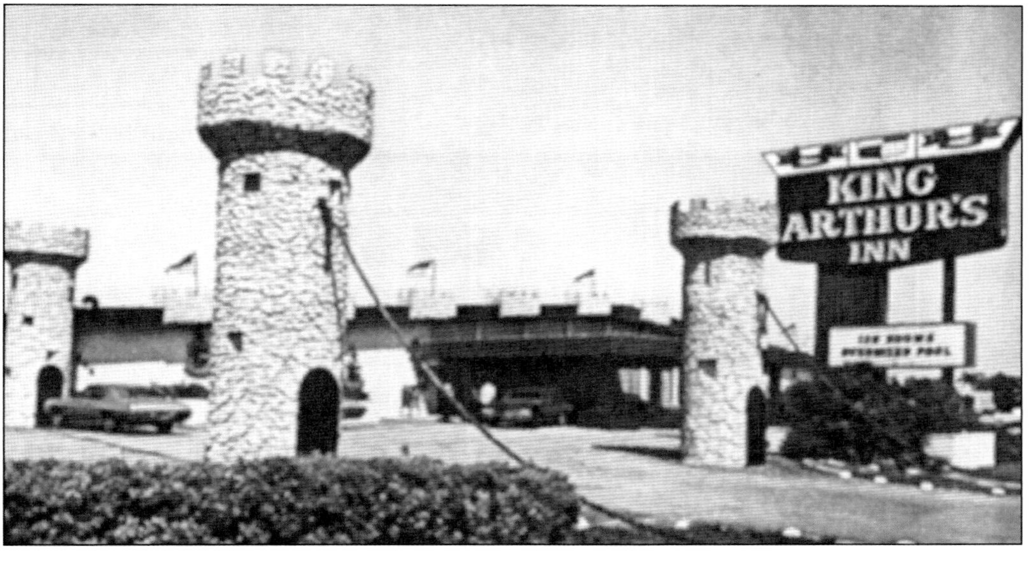

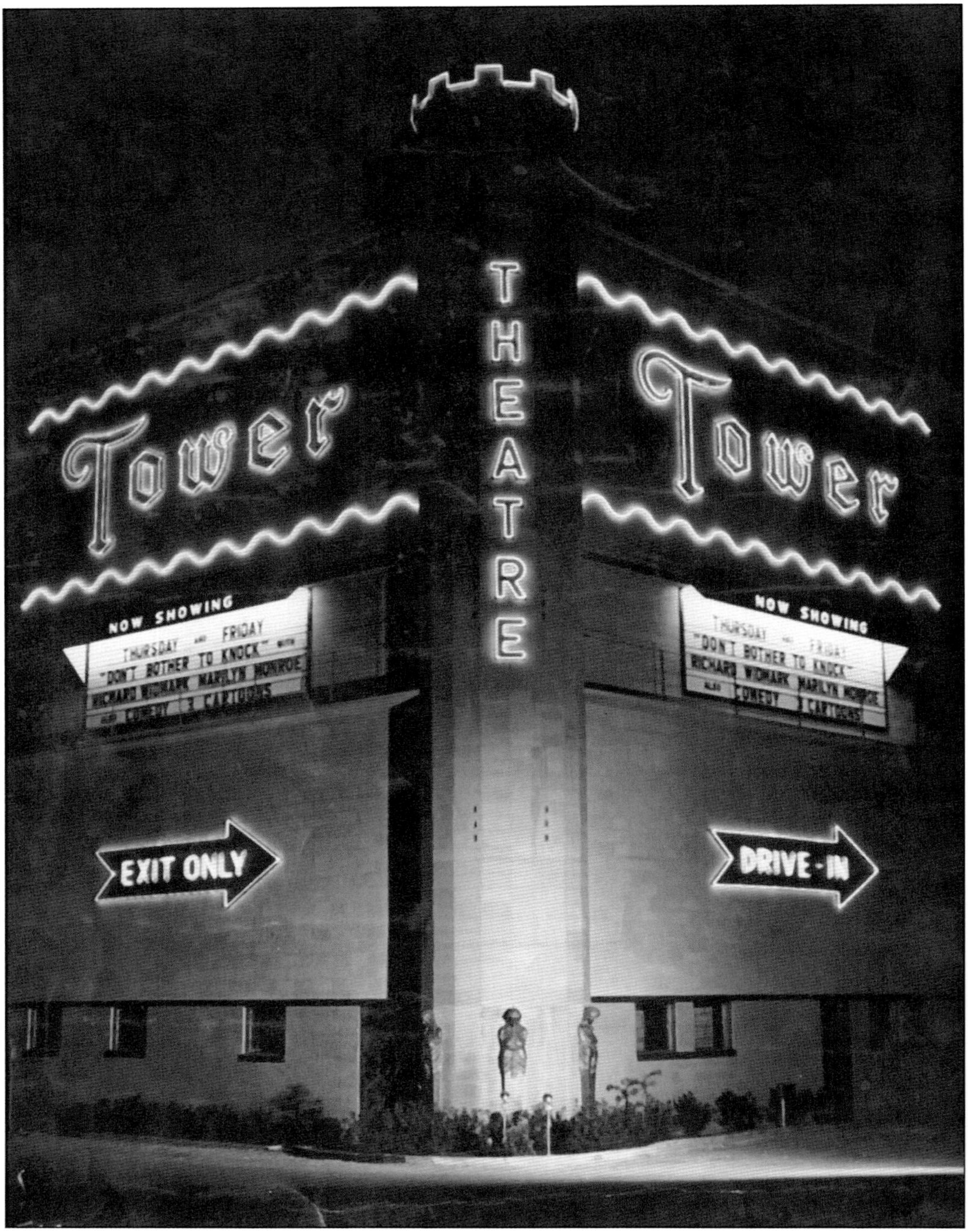

During the 1950s, the drive-in theater became a family favorite. This theater was a popular spot for Tampa folks looking for an enjoyable night of fun in 1952. The drive-in was next to the old Sulphur Springs Tower, a well-known Tampa landmark on property facing the Hillsborough River between Florida and Nebraska Avenues. This beautiful neon sign became another Tampa landmark and featured a neon tower that was designed after its nearby nemesis. Check out the movie promoted on the marquee: Marilyn Monroe's 1952 hit *Don't Bother to Knock*.

This beautiful image of the Sulphur Springs Tower was taken in 1945. The 1927 medieval-style tower originally serviced the nearby Sulphur Springs Hotel, pictured below. Considered to be one of Tampa's best-known landmarks, the tower inspired a drive-in theater on adjacent property that became another familiar icon. This local marvel still stands today as a proud testament to Tampa's glorious past.

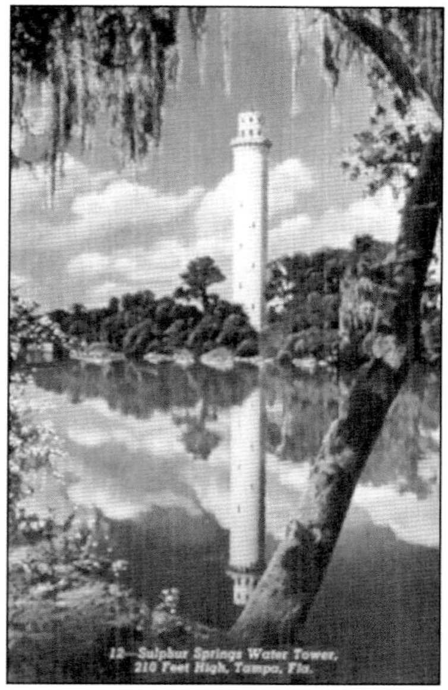

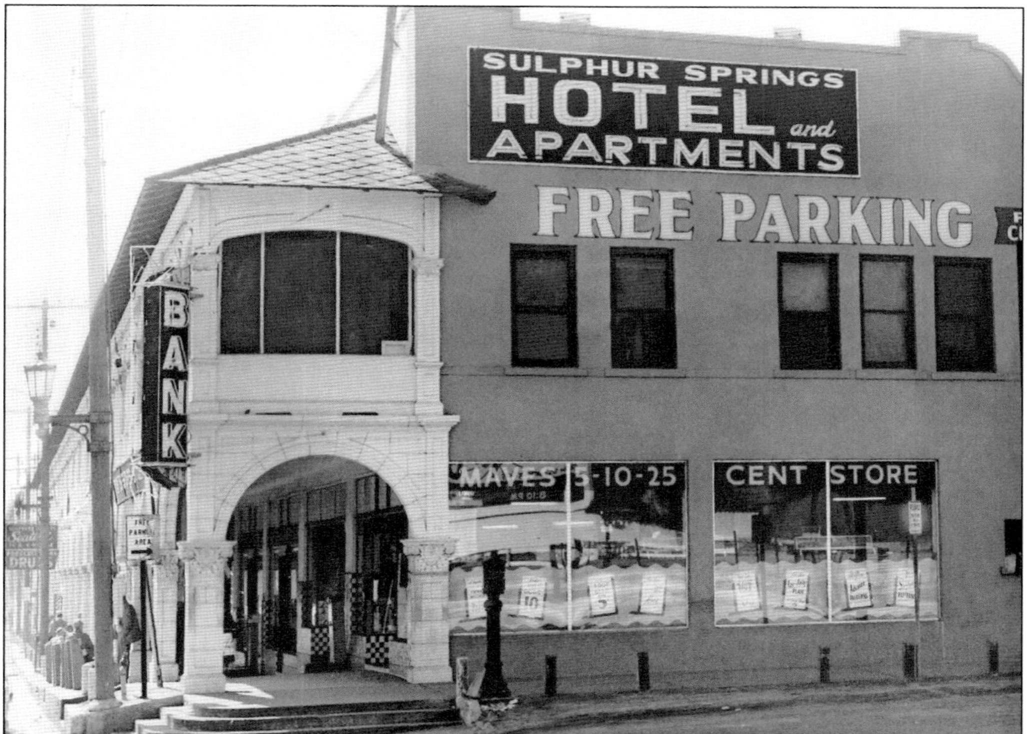

This is the Grand Sulphur Springs Hotel Arcade on Nebraska Avenue in 1956. Long before the arrival of plazas, this was a popular shopping destination for Tampa folks living in Seminole Heights and Sulphur Springs. This photograph was taken after Cinchett Neon Signs completed new neon work for the hotel. The 1926 Arcade Building was considered to be the first indoor shopping venue in the state. Look at the prices at the luncheonette: 10¢ for hot dogs and 5¢ for root beer.

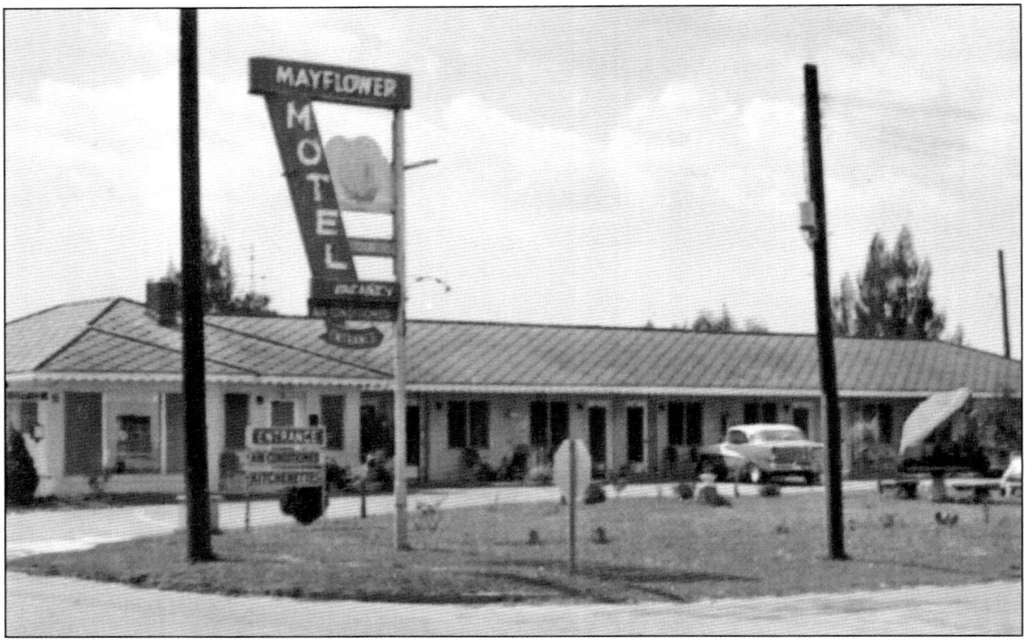

The beautiful Mayflower Motel, pictured in 1956, was built and owned by the Clemente family. The family's journey began on another ship though, one that embarked from Italy. Like many Tampa families, they reached their dream of having a successful family business. Cinchett Neon Signs designed this sign with a hand-painted portrait of the *Mayflower*.

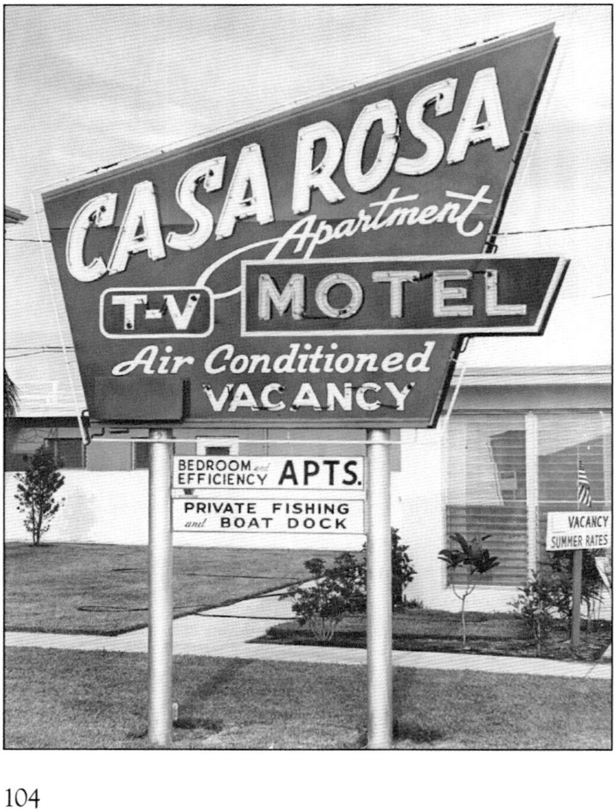

Welcome to the beautiful Casa Rosa Apartment Motel. Here is another neon beauty by Cinchett Neon Signs for the vintage waterfront motel in 1957. Notice that the sign says "Air-Conditioned" and "TV."

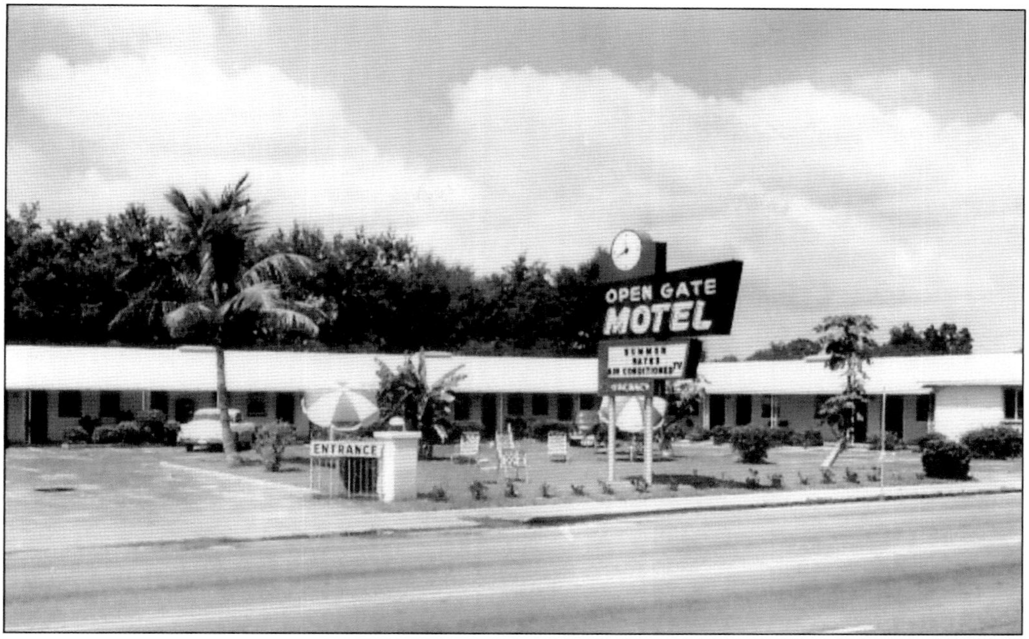

The beautiful Open Gate Motel, pictured in 1957, was one of many motels along Florida Avenue that welcomed visitors coming from the north along U.S. Highway 41 heading for downtown Tampa. This was before the interstate was developed, making Florida Avenue one of the main thoroughfares leading into the city.

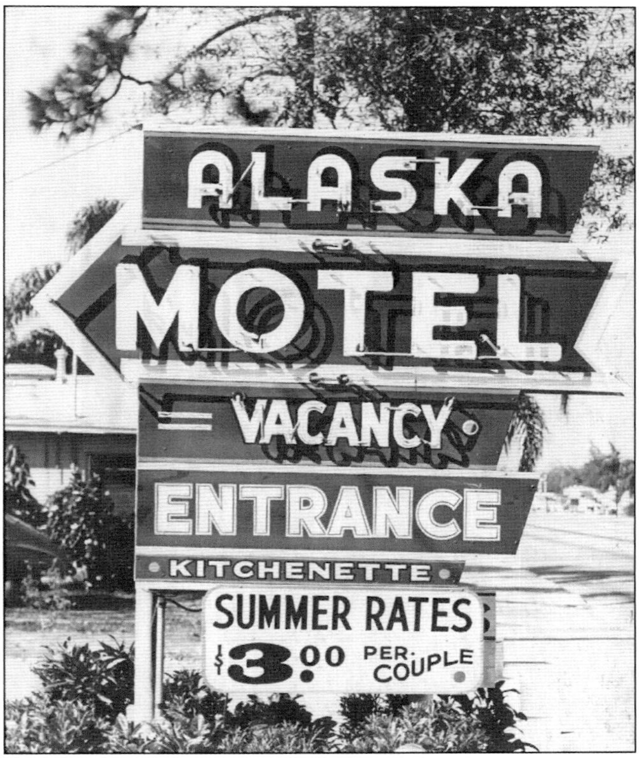

Welcome to Tampa's little Alaska—the owner must have been hoping to cool off his guests. This 1957 photograph was taken on Nebraska Avenue looking north at Hanna Avenue in Seminole Heights. One of many fine motels that popped up during the 1950s along Nebraska Avenue, this motel still operates today, as does the service station across the street seen in the background. Notice the price for a room: $3 per couple.

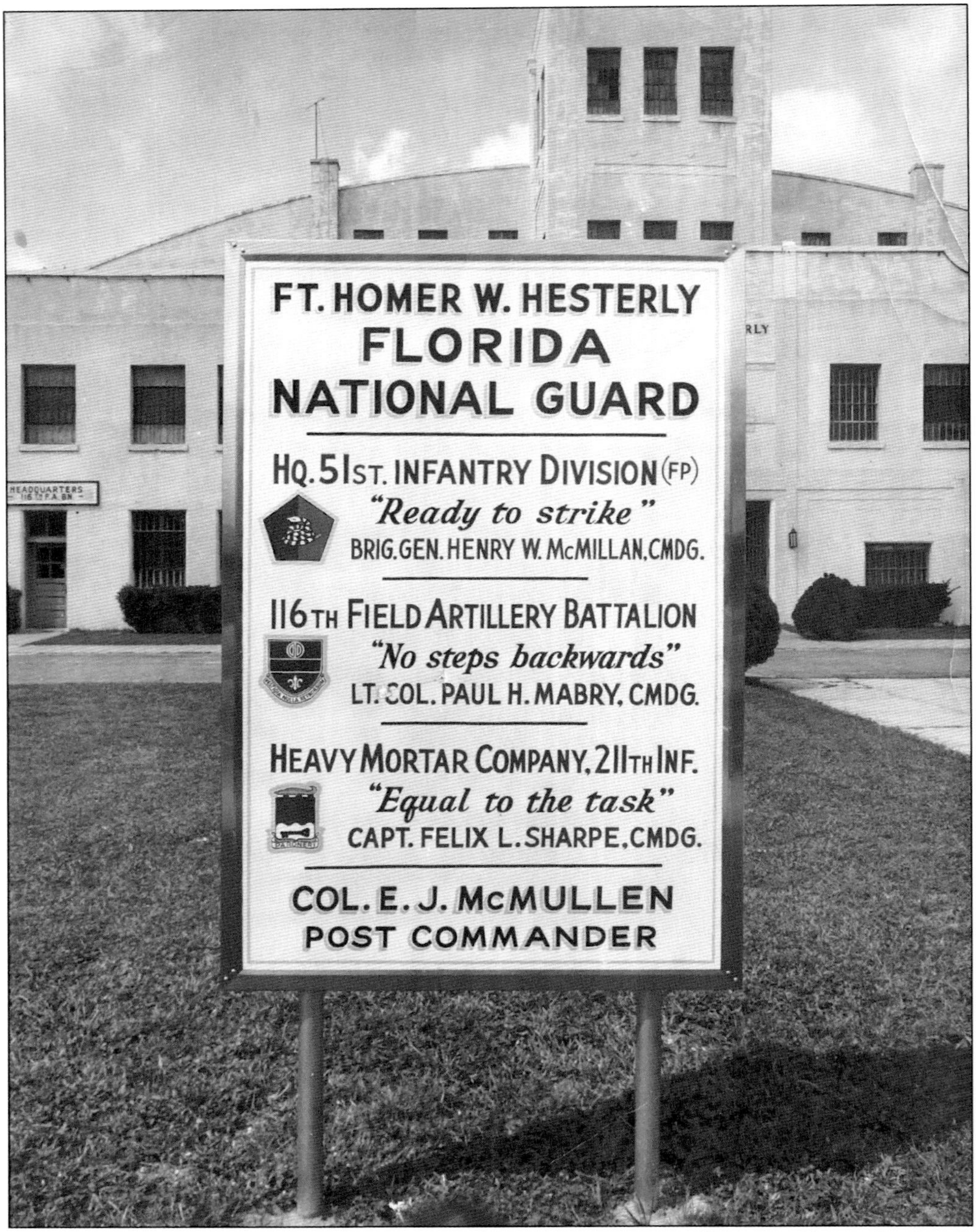

The Fort Homer W. Hesterly Armory, pictured here in 1956, is a well-known Tampa landmark located in West Tampa just north of Kennedy Boulevard on Howard Avenue. This building served as a popular venue for social functions, dances, and concerts before Tampa had a major civic center or auditorium. One famous concert held here has become a legend—the 1956 appearance of a young Elvis Presley to hundreds of Tampa fans. Another historic appearance here was in 1963, when U.S. president John F. Kennedy gave a speech during his reelection tour three days before his trip to Dallas.

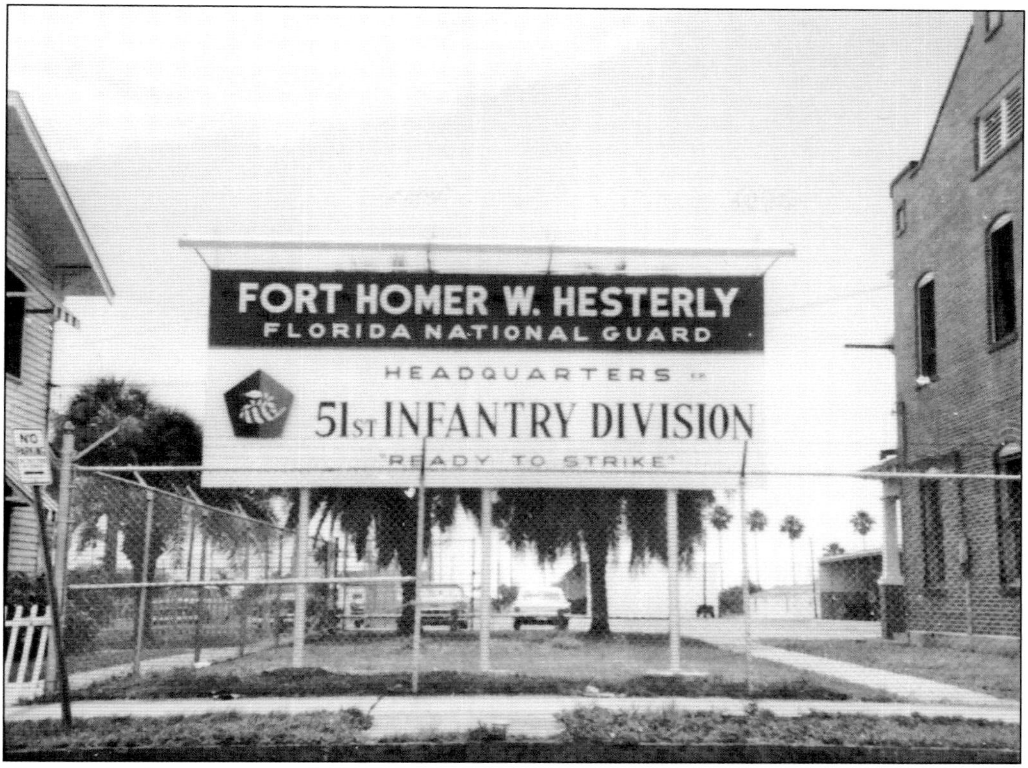

The sign for the armory stands as proudly as the fort itself in this 1956 photograph. In the 1950s, the armory was a popular destination for wrestling matches, boxing, dances, and ice-skating. Many happy memories were made here, and this art deco–style building still stands today. It is being considered for an urban development project.

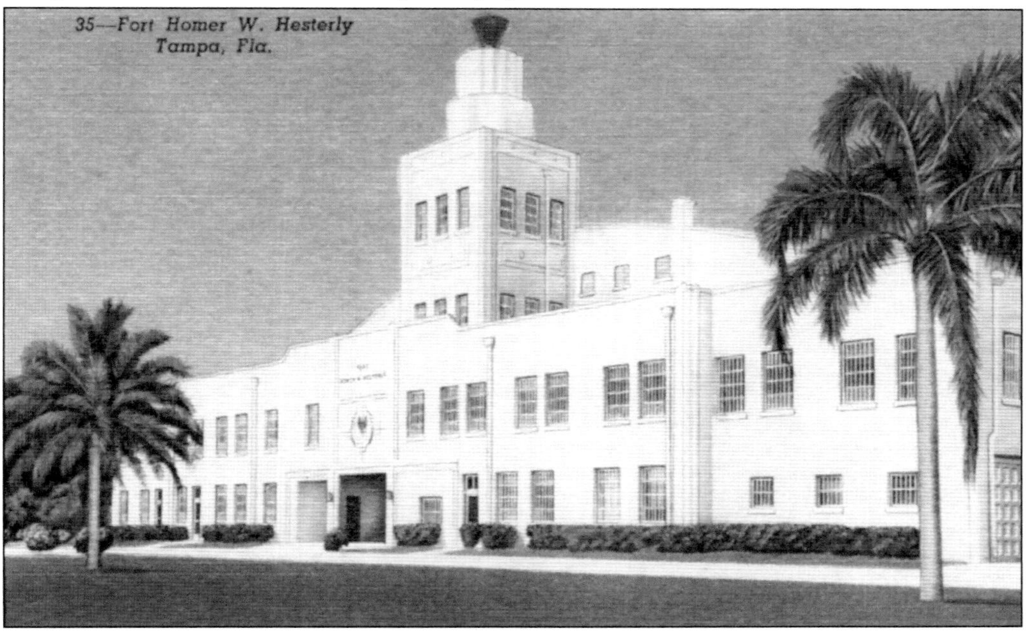

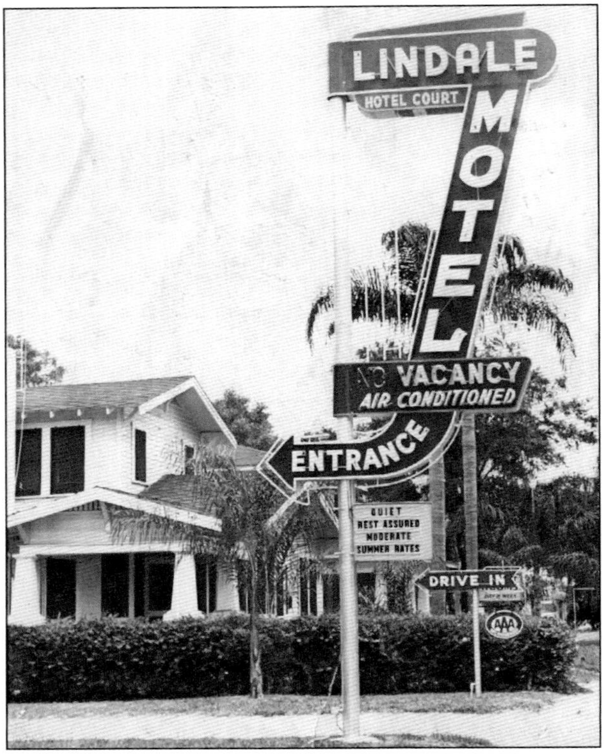

This is the Lindale Motel at 3102 Nebraska Avenue in 1956. With Tampa tourists arriving year-round, the popularity of motels could be seen on every major thoroughfare coming into the city. Two roads in Tampa that experienced this were Nebraska and Florida Avenues. Both brought travelers on busy U.S. Highway 41 into the city. This sign is actually a large arrow directing drivers into the motel. Another common feature of motel signs was to advertise air-conditioned rooms, a modern convenience many residents had not experienced yet in their own homes.

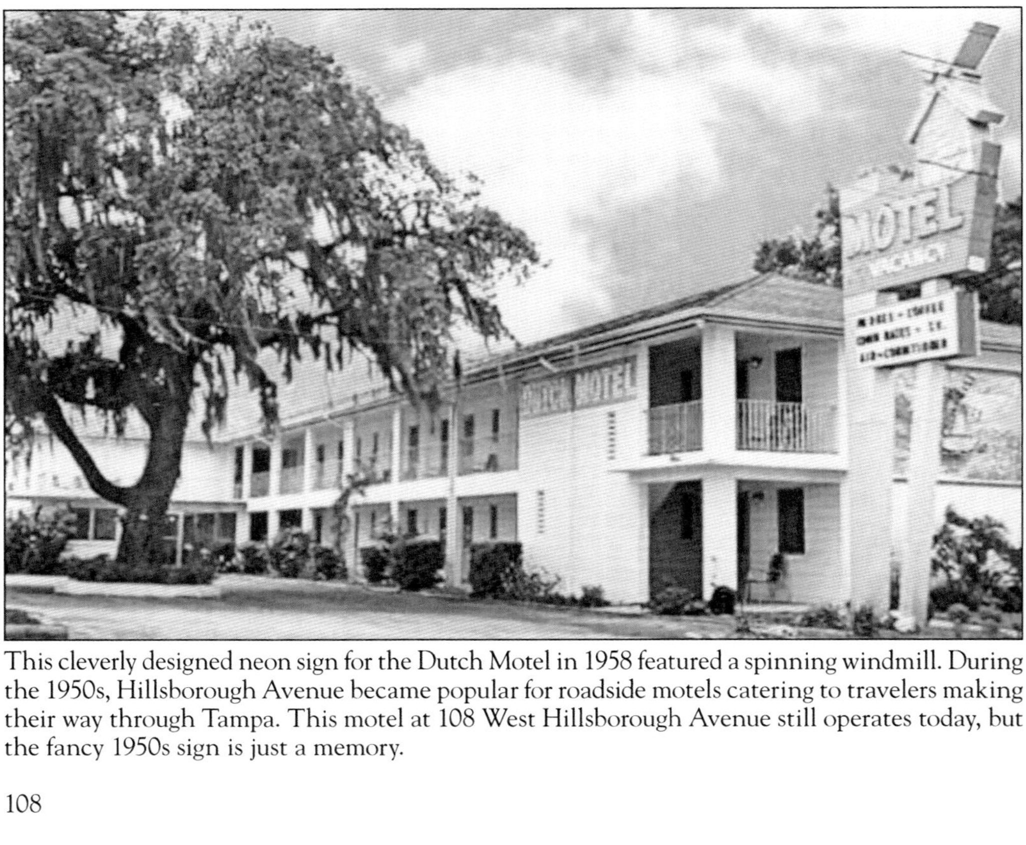

This cleverly designed neon sign for the Dutch Motel in 1958 featured a spinning windmill. During the 1950s, Hillsborough Avenue became popular for roadside motels catering to travelers making their way through Tampa. This motel at 108 West Hillsborough Avenue still operates today, but the fancy 1950s sign is just a memory.

Here is another classic symbol of an era long ago. Motels named after their owners is a nostalgic memory of family trips along the highway in the 1950s on holiday vacations. Travelers always felt welcome at family-owned motels that invited them into a warm and friendly atmosphere for their stay.

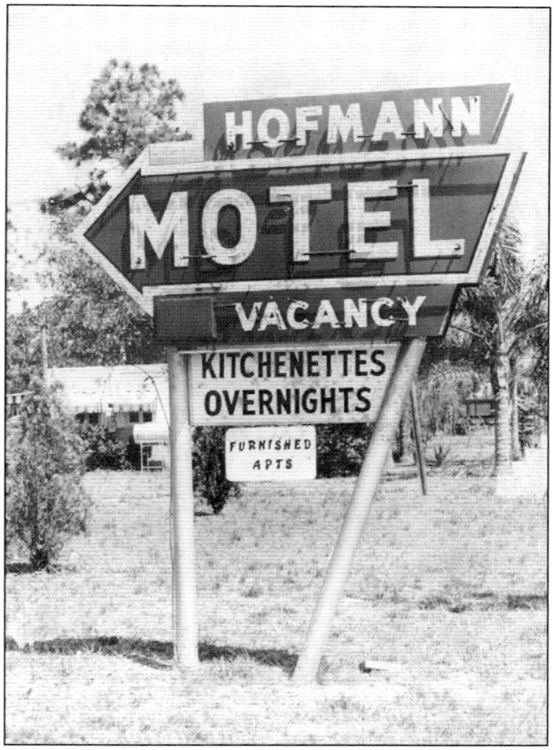

This motel was at 3319 West Hillsborough Avenue. This view looks west on Hillsborough Avenue toward Dale Mabry Highway in 1957. Notice the bright neon arrow to direct drivers into the motel. Flashing arrows became an iconic symbol of 1950s neon signs, taking a cue from actual highway signage that directed drivers along the road. The top of the neon sign seems to resemble the iconic 1957 Chevy's fin.

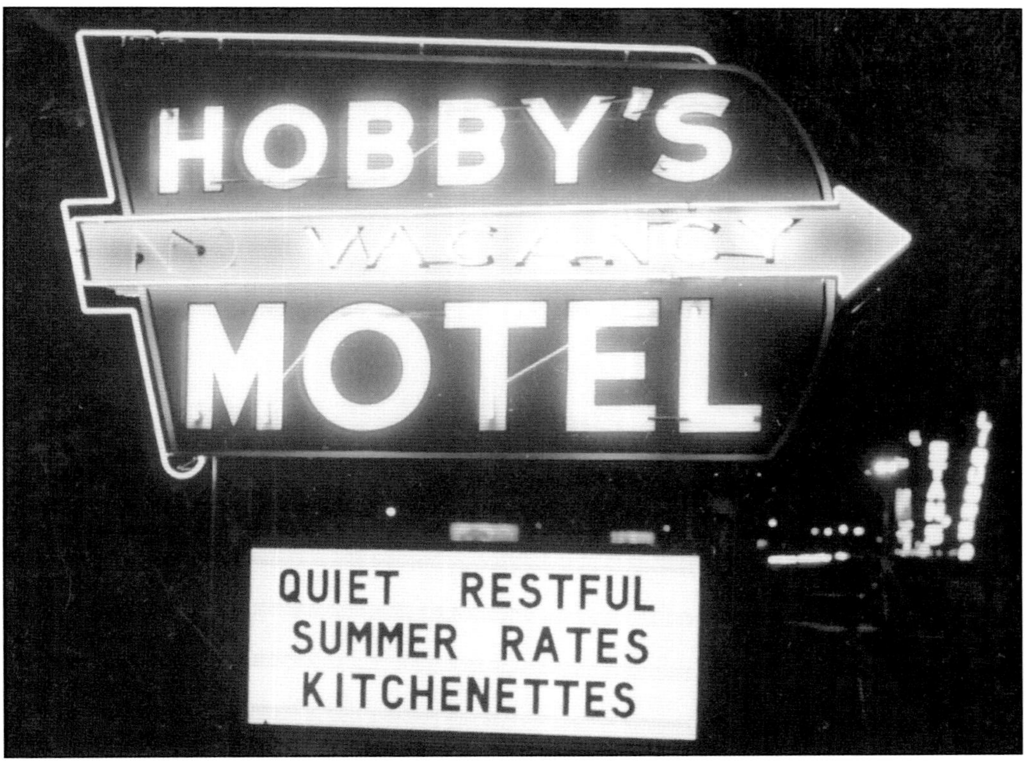

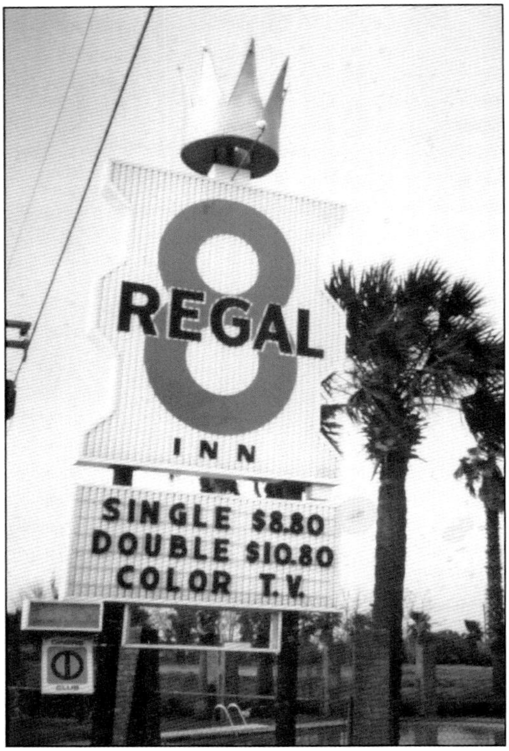

This 1967 hotel sign featured a giant revolving lighted crown. Take notice of the advertised rates, about $10 for a room with color television! Black-and-white television sets are another nostalgic memory of the 1950s and 1960s.

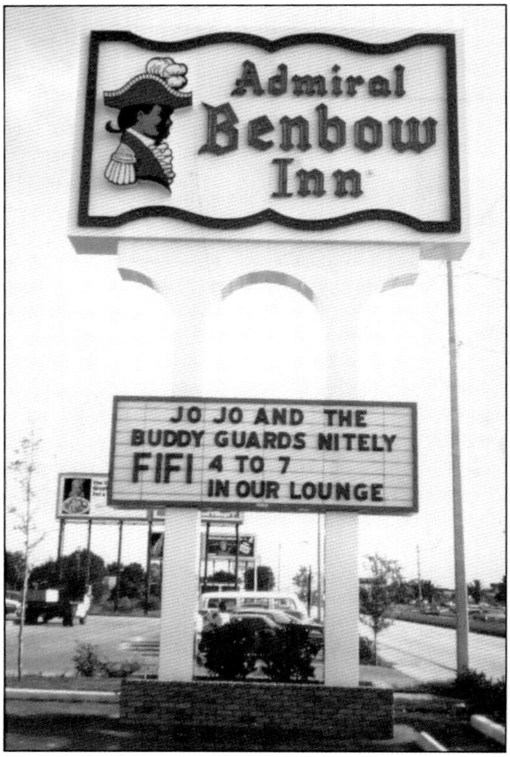

When this hotel opened in the late 1960s, it was considered one of Tampa's finest. The Admiral Benbow Inn was on Westshore Boulevard north of Cypress Street and is still standing today, but this beautiful neon sign sailed away long ago. This view is looking north at the undeveloped land along Westshore Boulevard. Today the east side of the street is lined with office towers in what is now the busy Westshore Business District.

Five

Neon Adventures for Commercial Ventures

Tampa's business community reached extraordinary heights during the 1950s and 1960s. With the city reaching record numbers in population growth and neighborhoods expanding every year, the commercial and industrial venture fields were wide open for savvy business owners with an entrepreneurial spirit. New construction in Tampa's broadening neighborhoods breathed new life into every type of industry and created opportunities for business owners that brought many of them an enduring legacy of loyalty from Tampa citizens.

Many of the well-known institutions that play an important role in the economic development of the city were established during this time period. In 1956, the University of South Florida was established in North Tampa, spurring major development in this section of the city and offering many new job opportunities. Tampa continued to expand, and new hospitals, schools, churches, and subdivisions all began appearing to accommodate the growth. Many business offices began moving away from the traditional downtown office building into more convenient neighborhood office plazas.

Tampa was a haven for small family-owned companies. During this era, thousands of people came to Tampa with high hopes of reaching their dreams of establishing their own businesses. Many aspiring young families saw the city as their path to success and reached for their goals with dedication and perseverance. Hard-working folks with a desire to secure their future often built their business from the ground up, and in many neighborhoods, young families with a desire for success constructed the businesses themselves. Tampa had everything to offer, including a warm Florida climate that would continue to attract new residents for years. Local building supply companies, hardware stores, realtors, and contractors all benefited from the city's tremendous expansion and growth.

These nostalgic photographs remind everyone of that passionate vision so many fine Tampa families held close to their hearts made into reality. The collective success of these enterprises has been captured through this historic collection of vintage images. This chapter serves as a photographic testament to the enduring work ethic of Tampa's business community, a tradition that continues today.

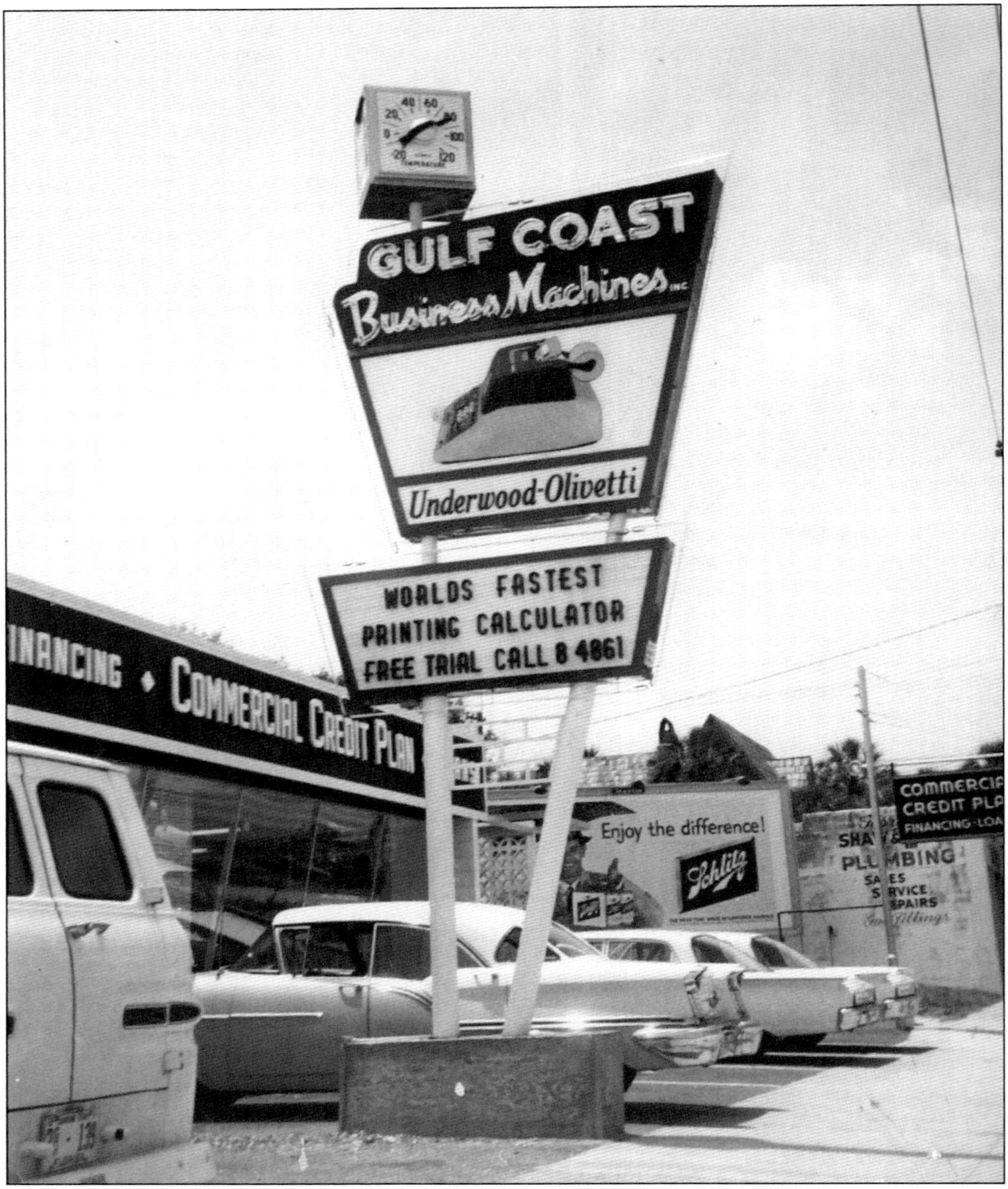

The Gulf Coast Business Machines building at 1700 Grand Central Avenue (now Kennedy Boulevard) is pictured in 1956. Take a moment to observe the details: the message board reads "World's Fastest Printing Calculator," with a picture of the latest model on the sign. On top of the sign is a revolving temperature gauge/clock so Tampans could see how hot their city was in 1956. Notice the five-digit telephone number on the marquee.

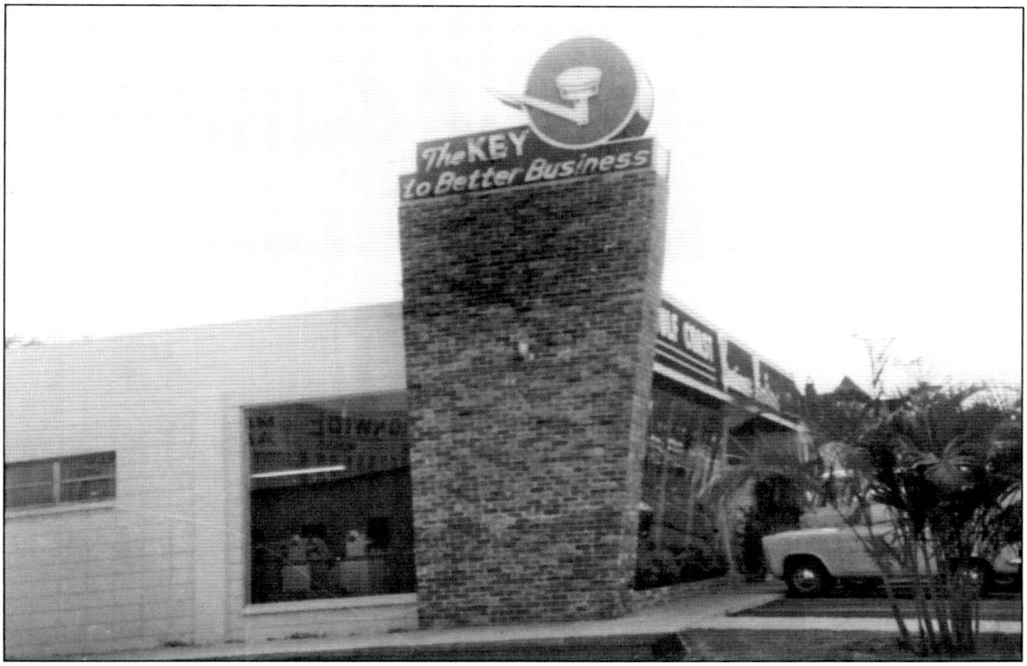

The big neon circle on top of the Gulf Coast Business Machines building featured a neon typewriter key in the circle above their slogan, "the Key to Better Business," in 1956—probably the only such neon sign ever made.

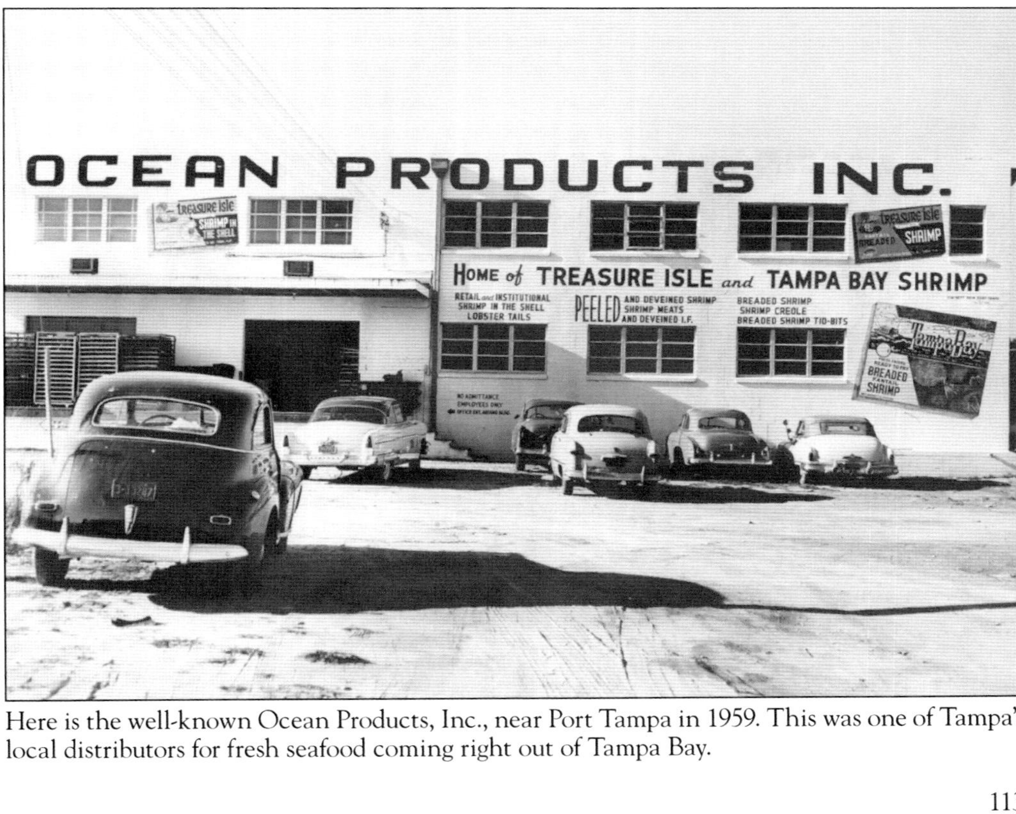

Here is the well-known Ocean Products, Inc., near Port Tampa in 1959. This was one of Tampa's local distributors for fresh seafood coming right out of Tampa Bay.

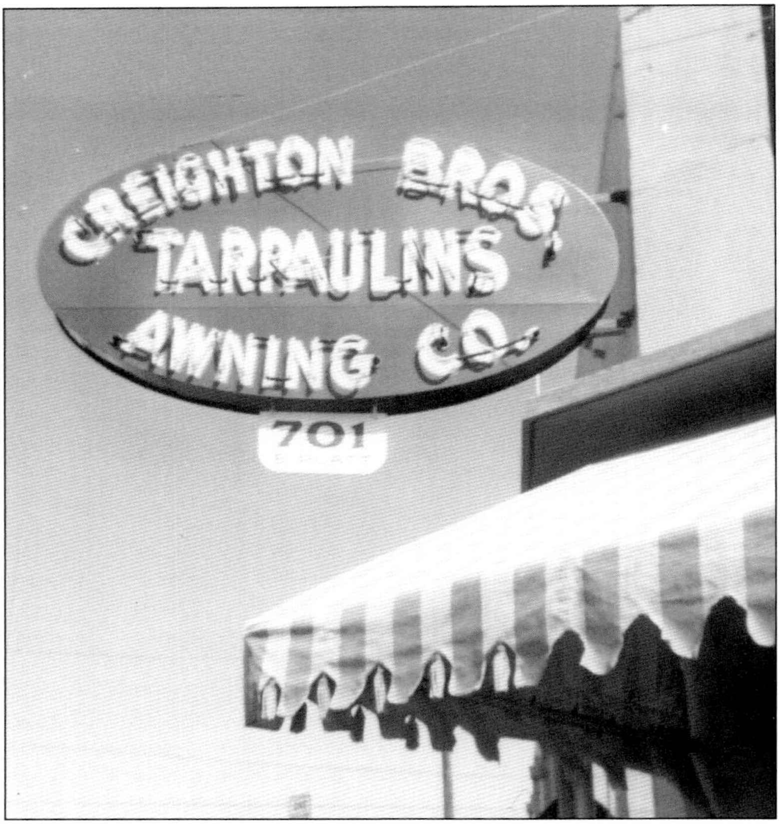

This is the Creighton Brothers Awning Company, Tampa's oldest and most well-known awning company, with its new neon sign downtown on Platt Street in 1955. This is another Tampa family that reached for their dream of owning a successful business. The picture postcard seen below recreates a beautiful evening view of the Creighton Brothers Awning Company that nicely frames the colorful neon sign above the awning in 1955. This family business was established in 1920 and still serves Tampa today.

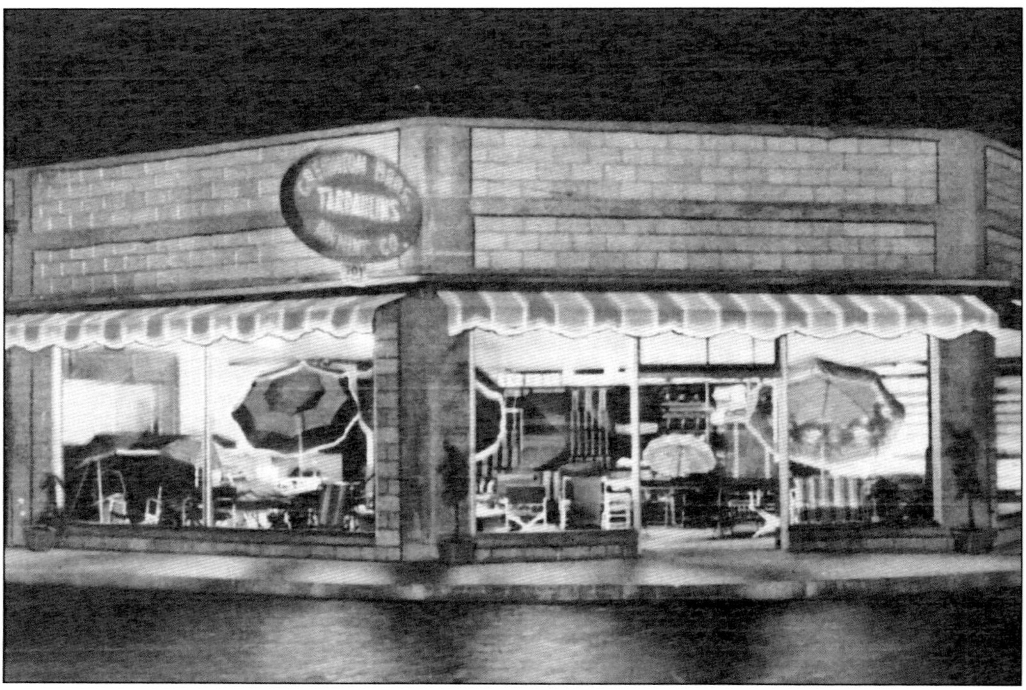

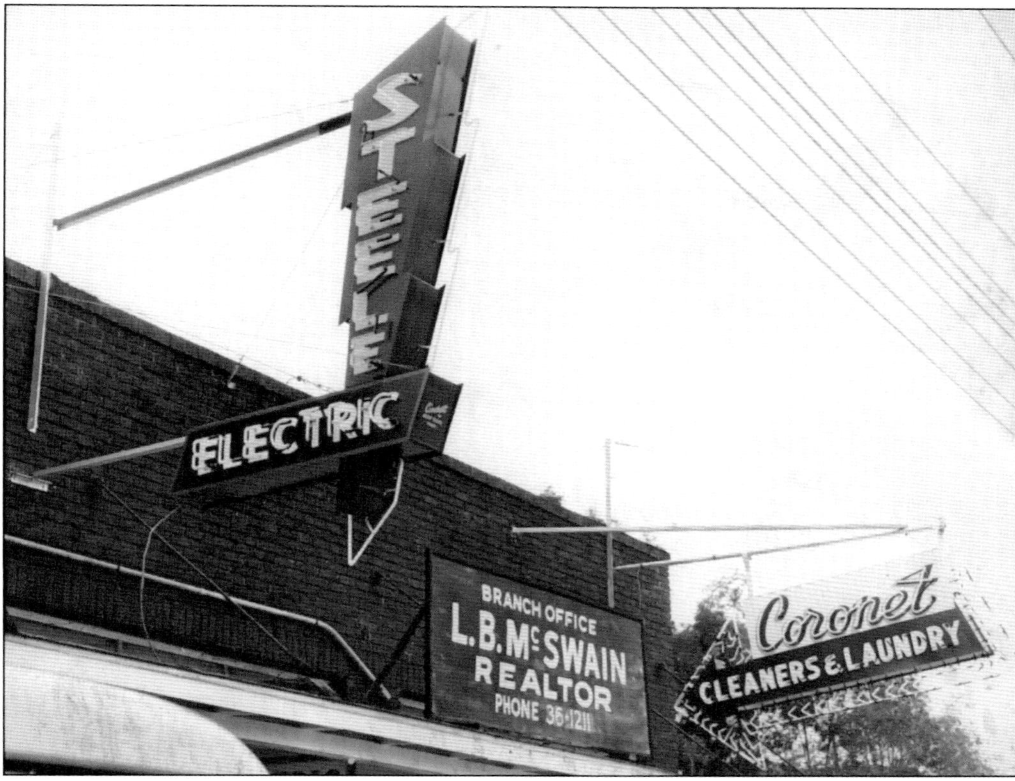

This striking neon sign for Steele Electric Company in 1956 is actually a giant neon lightning bolt—hopefully none of their customers were superstitious. Another flashy new neon sign is next door at Coronet Cleaners. The building pictured here in 1956 was at 4408 North Nebraska Avenue. Both of these signs must have brought a colorful glow to this Seminole Heights neighborhood.

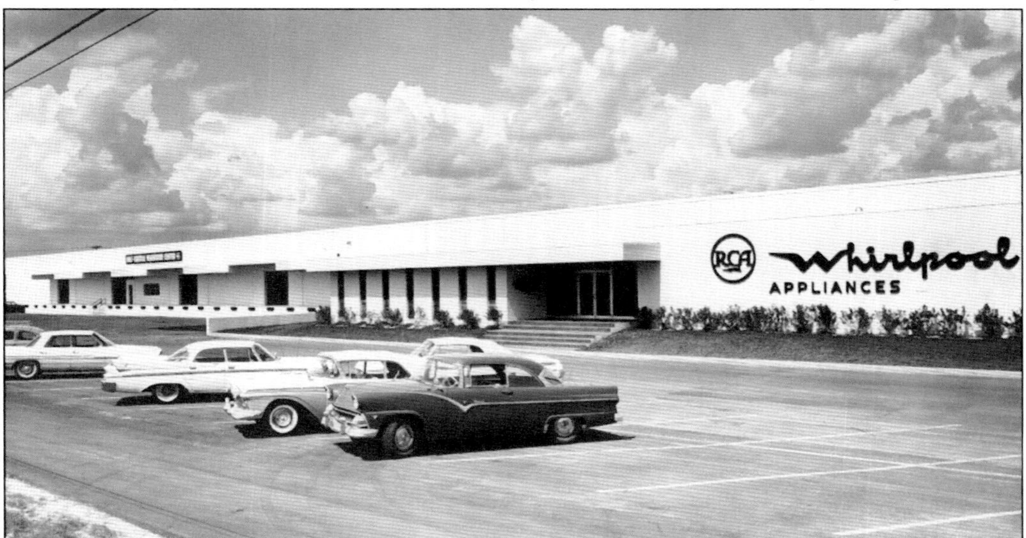

This is the new Whirlpool Distribution Center in 1958 at 6824 South Manhattan Avenue. This sprawling plant was another symbol of Tampa's expanding commercial industry in the 1950s.

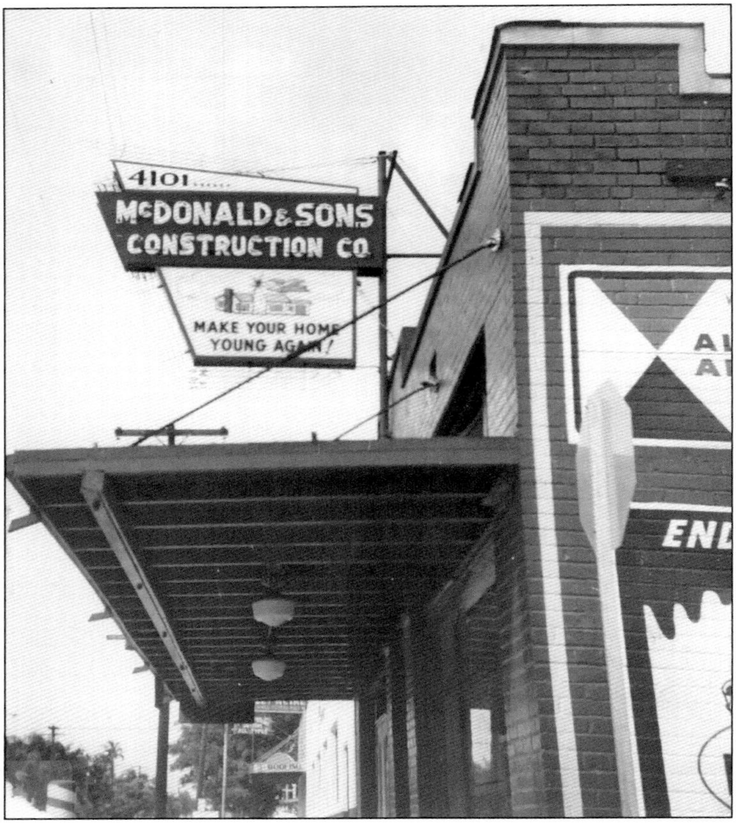

This construction company sign is quite animated, with a stork carrying the house to its new owners. Another feature of this sign that was a trademark for Cinchett Neon Signs was the street number (on this sign, 4101). This company was at 4101 Nebraska Avenue in 1960, and this vintage building still stands today.

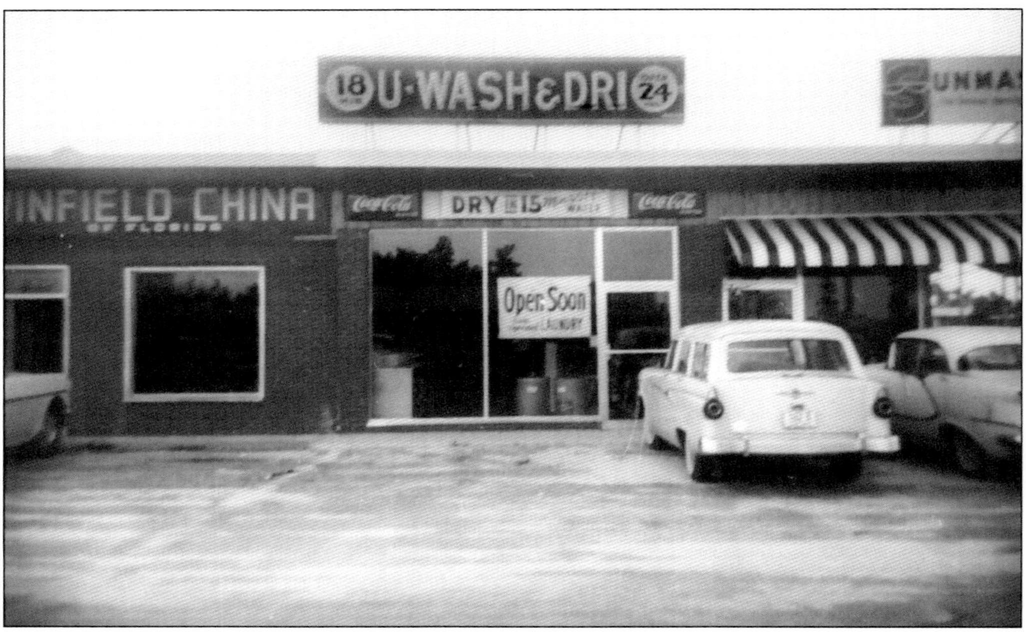

This 24-hour neighborhood launderette was located at 322 North Dale Mabry Highway in 1960. Notice that the sign says "Dry in 15 minutes" and "Soft Water."

Here is something not seen anymore. This company specialized in terrazzo floors, commonly found in homes built during the 1950s and 1960s. The cool floor was perfect for Tampa homes that did not have air-conditioning. Today terrazzo floors are considered a vintage feature of mid-20th-century homes. This shop was at 2708 North Armenia Avenue in West Tampa in 1960.

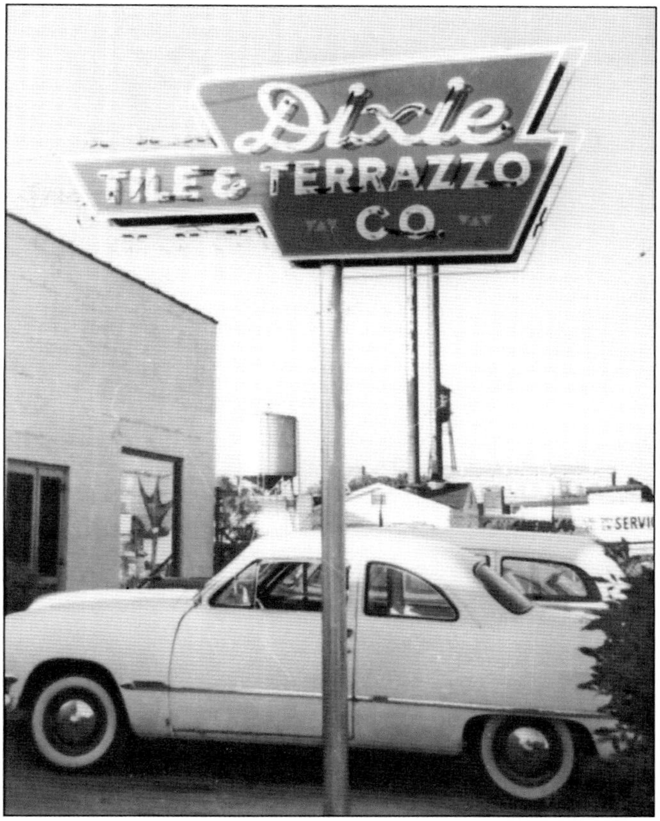

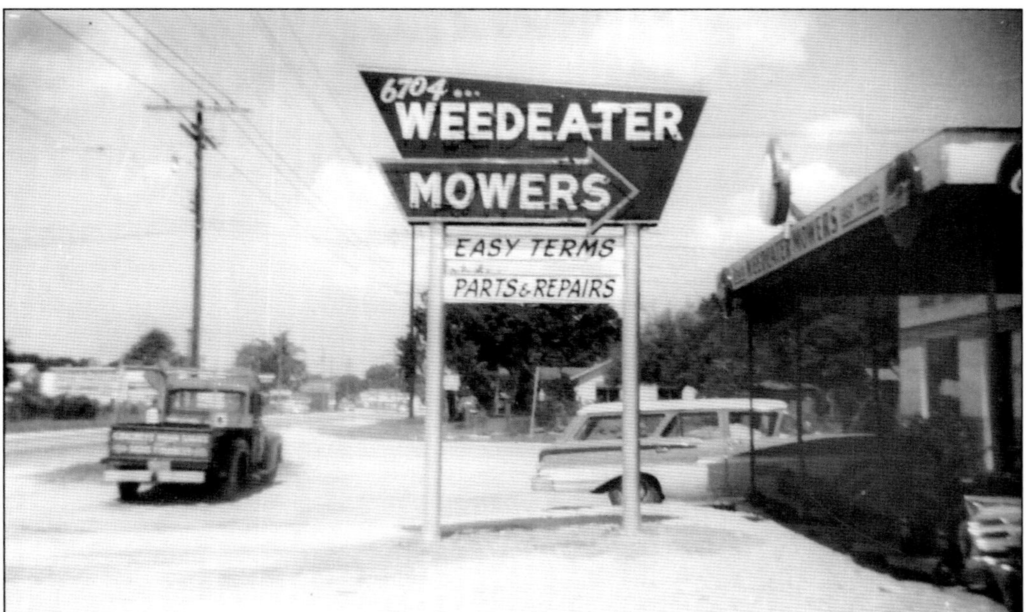

This lawn mower shop was at 6704 Broadway Avenue in East Tampa, and this view looks west in 1960. The sign featured a bright red flashing neon arrow.

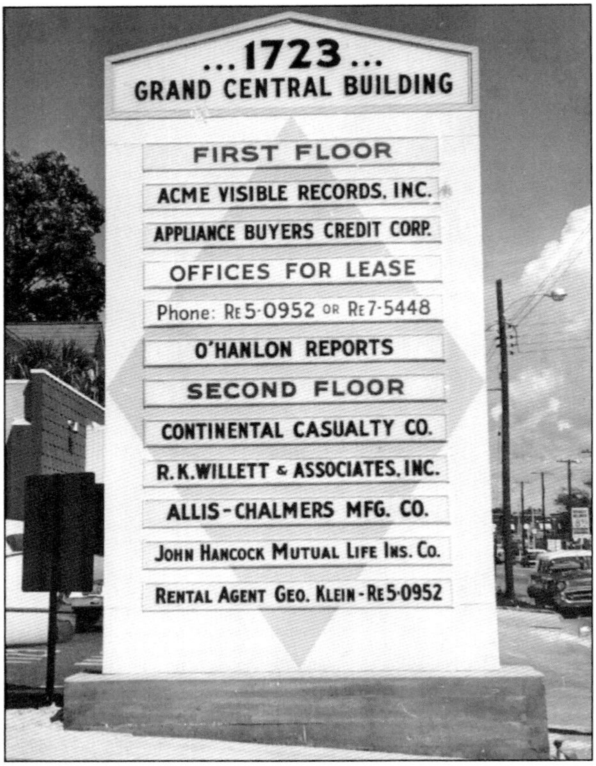

This monument-style sign was one of the first of its type in the 1950s and became popular as business complexes were created throughout the city, moving away from the traditional downtown office building. Notice the five-digit telephone numbers on the sign. The photograph was taken at 1723 Grand Central Avenue (now Kennedy Boulevard) looking east in 1959.

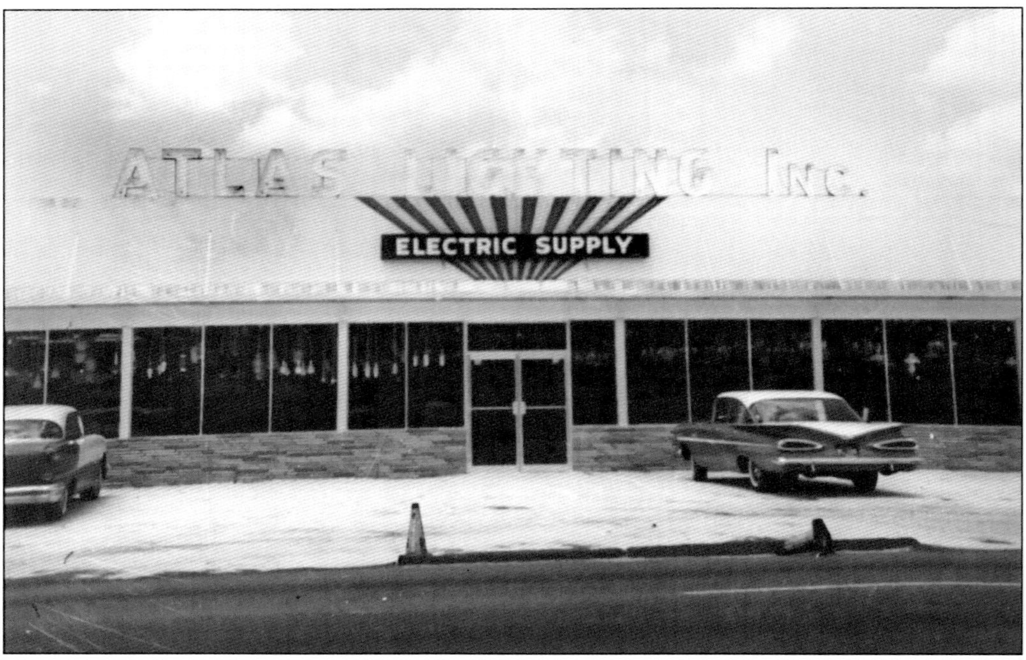

The Atlas Lighting Company at 7304 North Florida Avenue in Seminole Heights is pictured here in 1960 with its giant neon letters. This company was smart to select this location on the expanding northern edge of the city at that time.

During the 1950s, Mary Carter Paint Shops were Tampa's popular neighborhood stop for supplies and paints. This location was at 8219 North Nebraska Avenue in Sulphur Springs, and today it is a popular thrift shop. In later years, this paint company went on to become a multi-million-dollar development corporation with international success.

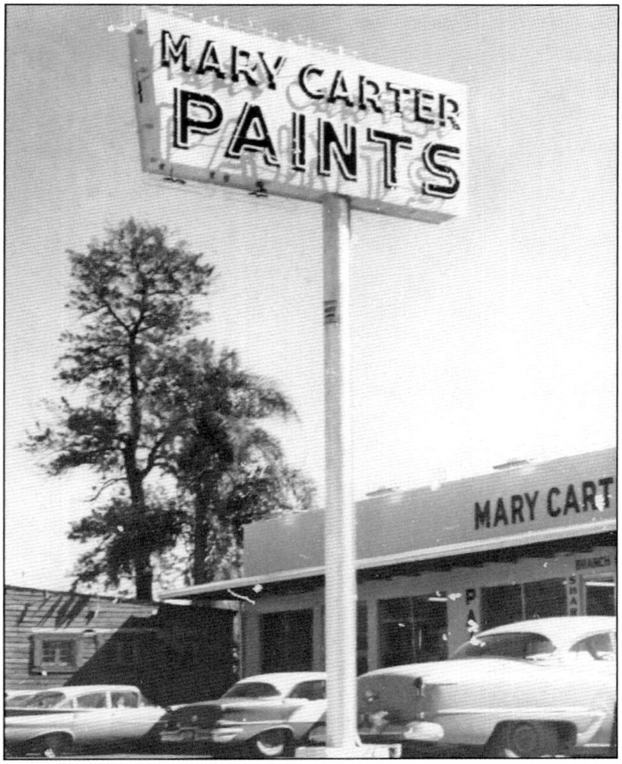

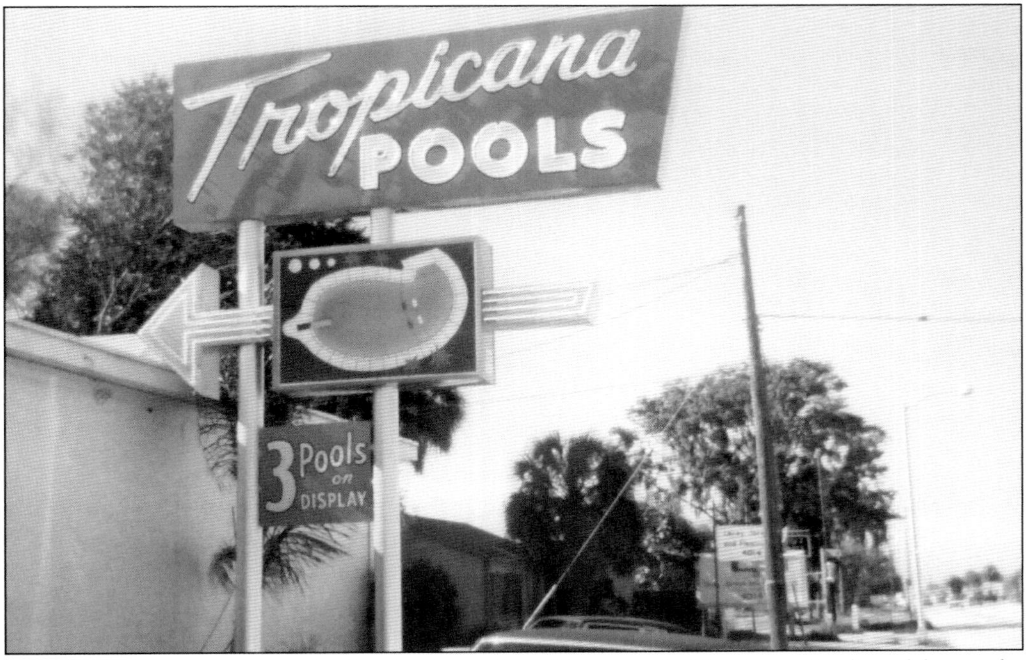

This beautiful neon spectacular by Cinchett Neon Signs was for Tropicana Pools and featured a hand-painted image of an in-ground pool with a bright yellow flashing neon arrow surrounding the artwork. This view is looking west from 4006 Kennedy Boulevard in 1968.

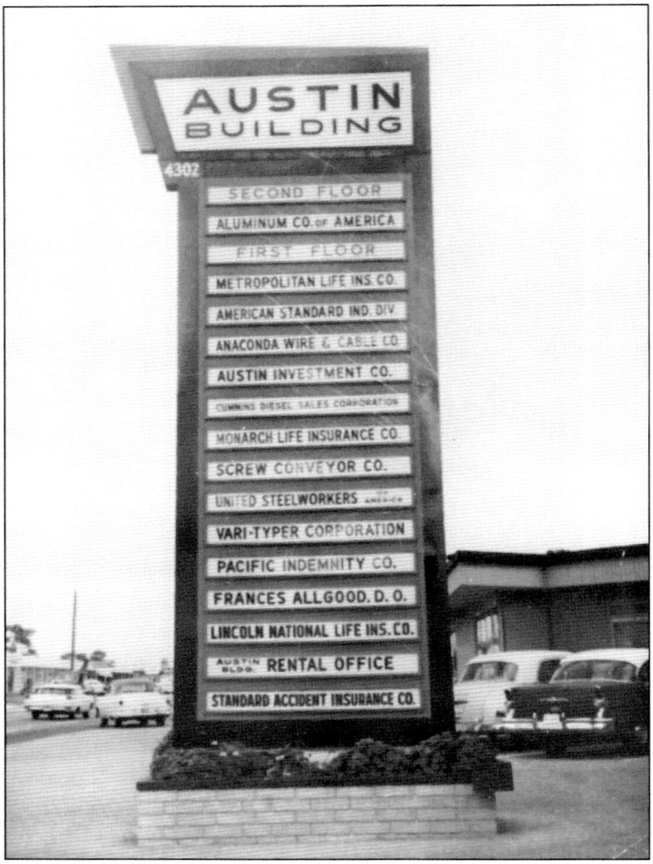

Another example of a monument-style office building sign, this was one of the first of its type installed in Tampa. This was a new concept in signage designed for an office complex similar to a shopping center with a parking lot in front of it. During the 1950s, Al Austin began development of what is now the Westshore Business District. This expansion near the west end of the city has proven to be a vital part of Tampa's success in the commercial arena. This 1958 photograph looks northeast along Henderson Boulevard, and this building is still occupied by the Austin Company today.

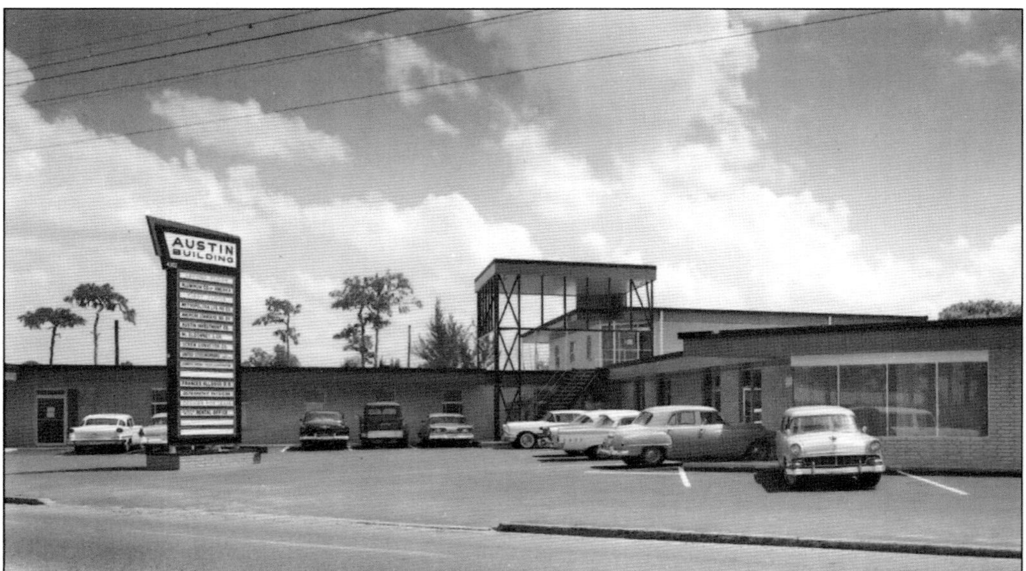

Here is another view of the new Austin Building sign in 1958. This type of sign was actually designed with white neon tubing behind the panels to light it up at night.

An early version of the U-Haul Rental Company's signage is shown in 1963 on East Hillsborough Avenue before its famous logo took hold. Notice the vintage 1950s-style travel-trailer parked near the sign. The nearby gas station advertised gas at 30¢ a gallon. This photograph was taken looking west along Hillsborough Avenue.

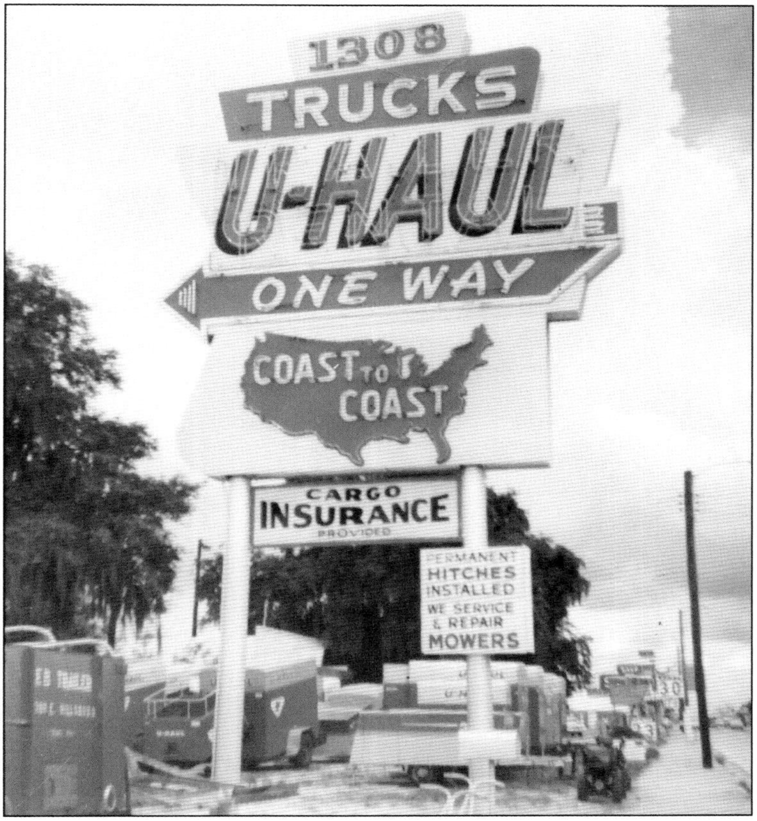

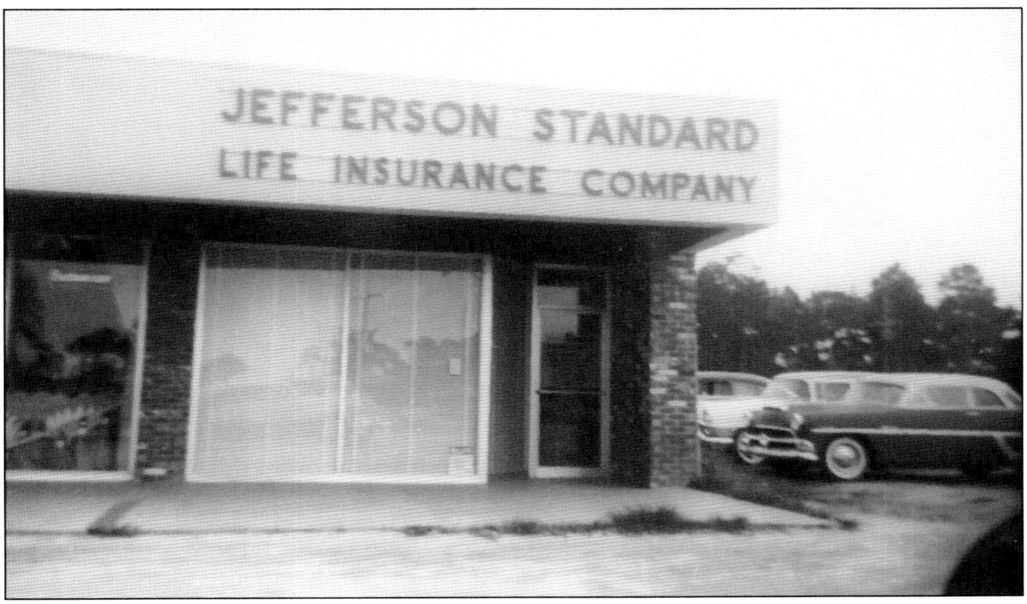

This insurance company was located at 1704 South Dale Mabry Highway just south of Neptune in 1958. The area in Palma Ceia along Dale Mabry Highway became a popular shopping and business district during the 1950s.

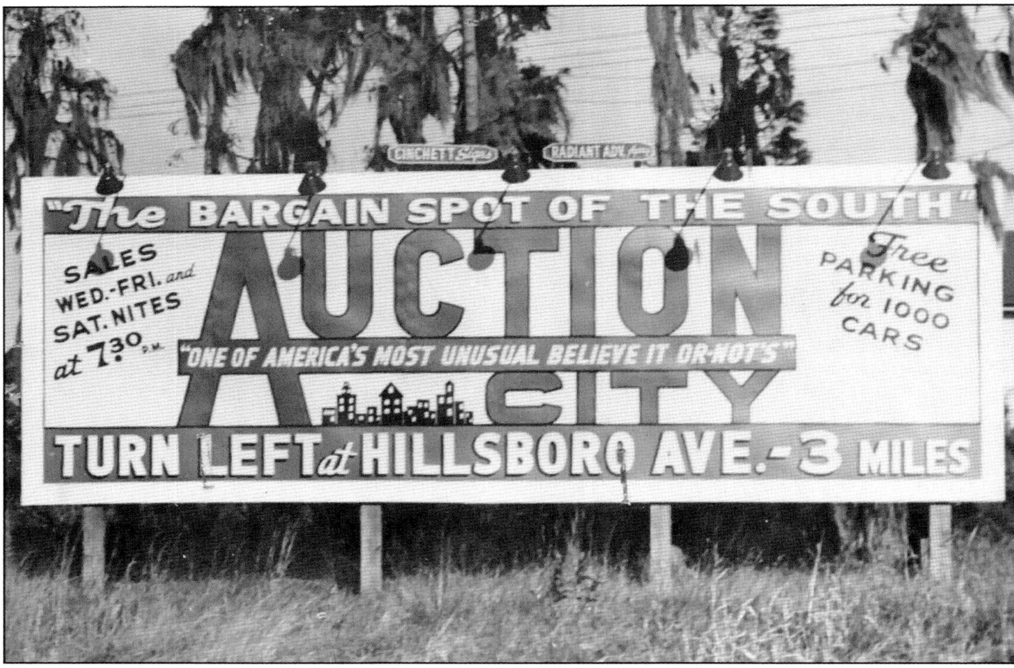

One wonders what was on the block at this popular auction house that advertises itself as being "one of America's most unusual believe-it-or-nots." This bargain spot was on Hillsborough Avenue around 1959.

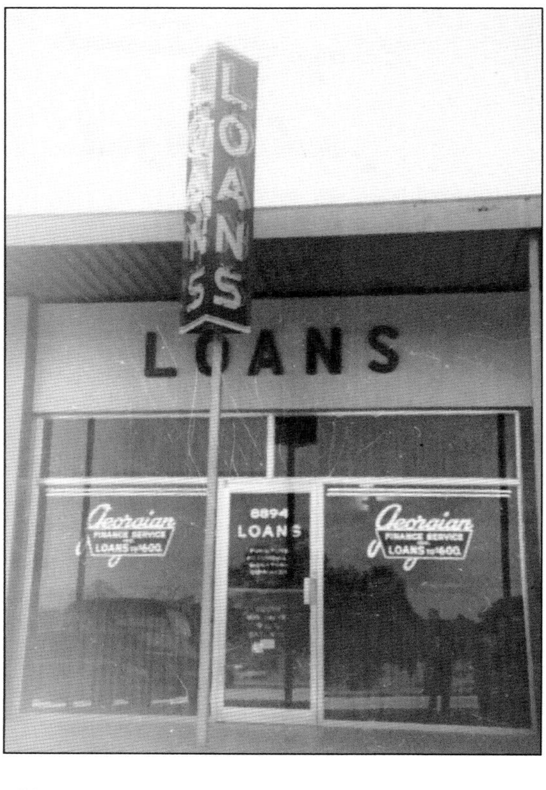

A $600 loan was the highest loan this company in Temple Terrace offered in 1959. Students at the nearby Florida College may have found their way here for help with a new car purchase.

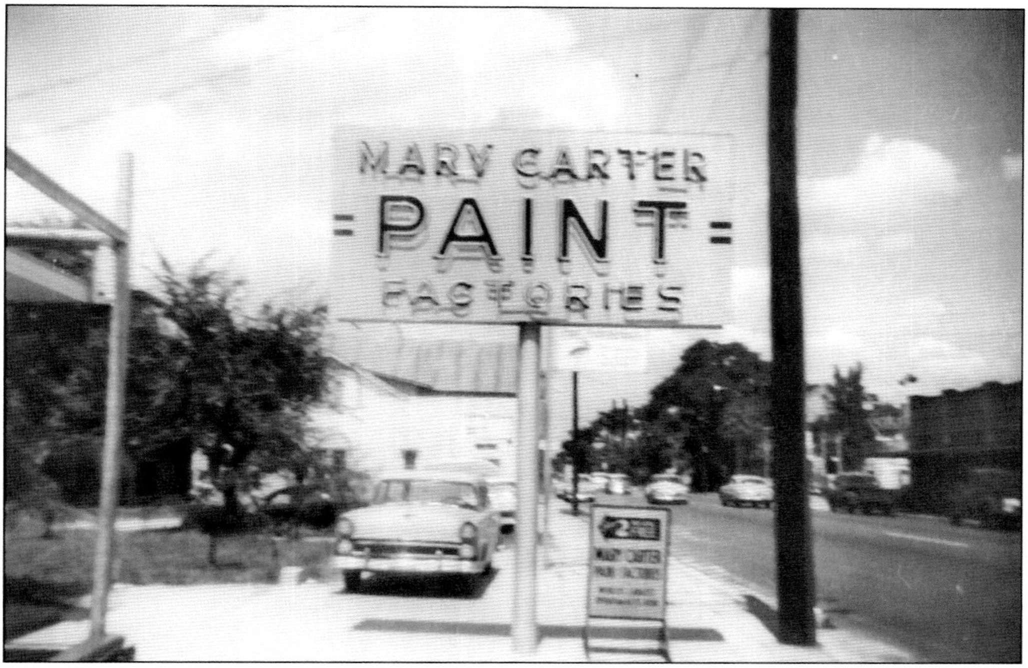

This popular paint store was at 3121 Broadway Avenue in East Tampa, and this 1962 view looks east along Broadway towards Ybor City.

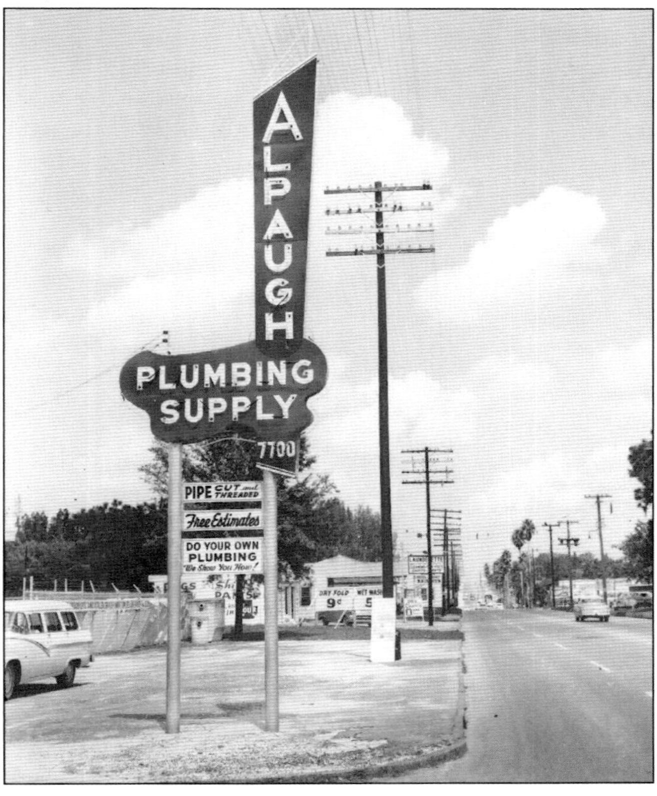

The Alpaugh Plumbing Company building at 7700 North Florida Avenue is pictured in 1959. This photograph was taken looking north toward the bridge over the Hillsborough River into Sulphur Springs. This well-known company still serves Tampa folks today.

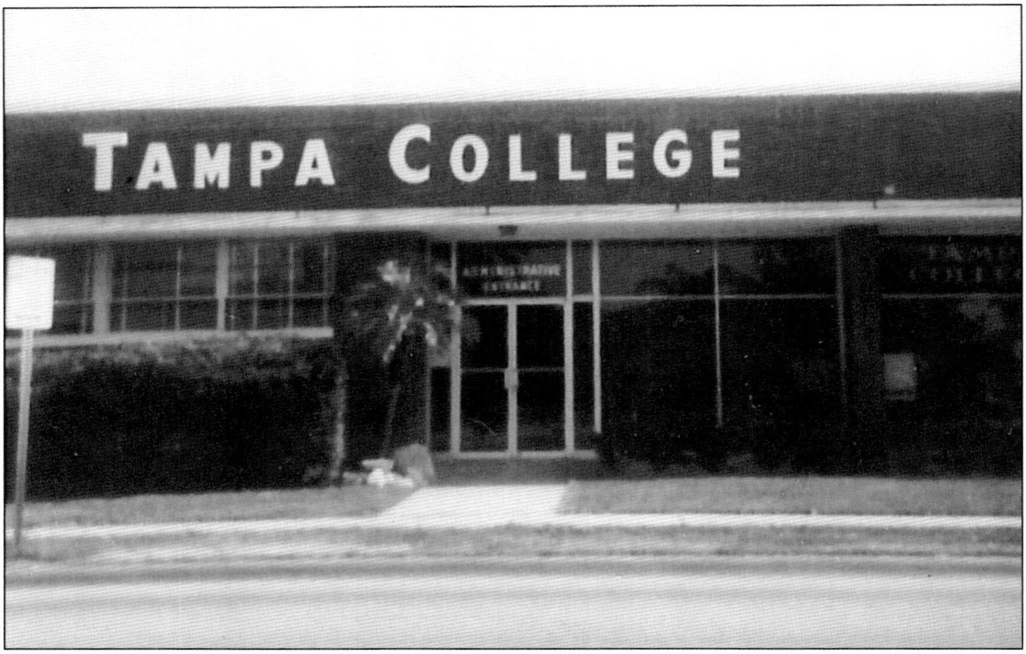

The Tampa College occupied the former IBM Building at the busy corner of West Kennedy Boulevard and Armenia Avenue near West Tampa around 1969. This was among Tampa's oldest colleges, founded in 1890. This building still stands today and was recently refurbished.

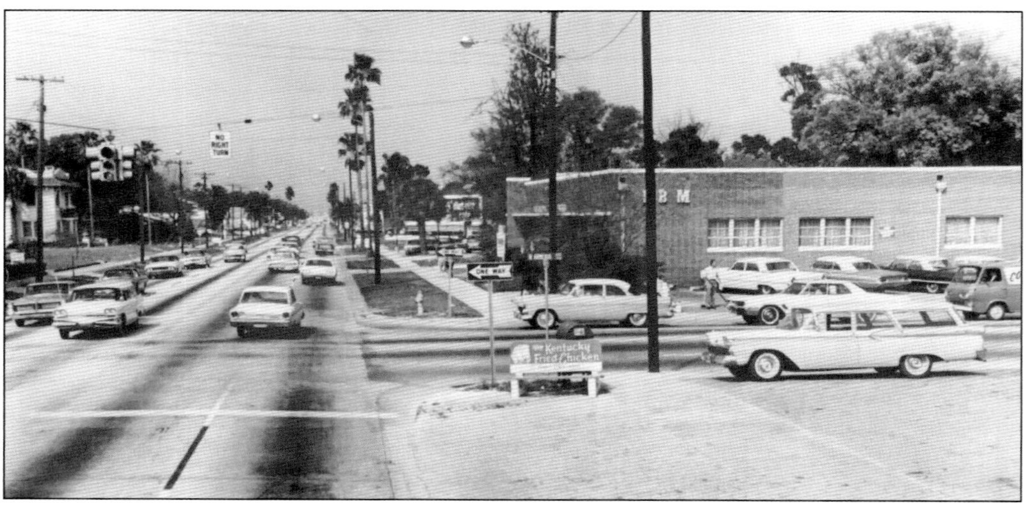

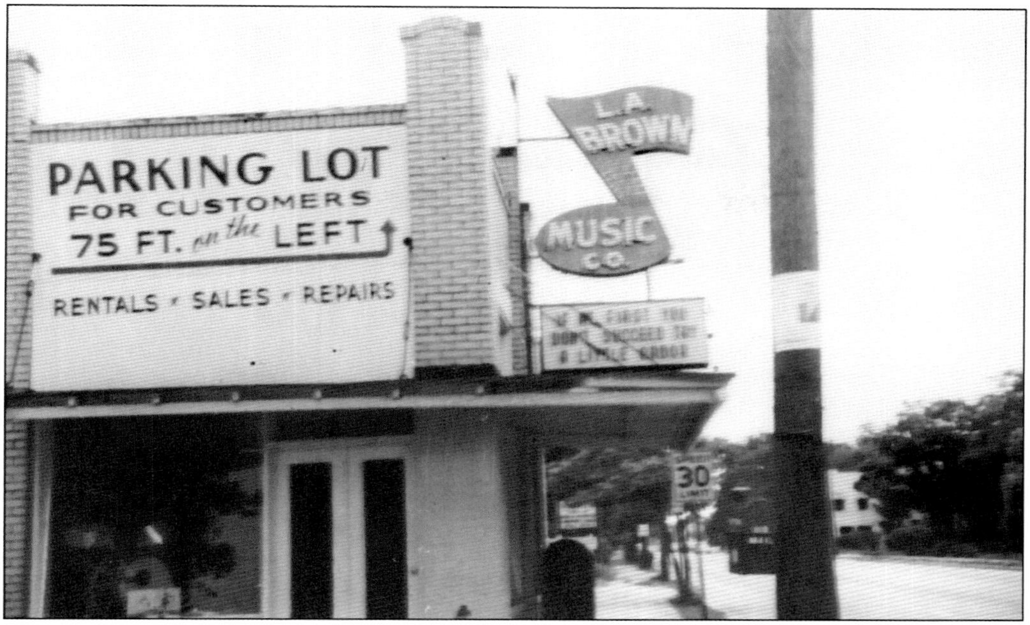

This corner music store cannot be missed by any musician driving by with that giant neon musical note and G-clef. Notice the message "If at first you don't succeed try a little ardor." This building was at Tampa and Plymouth Streets just north of downtown in Tampa Heights around 1958.

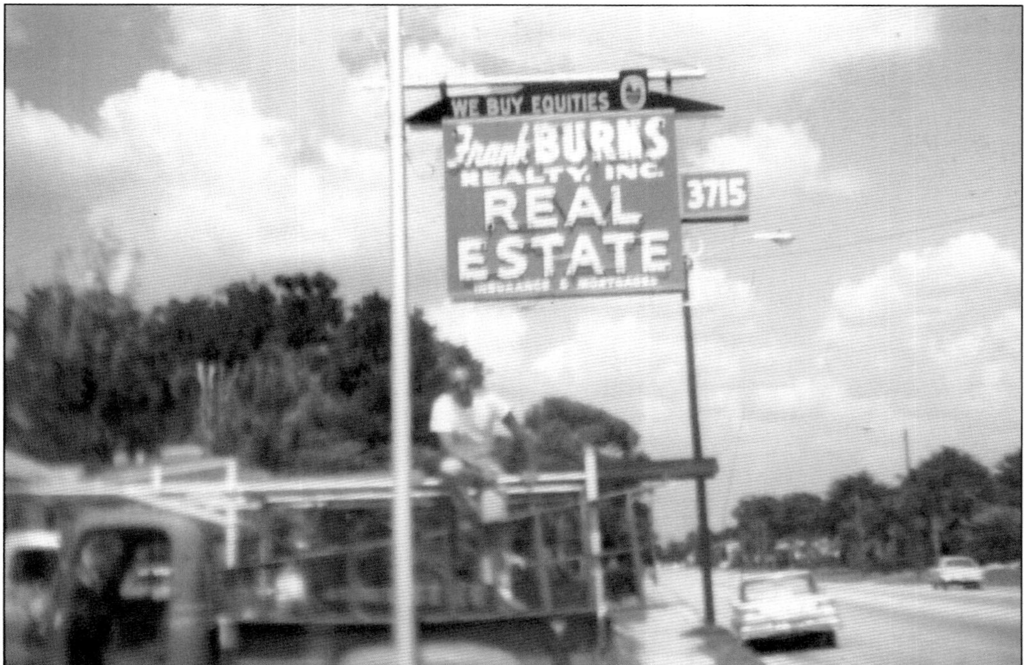

The Frank Burns Realty Company, one of Tampa's best-known realtors in the 1950s and 1960s, sold many homes during the city's population boom. Notice the rooftop design of this neon sign, proudly being used for a pose by one of Cinchett's employees. This view looks east on Azeele Street just past Dale Mabry Highway in 1961.

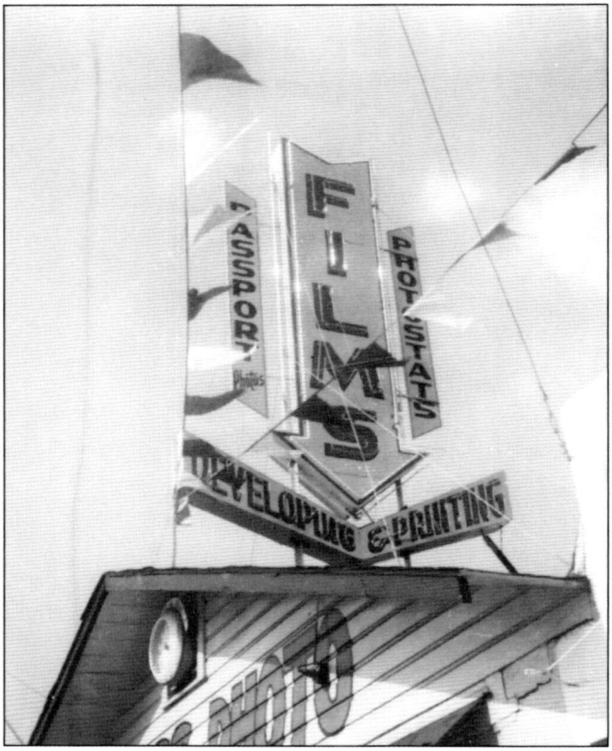

Here is something never seen anymore: shops advertising films. This photo shop seems to have a giant neon arrow falling on to it from the sky. Notice the vintage clock on the front of the building in this 1957 image.

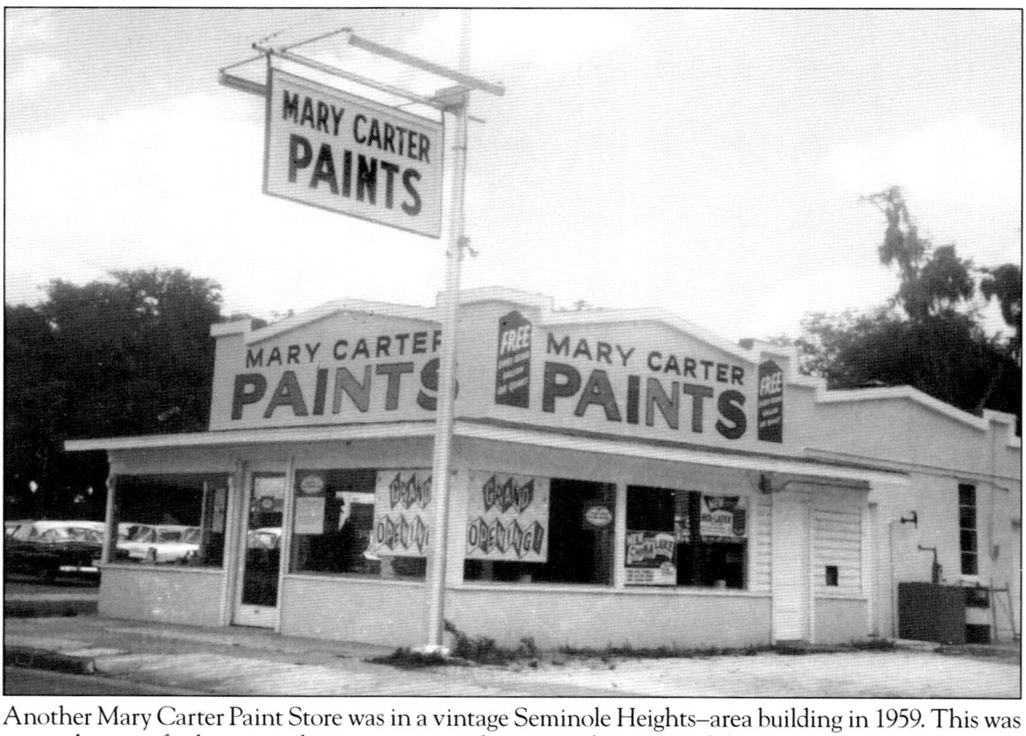

Another Mary Carter Paint Store was in a vintage Seminole Heights–area building in 1959. This was a popular stop for busy new homeowners in this expanding area of the city during the 1950s.

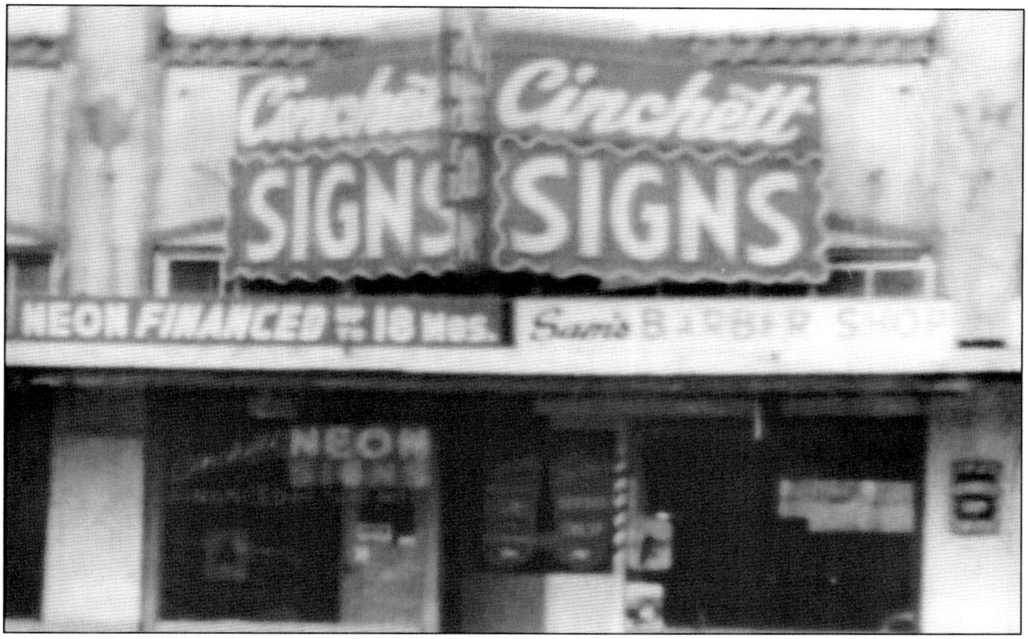

This 1957 picture shows the Cinchett Neon Signs Company at the corner of Florida and Osborne Avenues, where the company operated from 1948 to 1991. When Frank Cinchett's grandson, John V. Cinchett, came to work for the company in 1985, he marked three generations of the family operating the sign shop. Today this historic building is a popular antique mall.

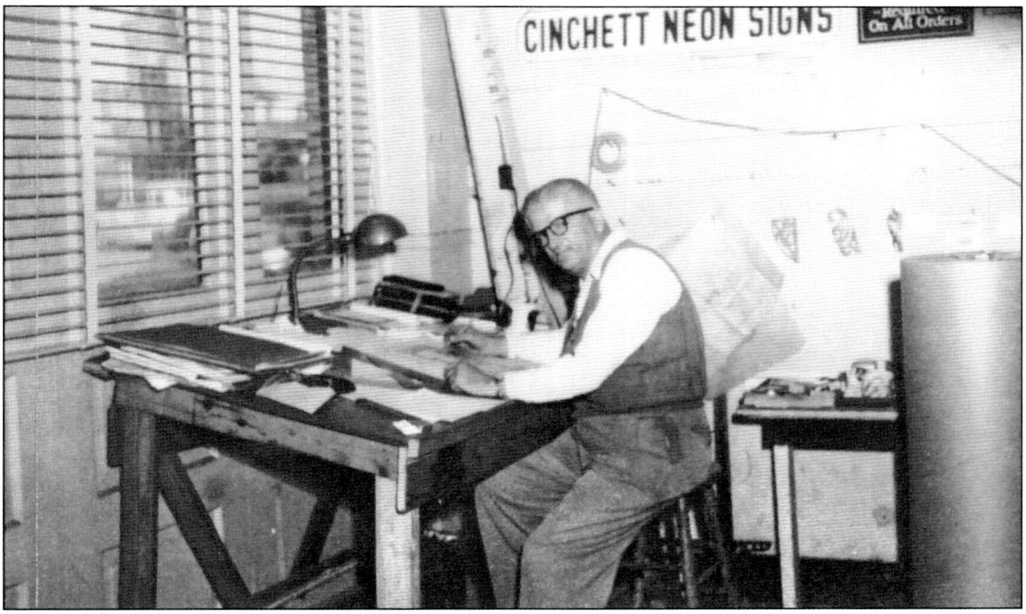

In this 1956 photograph, company founder Frank Cinchett is designing another neon sign in his office at 4707 North Florida Avenue in Seminole Heights. Frank was a pioneer in the neon sign industry when he opened his first sign company in 1927. When he died in 1963, his son John F. Cinchett became company president. The company was closed in 1997, when John passed away.